# Closing Correctional Institutions

# Closing Correctional Institutions

**New Strategies for Youth Services**

Edited by

**Yitzhak Bakal**

Massachusetts Department
of Youth Services

**Lexington Books**
D.C. Heath and Company
Lexington, Massachusetts
Toronto          London

**Library of Congress Cataloging in Publication Data**

Main entry under title:

Closing correctional institutions.

"Many of the articles . . . were written for a conference . . . sponsored jointly by the Massachusetts Department Youth Services (DYS), by the Institute for Social Research of Fordham University, and Boston College."
1. Correctional institutions—Addresses, essays, lectures.  2. Rehabilitation of juvenile delinquents—Addresses, essays, lectures.  3. Social work with youth— Addresses, essays, lectures.  I. Bakal, Yitzhak, ed.

HV9069.C518            365'.42            73–998

ISBN 0–669–86140–5

**Published simultaneously in Canada.**

**Printed in the United States of America.**

**International Standard Book Number:** 0-669-86140-5

**Library of Congress Catalog Card Number:** 73-998

# Contents

Foreword, *Benedict S. Alper*                                              vii

Preface                                                                    xi

Introduction                                                               xiii

**Part I**        **The Case for Deinstitutionalization**                 1

Chapter 1         The Politics of Change: Correctional Reform,
                  *Jerome G. Miller*                                       3

Chapter 2         The Creation of a New Network of Services for
                  Troublesome Youth, *John M. Martin*                      9

Chapter 3         Community Services and Residential Institutions
                  for Children, *Martin Gula*                             13

Chapter 4         Delinquency in Girls: Implications for
                  Service Delivery, *Carole Upshur*                       19

**Part II**       **Problems of Implementation**                          31

Chapter 5         Youth Service Systems: New Criteria,
                  *Robert M. Foster*                                      33

Chapter 6         From Institutions to Human Services,
                  *Herbert C. Schulberg*                                  39

Chapter 7         Alternative Models for the Rehabilitation
                  of the Youthful Offender, *I. Ira Goldenberg*           49

Chapter 8         Vision and Process: The Quality of Life in Community
                  Group Homes, *Howard W. Polsky*                        59

Chapter 9         Neutralization of Community Reistance to Group
                  Homes, *Robert B. Coates* and *Alden D. Miller*         67

**Part III**          **Strategies and Case Studies**                                85

Chapter 10       Effecting Changes in a Training School for Girls,
                         *Frederick Thacher*                                                          87

Chapter 11       The Teaching-Family Model of Group Home Treatment,
                         *Dean L. Fixsen, Elery L. Phillips,* and
                         *Montrose M. Wolf*                                                          107

Chapter 12       The University's Role in Public Service to the
                         Department of Youth Services, *Larry L. Dye*            117

Chapter 13       A Strategic Innovation in the Process of
                         Deinstitutionalization: The University of
                         Massachusetts Conference, *Robert B. Coates,*
                         *Alden D. Miller,* and *Lloyd E. Ohlin*                       127


**Part IV**          **The Massachusetts Experience**                            149

Chapter 14       Closing Massachusetts' Institutions: A Case Study,
                         *Yitzhak Bakal*                                                               151


                         **About the Contributors**                                          181


                         **Index**                                                                          183

# Foreword

There was a simpler time not so very long ago—in this country and in others with similar economic and social organizations—when the problems of the mentally retarded and disturbed, the aged, and the troubled young were dealt with in the communities where each of these people lived. A greater continuity or integration of the entire age spectrum seems to have prevailed in those days: those who were old were not euphemistically and evasively dubbed as in their "golden" years, and those who were deficient in intelligence or in emotional balance were not only tolerated but accommodated.

Since the age of Jackson, we have seen an increasing tendency to institutionalize persons in these categories, so that today we find an expensive, extensive and highly specialized network of places where those with conditions or abnormalities not easily dealt with at home or in the community are massed together in public or private custodies (see David J. Rothman, *The Discovery of Asylum* [Boston, 1971]). Regardless of diagnosis, they suffer a common fate—isolation of one degree or another.

The totality and the magnitude of such a system, with all its parts—programs, plant and personnel—stagger the imagination, and available budgetary resources as well.

When the penitentiary idea was launched at the close of the eighteenth century, a subordinate principle held that young people should not be confined with adult offenders in penal institutions. Until that time, with few exceptions, children were herded together with adults in penal stations, just as they were in places for confinement of the "lunatic." So when, in the 1820s, groups of citizens banded together to provide separate institutional care for young offenders, a major breakthrough in child care—harking back to the Rome of Clement XI—had finally taken place in the United States. Thereafter Massachusetts was the first state to establish a separate place for young offenders under public auspices, and such agricultural or industrial schools soon proliferated all over the country.

Today, 125 years later, these places—now called training schools—continue to receive youngsters and subject them to programs of restraint, brutality, and futility. Such institutions differ little from their original models, with one exception. Today the conviction has become almost universal that if they ever served any purpose other than as temporary places of restraint, their consistently high rates of failure to rehabilitate strongly suggest that the time has come to close them and replace them with more humane and effective measures of care, protection, and treatment for young people.

Nothing succeeds like an idea whose time has come. The institution as a means of coping with the problems of specific sectors of our population seems at this point to have run its course. Whether one is aged, below par intellectually or emotionally, delinquent, alcoholic, or drug-addicted, the source—and the remedy—of the problem lie in the communities where such people come from. By bringing them back into the community, by enlisting the good will and the desire to serve, the ability to understand which is to be found in every neighborhood, we shall meet the challenge which such groups of persons present, and at the same time ease the financial burden of their confinement in fixed institutions.

It is the contention of many of the contributors to this book that any drastic redesign of social policy or program inevitably arouses the antagonism and opposition of vested interests—legislators and civil service personnel who resent any change in accustomed practices; judges and court officers who sigh for the old days when tight warehouses were on call for retention of those who failed in the community; some public schools which deplore the absence of the institutional deterrent; the man in the street who is appalled at the thought of having "those people" housed across the street from him; the police who complain that their role has been reduced to that of operators of a perpetual revolving door.

Out of this experience has come a lesson we have been slow to learn: that penal institutions—whether for adults or juveniles—are subject to Parkinson's Law no less than other places. When facilities are available, they tend to be filled. Those who administer adult and juvenile corrections seem to resent vacancies in their warehouses. The result is what might be called the ramrod effect, whereby the institutional population is kept fairly constant and the rate of release is set by the rate of commitment—or vice versa.

The same kind of principle seems to be at work where the levels of security are set at minimum, medium, and maximum. Administrators always seem able to find enough "tough" kids to fill whatever maximum holes may be available, and so on down the line. If we had but two levels of security, we would have no difficulty in dividing the population in two instead of three.

The Massachusetts experience shows what happens when these three classical gradations of security are reduced to one; some alternative kind of placement in the community will be found. If you abolish maximum and medium security, you suddenly find yourself with only those who require minimum security.

Today's institutions for delinquents have failed, and nothing can alter that single fact. Even if what is to replace them is no more successful in the way of preventing repeated criminal conduct, the people who pass through these alternative facilities will—we may be sure—not emerge with feelings of worthlessness and degradation greater than when they first went into them.

The road back to community dealing with the problems of the young, the retarded and the mentally disturbed will not be easy. But the destination is a degree of community participation and effectiveness which has all but departed our lives as people living together. Part of the powerlessness and frustration which so many sense at this juncture will be resolved in this trend, to the benefit not only of inmates or clients or patients or criminals now in institutions—but of our citizenry as a whole.

As one who took part in planning and hosting the conference "The Closing Down of Institutions and New Strategies in Youth Services," from which many of the articles in this book were taken, I have the very positive conviction that truly effective intervention into the lives of troubled youngsters by programs based in their communities is bound to emerge from the skill and determination of those who chose the new alternative courses herein described.

**Benedict S. Alper**
Boston College

February 1973

# Preface

Many of the articles presented here were written for a conference, "The Closing Down of Institutions and New Strategies in Youth Services," sponsored jointly by the Massachusetts Department of Youth Services (DYS), the Institute for Social Research of Fordham University, and Boston College.

The conference was held six months after the Massachusetts DYS made a historic decision—to close all its training schools ("reform schools") and develop community-based alternatives for the young people involved.

A great many of the 500 conferees, including 250 from states other than Massachusetts, came to discover exactly what the Massachusetts DYS had done, how they had managed it, and how they planned to make it succeed. Most wanted more specific and detailed accounts of the alternatives devised for replacing the institutions.

As the conferees exchanged views, it became clear that people in and out of the youth services field were deeply concerned and hungry for more information about the entire process of closing our correctional institutions.

This book was compiled and written in the belief that there are many people who have a similar interest in discovering why and how correctional institutions are closed, and the more humane, profitable, and meaningful alternatives there are for treating previously institutionalized people—especially the young—in twentieth-century society.

Any book that has its starting point at a conference involves so many individuals, colleagues, and friends deserving acknowledgment that the task becomes impossible. All those who contributed their time, effort, and support, therefore, have my sincere thanks. There are, however, four people who must be given individual thanks for their support throughout this project. They are Elaine Bakal, Joseph Beckman, John Butenas, and Howard Polsky.

# Introduction

The large correctional institution has failed to achieve its purposes. Placing people who do not follow the established rules of our society—especially the young—into environments set apart and distinct from society, has served neither the public nor the person confined. Whether the intent has been to punish or to rehabilitate, the experience of over a hundred years has shown that institutionalization is not the answer. The learning process has been expensive not only in monetary terms, but in human cost as well.

Even as larger institutions are being built, more and more professionals in youth services, mental health, and the correctional field in general have come to believe that society can be better served by alternatives that include a setting within the society to which the person in trouble must ultimately return.

The correctional institutionalization of young people has undergone essentially three stages of development:

1. The first stage was based on a belief in the value of placing offenders or disturbed young people in a wholesome setting, away from the negative influences of their home and community environments. The plan was to cultivate proper values, attitudes, and behaviors through a regimen of discipline and inspirational character-building. To that end, the first public reform school, the Lyman School for Boys, was established in Massachusetts in 1846.
2. The next stage was the introduction of clinical services within existing institutions, providing individualized attention to motivational and psychological aspects of the residents.
3. The third stage followed from the introduction of therapeutic community concepts into the large institution. Groups of doctors, social workers, attendants, and inmates openly discussed their problems and grievances. This was intended to create a more responsive climate for the joint working out of differences. But there was a basic contradiction between the traditional closed institutional setting and the new style of open meetings. This contradiction resulted in tension that could not be satisfactorily resolved. To sustain trust between worker and inmate during those hours not spent in open encounters proved difficult. It became apparent that polarized subcultures invariably resulted from placing trained personnel in authority over residents who lived under severe restrictions. This polarization prevented the emergence of a common transcending culture of mutual caring and aid. And the larger the institution, the more pronounced the polarity.

Life in the closed institutionalized setting is prey to peer-group pressures on residents and staff members as well. At the level of the basic living unit, untrained, underpaid, immobile personnel are isolated from the administrators and professionals in charge of the institution. They make deals with residents, with whom they have to form some kind of underground *modus vivendi*. Thus the whole institutional enterprise becomes manipulative, encouraging self-serving anti-system behavior. Researchers have found that a high rate of recidivism persists among youth and adults discharged from institutions. Staff, it was also found, in many cases became institutionalized themselves.

Many practitioners in the corrections field began to see that rehabilitation consists not of therapists "curing" offenders, but rather of worker and resident creating a culture of trust and a problem-solving climate where all grow together or regress together, but this technique requires a totally noninstitutional social structure, capable of supporting the residents' functioning in the home and in the community. Thus the idea was born that the institutions themselves should be eliminated.

It is the closing of large institutions that actually stimulates new thinking about community-centered programs for helping those who cannot fit into conventional community structures. The closing of the large institutions presents new opportunities for diverse people in the community, professional and nonprofessional, to become involved and come forward with their ideas about how troubled people can be helped within the community, without the ultimate recourse of sending them away to a large institution, cut off from society. Only when the decision for closing institutions is made are ways then found to effect the transformation and to open new directions for helping people in trouble in the community.

But ideas for change always meet opposition, and any institution creates a bureaucracy that will fight to maintain its own existence. Administrators and professionals associated with large training facilities reveal a peculiar blend of realism and rationalization in their rationale of "yes, that's a good idea but...." There is a whole system of "buts" as to why it is not feasible to close the large institutions. Some of these "buts" come from forces outside the corrections field relating to legal and economic considerations, to "buts" relating to an entrenched bureaucracy, to "buts" about communities that will not accept delinquent and disturbed youngsters in their neighborhoods. These "buts" are impressive not because very effective arguments have been made in their favor, but because they are so frequently heard in discussions with staff and administrators familiar with the large residential institutions. Their unchallenged acceptance is gospel.

Whatever the truth of this system of "buts" is, its latent function is to justify the institutional system. Without the actual decision to close the institution, all progressive solutions are stillborn. Creative ideas remain locked in the system of the large institutions, and energy is siphoned off both in defense of the existing institutions and to block their closing. Instead of facing the "buts" in the context of eliminating the system that gives rise to and supports them, these "buts" are fallen back on so that no significant change occurs, or only half-hearted community-based alternatives are ventured. The large institutions create larger and larger "buts," which in turn become the ideological mainstay of those institutions.

The articles in this book speak to many of these arguments against closing our institutions. The papers in Part I give the general concepts and rationale behind the belief that deinstitutionalization must take place, detailing the disadvantages of the institutional setting and sketching the broad outlines of alternative solutions. The papers basically tell why new alternatives must be found.

The papers in Part II are more specific in their presentation of the alternatives that are available. They describe the methods involved in achieving success as the institutions are closed and community-based service structures take their place. In doing this they tell what can and should be done.

Part III becomes still more specific, in that actual case studies are presented, showing what has been done in individual situations to implement alternatives.

Part IV details the Massachusetts experience, in that it is the first state to close all of its correctional institutions for youthful offenders, and thus reflects the culmination of all the factors presented earlier—theoretical and practical—in action.

Based on the material presented in this book, it will become clear that there is widespread acceptance of the basic principle that community-based programs must replace the institutionalization of young people. Those who read this book in hopes of finding a blueprint for success may feel a sense of frustration. For we have only begun to find our way.

Evaluating individual alternatives to incarceration must be a constant and long-range process. Great caution must be taken to see that community-based alternatives do not transfer to the local level the same attitudes and practices that characterize the institutions they replace. Methods must be found to evaluate how effective these new alternatives are in reducing delinquency, in lowering the recidivism rate, in cutting down street crime. And those concepts and techniques that fail must be cast aside and new ones found.

It is hoped that this book will contribute in some way to finally convincing people that institutionalization does not work, that there are real alternatives that have proven successful on a small scale in the past, and that Massachusetts has shown clearly that it is possible to carry on the process on a large-scale basis. Perhaps then we will stop incarcerating our young—and eventually our adult—offenders, and discover the rewards of humane treatment.

# Part I
## The Case for Deinstitutionalization

# 1

## The Politics of Change: Correctional Reform

Jerome G. Miller

*Society and the Labeled Inmate*

There are serious problems in dealing with the realities of reform in correction, since people often prefer to hear myths—and the truth in this area reflects so deeply in ourselves. There is no such thing as objectivity in talking of "treatment" of the offender—since any such treatment redounds immediately to one's own personal self-concept—and ultimately affects the fabric of cohesion in the society.

When discussing the dilemmas involved in the diagnosis, treatment, or rehabilitation of those we call "delinquent," one should look not only at the roles played by administrators and the helping professions, but also at the role played by society. Social and political considerations are basic to any discussion of correctional reform. The very nature of labeling youth as "delinquent," "wayward," or "stubborn" is related to the power of the definers and the powerlessness of the defined. Society views the deviant as an outsider and prefers to isolate him in the abnormal setting of an institution. Administrators and the helping professions administer "treatment" based on arbitrary definitions, thereby fulfilling social or moralistic functions for the society other than that of rehabilitation. The defined cannot escape these definitions, which results in self-defeating social roles and delinquent self-concepts.

The injustices of our correctional system by far outweigh the injustices perpetrated upon society by the inmates. We must recognize that, although we have preached rehabilitation, we have been involved in producing scapegoats who present ever greater dangers to all of us. The basic latent functions of our correctional system tell us more about our society than about those we are treating. It reveals an abiding and persistent need to punish, in a spirit of hostile retribution, those who break our norms and thus challenge our roles. In this sense, one can understand George Herbert Mead's comment that the criminal basically does not challenge the cohesiveness of a society, but may, in fact, contribute toward that cohesiveness by uniting the members of the society against the rule-breaker, as defined by his action as an outsider.[1]

From the beginning one wonders if it is feasible to treat the delinquent through society's official agencies. For if the truth were known, there are few private and fewer public treatment agencies that honestly deliver what they say they do. Our best efforts to treat the delinquent for the most part have begun in incompetence and have built to a climax of punishment and physical or psychological violence toward the offender—a process that insures the intensity of his bitterness and the escalation of his crimes. Statistics compiled by the FBI show that 74 percent of adults who are imprisoned return within five years. The same pattern is found among our juveniles. We continue, however, to harbor the myth that the longer we imprison the offender, repetition of his delinquency will be less likely. The only need we serve is our own need for false reassurance—and in these days of a rising crime rate such reassurance is a luxury beyond our means.

Class and racial prejudice is pervasive in the functioning of our correctional system. Increase in sophistication of the society with reference to diagnosis and treatment of delinquency seems to be in more or less of a ratio to the relative power and affluence of those defined as delinquent. It may be, for example, that the experience of middle-class youngsters with drugs will have an indirect salutary social effect upon the poor who have been involved in the same problem for years, since it is difficult to accuse as scapegoat those with access to the power structure.

### Administrative and Bureaucratic Dilemmas

There are a number of bars to substantive change and reform in the correctional system. Many of these lie in the system itself, which is designed to endure despite failure in its manifest task, i.e., the rehabilitation of offenders. Others lie in the contradictory roles the correctional administrator must play.

The knowledgeable correctional administrator finds himself torn asunder by his own agency. The common escape procedure for the administrator is to avoid knowing the agency well and to survive by avoiding contact with the "stuff" of his agency, i.e., the inmates. One can relate easily to the mechanisms of the bureaucracy and keep it smooth running with virtually no feeling of moral dissonance provided one keeps ignorant of his population. Diagnosis and classification feeds and fortifies the studied ignorance and selective inattention of the administrator by validating his withdrawal to bureaucratic tasks. He can ensure, thereby, that his contacts with his clientele fit well whatever diagnostic, moral, or legal categories are provided to justify the apathy and ultimate violence of the system.

The arrangements upon which the correctional system rests, such as civil service protections, political patronage, and institutional bureaucracy, insure that there can be no quick or meaningful reaction to a specific inequity. The kinds of "reforms" that come through the bureaucratic, self-protective system, are made without confronting the issues. In many ways they are less a substantive change than merely an absorption of contradiction. There may be some progress, but it may easily lead to more basic and deeper injustice of the captive "deviants" if those with the defining power are not impelled to question their own stances and definitional categories.

One gets an uneasy feeling looking at the banal and mediocre level of corrections, to observe administrators and staff rushing to embrace classification centers, simplistic behavioral diagnostic models, operant conditioning and aversive therapies. The embrace is a solution and an escape—a solution to the problem of controlling difficult behavior of the deviant and an escape for the society from confronting or understanding the "rationality" of a delinquent or criminal act. It is in this context that Edmund Leach defines a "cure" as "the imposition of discipline by force; it is the maintenance of the values of the existing order against threats which arise from its own internal contradictions."

An administrator has to have a sense of process and a capacity for informed loneliness. He faces the problem of maintaining his integrity and not believing or internalizing the roles he is forced to play. Otherwise, in constant interaction with staff, bureaucrats, and politicians who may all hold conflicting views of methods of correction, the administrator begins to be socialized to a system that at its core cannot tolerate the ends for which it must strive.

*Professional Dilemmas*

In much the same way as administrators, the helping professions are caught up in the social processes of subjugation and scapegoating. By their very existence, the professions come to assume latent functions of social control. The practice settings, roles, and skills of the helping professions are part of the social processes of control. In this sense, they represent a response to belief systems (families, communities, societies) and to definitions made by those systems.

The diagnosis relieves strain on the system by allowing focus on the deviant who is in large part a product of the inconsistencies existent in the system. The clinician who identifies with the humanity of his patient or client is unusually vulnerable, in that to play the game with other rules (e.g., to demonstrate the reasonableness of the client in response to a contradictory or unreasonable social system) will likely insure the retribution of the system in punitive handling of his unfortunate client.

R.D. Laing notes that the diagnostic process that denies social intelligibility to behavior,

sanctions a massive ignorance of the social context within which the person was interacting. It also renders any genuine reciprocity between the process of labeling (the practice of psychiatry) and of being labeled (the role of patient) as impossible to conceive as it is to observe. Someone whose mind is imprisoned in the metaphor cannot see it as a metaphor. It is just obvious.[2]

Laing succinctly outlines the dilemma and the paradox:

The unintelligiblity of the experience and behavior of the diagnosed person is created by the person diagnosing him, as well as by the person diagnosed.[3]

One can see why Laing reaches the conclusion that diagnosis is a social fact that is, in turn, a political event—a "social prescription" that imposes definitions and consequences on the labeled person and provides a sanction for a set of social actions.[4]

Until the ideology underlying corrections changes, such procedures as diagnosis and classification will be of questionable merit. It matters little to the person locked alone in a stripped cell whether it is called the "hole" or the "adjustment center" or whether he is classified as a sinner, a constitutional psychopathic inferior, a defective delinquent, or a sociopath. Their ideology of correction will not change until those labeled by it have some say in that defining process. Unfortunately, the diagnostic system is so rigid that the diagnosed cannot influence the categories used to define them. When one approaches the vast range of social problems relating to those persons defined as "outsiders"—the "delinquent," the "mentally ill," the "criminal," and so on, the use of treatment techniques flowing from these arbitrary categorizations has serious implications. The changing of the "scientific" label or theory is almost peripheral to the actual handling of the deviant—the particular theory providing the social sanction to treat in ways that tend to insure the status quo of the society.

*The Process of Change*

In terms of ideology, the question of correctional reform is not whether we can break out of previous definitions to more up-to-date definitions. It is rather whether we can (1) effectively break the vicious circle of definitions calling for institutional arrangements which, in turn, revalidate the definitions and; (2) build into new definitions (since they will come) enough categories that show the social and psychological strengths and the life-space of those defined as delinquent or criminal.

We must realize that no amount of reform funneled into our present institutional system will basically change it. To insure fundamental and lasting reform, therefore, our institutions must be closed. There must be a move to greater integration of correctional programs with the local community. It is my hope as a Commissioner of Youth Services, that Massachusetts will become the first state to have a regionally-based correctional treatment program.

In approaching correctional reform in Massachusetts, it seems evident that one has to move in three different ways. The first step is to win public support for reorganization. Someone from the department's central staff regularly travels throughout the state, talking about the old system and what needs to be done to change it. Through this public educational process, it is believed that the public will move dramatically. If community integration of correctional programs can be established, they have a potential to reeducate the public as to who and what "criminals" and "delinquents" are in a variety of social roles other than those of "inmates." Community settings can provide the environment for the beginnings of a democratic process within corrections.

Second, administrators must try to do as much as possible within the law to change the system. A great deal can be done administratively in correctional reform. Administrators must be cool and in a sense manipulative and must use the laws as creatively as possible. They should also take the initiative to integrate correctional programs as closely as possible with local communities.

Third, legislatively, attempts must be made to enact and codify some of the changes being made. Administrative changes last only as long as the administrator making them, or as long as he is there to implement them. It is important, therefore, that administrative changes are codified into law.

In order to change the present political nature of diagnosis, the helping professions will need to develop a philosophy of diagnosis and treatment that is consistent with a democratic society. This should include a feedback role for the professional as he brings the perceptions of the client to the larger society. In this sense, the clinician should be wary of any treatment of criminal behavior without having to consider or deal with its causes.

Finally, crucial to significant reform of the correctional system will be the growth and development of the inmate and ex-inmate organizations. Despite their newness and limited influence, these movements hold the most promise for reform of the system. They provide the beginnings of participation of the inmates in their own future. Inmate organizations could provide the first effective "inside agitators" who will bring pressure for substantive change and movement out of institutional settings. The future of corrections will be set by its ability to use the best structures rather than the worst impulses of our society. If this can be allowed, not only will we see basic reform, but we will possess a correctional system which enhances our own humanity.

## References

1. G.H. Mead, "The Psychology of Punitive Justice," AMERICAN JOURNAL OF SOCIOLOGY 23 (1918): 577; Talcott Parsons et al., eds., Theories of Society (New York: Free Press of Glencoe, 1961), II, p. 876.

2. R.D. Laing, "The Obvious," in D. Cooper, ed., TO FREE A GENERATION (New York: Macmillan, 1968), p. 18.

3. Ibid., p. 18.

4. R.D. Laing, THE POLITICS OF EXPERIENCE (Middlesex, England: Penquin 1968), p. 100.

# 2

## The Creation of a New Network of Services for Troublesome Youth

John M. Martin

For almost two hundred years in the United States the large congregate institution has been the hub around which the rest of an essentially coercive and punitive penal apparatus has rotated. Beginning in the middle and late 1800s, probation and parole began to be used more and more as substitutes for incarceration, but the central feature of penal life remained the large residential institution where offenders were isolated and removed from the general community.

In more recent decades, of course, penology has been renamed corrections, and children and adults have been confined separately. Separate probation and parole services for children have also been established, as well as a separate court and trial procedure. Lately, half-way houses, group homes, and various types of work camps have been developed for delinquents, both youthful, and, to some degree, adult offenders. Yet the large residential institution has continued to play a major role in both juvenile and adult corrections.

Very recently, however, a social movement has evolved which, gathering headway, is seeking to reduce drastically the proportion of adjudicated court delinquents committed to training schools and other large institutions for care. Significantly, the same movement is trying to reduce sharply the absolute number of children who are dealt with by the juvenile court in the first instance.

It is important to note that this movement is national in scope, and that convincing evidence of its progress may be found in many different jurisdictions across the country. At the federal level, the Youth Development and Delinquency Prevention Administration of the Department of Health, Education and Welfare, one of the sponsors of this conference, has given special priority to the development of what are called *youth services systems*. These are systems at the local level designed specifically to cut down drastically on the number of youth entering the juvenile justice system or being dealt with by means of traditional correctional programs.

The first stages of the movement being described have been linked by some commentators to the early 1960s when the federal government first began to spend larger and larger amounts of money in the delinquency field on demonstration and other projects geared to improving conditions in local jurisdictions. Other observers have noted that the movement seemed to evolve as social scientists, as distinct from psychiatrists and other clinicians, began to play more significant roles in policy-making decisions in the field at the federal and local levels. Certainly the vigorous interest lawyers have shown in recent years in the reform of the juvenile court has been an integral part of the movement.

A growing awareness that faults lie in the basic models upon which the juvenile court and juvenile corrections are built forms the intellectual backbone of this movement. Thus its ultimate goal is the abandonment of existing models and the development of radically different and new ones to take their place. This is drastically different from the goals that formerly dominated criticism in the juvenile justice field, which, for example, for a long time tried to decide such problems as how many cases should constitute a maximum parole caseload and whether or not probation was social casework.

At the risk of oversimplification, it may make some sense to try to identify several of the premises out of which the new movement for the reform of the juvenile justice system has emerged. First, critics of the juvenile court and of juvenile corrections are now aware that they must look at how such organizations actually function and at what the consequences of such functioning are for the children involved, rather than at how such systems declare they are supposed to function, and at what they say their results are supposed to be. In brief, critics have learned to look at the realities of such systems, and not to be put off by the partisan rhetoric used to justify their existence. This rigorous and empirical type of examination has raised serious questions about due process and other legal issues as they relate to the juvenile court. And it is from this perspective, too, that critics have become concerned about the unanticipated, but nonetheless stigmatizing, consequences of official action against any child.

Second, a sharp shift in orientation regarding the causes of delinquency has taken place as environmental conditions impinging in a destructive way upon youth have become accepted as more significant for policy-making than views which focused essentially on the so-called inherent defects of delinquents. As a result, emphasis has been placed on the various social processes, including those characteristic of the juvenile justice system itself, which serve to isolate and to deny access to socially acceptable roles to many young people, especially those who become labeled as society's misfits.

Third, the movement has accepted the view that underlying social conflict is characteristic of a wide variety of adult-child relationships in modern society. Further, the movement seems aware that perhaps no better illustration of how adults dominate and coerce young people can be found than in the day-to-day workings of the juvenile justice system. Here the ultimate sanction of the state is applied to youth who have been defined by the adult world as troublemakers.

Fourth, critics and skeptics of traditional juvenile justice programs and practices have accepted as fact that, based on the best existing evidence, no effort to rehabilitate delinquents or to prevent delinquency seems to work very well. Further, it is believed that the deeper young offenders are brought into the juvenile justice system, the fewer are their chances for eventual rehabilitation.

Within this framework, of course, commitment to a training school for a juvenile is considered the very end of the line, and the most harmful disposition a judge can make of his case.

Fifth, and lastly, critics have recognized the social class and racial dimensions of the juvenile justice system. That is, they realize that juvenile courts and juvenile correctional agencies deal essentially with the children of the poor and with minority group children. This occurs not because such children commit more illegal acts than the children of more affluent and influential groups, but because the latter possess alternative child-care systems which largely eliminate the need for the intervention of the juvenile justice system. By definition, the poor and the minorities have no such assets, or if they do, are seldom in a position to have them accepted by officials as suitable alternatives to official care.

In sum, critics of the juvenile court and of juvenile corrections are aware that these systems as presently constituted have gross and serious deficiencies which work great harm on the young people touched by them; that the greatest damage of all is done to those juveniles who are committed to training schools, which constitute the custodial heart of the juvenile corrections system; and finally, that both systems deal essentially with the children of the poor and disadvantaged, while other child-care systems are activated to meet the needs of troublemaking juveniles from the more influential classes.

Based on these definitions of reality, a national effort has commenced to find new strategies to provide services for the clientele of the juvenile court and of juvenile corrections. Two ideas dominate this effort. The first is that as many cases as possible should be prevented from entering the juvenile justice system before they make a court appearance. The second is that, subsequent to court, as many cases as possible should be dealt with by a variety of community-based alternatives rather than by being processed into the traditional system and, perhaps, ultimately being committed to large congregate institutions. By following these two policies, a maximum number of youth would be diverted from entering the system at all, while at the same time a maximum number of those who have reached court would be prevented from penetrating too deeply into the core of the system.

Both policies obviously require that satisfactory alternative arrangements be made for those juveniles requiring some sort of service who have either been diverted from court or prevented from penetrating too deeply into the corrections system. And this has not proven to be an easy task. Yet the challenge is being picked up in a variety of jurisdictions. Here in Massachusetts, for example, the need to meet this challenge immediately and in a large-scale way was precipitated by the calculated decision to close down the state training schools and to develop less destructive alternatives on a crash basis.

Clearly, any such drastic restructuring of the juvenile justice system, whether done over time or on a crash basis, raises many questions. Problems of funding and of staffing alternative programs come immediately to mind, as do problems concerning program substance and sponsorship. Then there are questions bearing on strategies for handling the various types of opposition which is bound to arise—for example, opposition from the staffs of institutions which are phased out or closed, opposition from those who believe in close custodial care for offenders, both adult and juvenile alike, and opposition from various legislative and other governmental factions which may disagree for any number of reasons, including those of party interest. The list of questions becomes very long indeed.

One limitation involved in improving the present juvenile justice system seems, however, to warrant special mention. Basically this system provides care to the children of the poor and the disadvantaged who have been officially defined as troublesome. Similar children from more influential groups receive care from alternative child-service systems and are shielded from the consequences of contact with a publicly operated justice system. How can any publicly operated system afford the same advantages to the children of the poor who have been defined as troublemakers as those offered by the alternative systems used by more influential groups to their clientele?

The very statement of the question suggests the inescapable answer. No real solution seems possible. Public care for the poor seems inevitably to work more hardships on its recipients than private care for the rich. The juvenile justice system is inherently discriminatory, not by design but by consequence. These realities underscore the wisdom of a public policy that stresses diversion from the juvenile justice system and the avoidance of penetration into the system for as many children as possible. Viewed from this perspective, unless designed as an instrument of social repression, any policy which does not seek to establish less ruinous substitutes for traditional juvenile correctional programs, especially those represented by large congregate institutions, is simply unacceptable.

# 3

## Community Services and Residential Institutions for Children

**Martin Gula**

Community services have always lagged for troubled and handicapped children in the United States. The consequences of this lag have been many. Most awesome has been the growth of large, custodial public residential institutions for so-called dependent, delinquent, retarded, and emotionally disturbed children—children who come to these institutions frequently because services are missing in the community.

Can this lag be turned around so that community services become an effective base for screening, planning, and programming for handicapped children, and, as a consequence, modify, reduce, or eliminate congregate public institutions?

We will never know unless we try. And the first vigorous efforts to make this turnaround are showing promising results in mental retardation, delinquency, mental health, and child-welfare programs.

### Problem

Almost a half million children and youth spend some time in 24-hour residential institutions each year. The cost to taxpayers and parents is at least three billion dollars annually. The benefits to children, families, and communities are uncertain, even when measured by private, well-staffed institutions with individualized programs for children.[1]

The consequences for children in public custodial institutions are alarming, when one considers the gross delinquency recidivism in state training school graduates and prolonged dependency in retarded youngsters in state schools. These are hardly indicators of cost benefits.

To be sure, there are some fine public residential schools, but they are comparatively few in number.

This multi-billion-dollar annual expenditure for custodial institutions increases each year, an expenditure that relentlessly diverts funds from potentially more constructive community services and alternative community resources for 24-hour care, such as group homes and foster homes.

### Precedents

In the early part of this century, a few communities began to establish alternatives to institutions. The landmarks are worth noting.

13

In 1916, a New York Jewish orphanage established a group home for adolescent girls on a residential street to help prepare "orphanage" girls for community living.

In the 1930s, social security legislation established financial aid to families with dependent children, child-welfare services, and public adoption and foster-family care as alternatives to orphanage care for neglected and dependent children. The alternatives worked. Orphanages emptied half their beds in the next few decades. However, institutional beds for delinquent, retarded, and emotionally disturbed children continued to increase.

In the 1940s, Michigan and New York State delinquency leaders prepared plans for decentralizing custodial state training schools by establishing regional and local services, group homes, and small residential facilities. But the plans died as paper plans because society, its legislators, and its organizations were not ready for this reorientation.

In the late 1950s and early 1960s, the Federal Children's Bureau, in cooperation with other national organizations, launched a drive to develop group homes and related community services as alternatives to custodial institutions.[2] Since then, residential group homes, serving seven to twelve children and located in community neighborhoods, have multiplied rapidly under child welfare, delinquency, retardation, and mental health organizational auspices. There may be as many as 50,000 children currently living in such community facilities, who might otherwise be in congregate institutions.

## Community Service Systems

Now, in the 1970s, the time may be right for establishing community-based service systems that have never rooted before. These include community mental health centers, regional mental retardation centers, the eight "impact" cities designated by the Law Enforcement Assistance Administration for delinquency prevention and institutional alternatives, and the newly conceived social service delivery systems and health delivery systems. Each is challenging and urging traditional services to combine their efforts to establish comprehensive, community-based service systems. Perhaps the most ambitious of these efforts has been launched in Palm Beach County, Florida, where a combined health and social service system is being tested as a national pilot experiment.[3]

The Golden Gate Mental Retardation Center in San Francisco is a dramatic illustration of a community retardation service system displacing custodial state institutions. This center is state-financed and provides about fourteen community services including screening, counseling, referral, monitoring, purchase of services from private or public facilities, and stimulation of new services. The center determines which children need care in the existing state institutions. Referrals to these institutions have been reduced by 25 percent in the last two years. In fact, no referrals are made to state institutions unless the institution can prove in advance that it has a desirable program for a given child being considered for residential services.

Similar community service systems for retarded children are being affected in Michigan with special legislative appropriations to demonstrate the feasibility of filling gaps in community services including counseling for parents, foster family homes, sheltered workshops, and residential group homes. Montana has established its Eastmont Training Center, a pioneering project that combines day services and five-day residential programs to permit children to maintain strong ties to their families and home communities on weekends.

The Tennessee Department of Corrections, in cooperation with the Kennedy Research Center at Peabody College, is establishing a model community-based program to serve as a constructive alternative to "incarceration" of mentally retarded adolescents in juvenile correction facilities. Records of over 1,000 adolescents placed in Tennessee correction facilities revealed that 52 percent of the residents achieved IQ scores of 85 or below and 18 percent had scores of 70 or below on group administered tests.

Community service delivery systems are being promoted under mental health auspices in order to reduce the numbers of emotionally disturbed children and youth placed in state and county public mental hospitals, sometimes in wards with adult patients in advanced states of mental deterioration.[4]

Prior to the 1970s, local and state efforts at establishing preventive community services as alternatives to institutionalization were accelerated by a variety of federal grants under such legislation as the Mental Retardation Facilities and Community Mental Health Center Construction Act of 1963; the Community Mental Health Centers Act of 1965; the Neighborhood Facilities Program of the Housing and Urban Development Act of 1965; and the Juvenile Delinquency Prevention and Control Act of 1968.

However, at the time of this presentation, fragmentation and proliferation of human services prevail in the nation, complicated by vertical-categorical funding of separate programs by federal, state, and local appropriating bodies. An effective local human service system is still in the conceptualization stage.

The late 1970s and early 1980s may witness beginning efforts at interlocking categorical service systems (delinquency, mental health, etc.) into allied service systems. This move may be strengthened by current class action suits establishing constitutional rights to services for handicapped children and youth, as well as current efforts to ameliorate harmful labeling and categorization of children for service purposes. Federal, state, and local advocacy groups for handicapped children and youth may eventually combine their efforts in behalf of allied service systems.

## Opposition to Community Service Systems

A community-oriented service system does not root in a community unless some very favorable forces accompany the initiation.[5] This includes: dedicated leadership; support by legislative or executive commitment; sufficient funds to effect quantitative services; and a public strategy that gradually wins more supporters than opponents. Opponents will protect custodial institutions because of tradition, habit, protection of institutional jobs, fear of what impact handicapped children will have on neighborhoods, or reluctance to surrender the segregation and punishment that institutions provide. Perhaps the basic fear is that the community service system will put all aggressive, disturbed, and multiply handicapped children back on the streets with no consideration or protection for their neighbors.

For this reason, a viable community service system must, in advance, prepare its 24-hour residential alternatives to custodial institutions for the relatively small but real proportion of youngsters who need residential care, specialized services, and controlled conditions. To ignore this component of the community system, one invites the most aggressive pressure to return to old institutional systems when the first few youngsters under a new system commit some flagrant acts in the community.

*Group Homes and Residential Facilities*

Group homes are being used for dependent, delinquent, retarded, and disturbed children and youth. They are variously described as "halfway houses," "hostels," and pre-institutional and post-institutional resources.

The group home must be disengaged from the pre- or post-institutional "axis" to find its proper identity and role in a community service system. The group home must be well conceived, staffed, and programmed or it becomes another custodial, ineffective 24-hour facility.

Moreover, the group home is not a substitute for the 24-hour care that some children need in their own homes, with relatives, with adoptive families, foster families, in small residential treatment facilities in the community, or in specialized hospital centers.

A new group home is probably established each day somewhere in the nation, under public or private welfare, mental health, mental retardation, or delinquency auspices. Family dwellings, apartments, high-rise and public housing units are being used for this form of 24-hour care.

Group home costs vary with the quality of staff, program, and regional cost variations. Operating costs for group homes of good quality can be higher than costs for congregate custodial institutions, although the difference is reduced when costs of capital expenditures and maintenance in state institutions are included.

There is no justification for spending $20 a day for group home care for a youngster who more properly needs foster family care, at perhaps half the cost to the taxpayer; or, care in the home of a relative on a fee basis.[6]

*The Look Ahead*

Today, no more than a dozen states have established the basic components of viable community service delivery systems for dependent, retarded, delinquent, or disturbed children. Will the 1970s and 1980s really effect a moratorium on expanding custodial institutions in favor of such community service systems?

There are reasons to be optimistic, including (1) increasing television and newspaper exposure of the evils of custodial institutions; (2) legal challenges to commitment of youngsters to institutions; (3) the higher quality and costs inherent in a child's right to treatment when separated from the community; (4) the successful precedent of closing orphanages for dependent children; (5) the beginning successful testimony of regional mental retardation centers in reducing commitments to institutions; (6) the persistent federal emphasis on institutional alternatives for federal funding; (7) state appropriations redirected toward less costly community alternatives from large custodial institutions that drain state revenues;[7] (8) disenchantment with traditional medical modalities and the use of professional personnel in favor of paraprofessionals, as well as group approaches and behavior-modification techniques; (9) a slow but growing inclination of taxpayers and citizens to open more community possibilities for helping handicapped children; and (10) the expansion of child advocacy groups.

If the nation experiences a stabilization or modest growth in child population in the 1970s and 1980s, community service systems may well reverse the increasing number of retarded and disturbed children coming to public and private institutions and hospitals, and reduce the numbers of children in all custodial institutions by at least one-third.

This in itself will be a considerable achievement. It is to be hoped that expanded community service systems will go a long way toward improving conditions in the present-day institutions and alleviate the need for many of them in the future.

**References**

1. Allerhand, Weber, and Haug, ADAPTATION AND ADAPTABILITY: THE BELLEFAIRE FOLLOWUP STUDY (New York: Child Welfare League of America, 1966), 188 pp.

2. Martin Gula, CHILD CARING INSTITUTIONS—THEIR NEW ROLE IN COMMUNITY DEVELOPMENT OF SERVICES (Washington, D.C.: Children's Bureau, D/HEW, 1958), 27 pp.; AGENCY-OPERATED GROUP HOMES, 1960, 35 pp.; AGENCY-OPERATED GROUP HOMES—A CASEBOOK, 1965, 89 pp.; Kenneth Carpenter, HALFWAY HOUSES FOR DELINQUENT YOUTH, 1963; Michael Begab, THE MENTALLY RETARDED CHILD—A GUIDE TO SERVICES OF SOCIAL AGENCIES, 1963.

3. Comprehensive Service Delivery System, sponsored by Social and Rehabilitation Service, HEW, and Florida Health and Rehabilitative Service Administration.

4. Joint Commission on Mental Health of Children, CRISIS IN CHILD MENTAL HEALTH: CHALLENGE FOR THE 1970s (New York: Harper & Row, 1970), p. 269.

5. Seymour Sarason; George Zitnay; and Frances Grossman, THE CREATION OF A COMMUNITY SETTING (Syracuse University, Division of Special Education and Rehabilitation, 1972), p. 9.

6. David Fanshel, and Eugene Shinn, DOLLARS AND SENSE IN THE FOSTER CARE OF CHILDREN: A LOOK AT COST FACTORS (New York: Child Welfare League of America, 1972).

7. Robert Smith, A QUIET REVOLUTION—PROBATION SUBSIDY (Washington, D.C.: U.S. Department of Health, Education and Welfare, Social and Rehabilitation Service, Youth Development and Delinquency Prevention Administration, 1971), 90 pp.

# 4

## Delinquency in Girls: Implications for Service Delivery

Carole Upshur

The study of delinquent behavior in adolescent girls has long been neglected, both because of the absence of general interest in women's studies until very recently, and because girls make up only about 20 percent of the juvenile court population. Recent theories propose that there are two basic reasons for delinquent behavior, (1) the lack of opportunity for certain minority groups of youth to obtain desired educational, recreational, and vocational achievements legitimately, and (2) the existence of a criminal subculture in which deviant acts become the norm (Glueck,[1] Kvaraceus,[2] Cloward and Ohlin[3]). Girls' crimes, however, rarely indicate the striving for power, status or money which disadvantaged boys seek through forming gangs, stealing cars, and committing burglary. Rather, girls most commonly act-out by running away, refusing to obey parents, truanting from school, and engaging in promiscuous behavior.

Further, girls rarely form gangs except as auxiliaries to boys' gangs, and they generally perform passive roles such as providing alibis, sexual favors, or hiding weapons; they are usually not directly involved in the criminal gang subculture. Neither of the recent delinquency theories thus adequately explain the patterns of female acting-out. There remains widespread lack of understanding about the causal factors in female delinquency and inability to provide adequate rehabilitation services for those girls who are before the nation's juvenile courts.

### An Emerging Theory

In developing a theory of female delinquency, one must draw from a few inadequate studies, sparse statistics, and unsystematic personal experience. When these are combined, however, they point to three major causal factors: disturbed family dynamics, the unfulfilling nature of the traditional role of women in a male-dominated society, and the negative social reaction given to women who do not conform to the traditional roles. Difficulty in achieving healthy heterosexual relationships and satisfactory sex role behavior may be due to disturbed family patterns such as absence of a father, the existence of a criminally or mentally deviant father, or a mother who pushes the girl into premature sexual activity as a fulfillment of her own fantasies.

This difficulty can be overcome if a girl has the opportunity and is reinforced

19

for exploration of talents, skills, and special interests around which to focus her identity. However, many girls are taught that their major life task is to find an acceptable marriage partner and raise a family. Activities that do not fall in the traditional pattern of preparation for these roles are regarded as "unfeminine." The girl is then in a double bind, unable to express her interests and talents on one hand, and on the other hand forced into a role that is uninteresting and unfulfilling.

Fewer boys meet this same problem at puberty both because social expectations of their heterosexual conduct are less confused and because they are encouraged and reinforced in developing many skills and talents around which to base their identity. Thus adolescent girls may turn to acting-out when they cannot, or will not, conform to normal expectations of female heterosexual behavior and *also* are not reinforced in developing other skills or activities around which to build an identity.

The third factor comes into play when once a girl has stepped out of the boundaries of acceptable behavior, she is not given a "second chance." Delinquent behavior on the part of boys is often dismissed as just "being a boy" or "sowing wild oats." A girl, however, is condemned by peers, parents, officials, and potential teachers and employers alike, leaving her with little incentive to strive for more acceptable behavior.

These three factors, disturbed family patterns, the unfulfilling nature of the traditional female role, and sexist attitudes, are added to any racial or socioeconomic disadvantages a girl may also bear. Thus they explain why work with delinquent girls is much more difficult than with boys. A delinquent girl's attempt at development of a meaningful lifestyle is more complex: she is told by a sexist society that she is no longer fit to assume traditional roles of being a wife and mother, yet she is given fewer acceptable alternatives for new behavior. Once it is understood that sexism plays a significant role in female acting-out, however, the matter of developing rehabilitative services that will meet girls' needs is relatively simple.

*Supportive Data*

**Disturbed Family Dynamics.** Family dynamics plays a more important role in female than male delinquency because, as mentioned above, the male's development of heterosexual relationships and a fulfilling sex role identity is easier. Psychoanalysts postulate that since the male's original love object, his mother, is the same sex as his potential adult love objects, he must merely transfer the love for his mother to other appropriate females beginning at puberty. A girl, however, must complete a complicated process of breaking the tie to her mother, and transferring it to her father, so that she may eventually have normal heterosexual impulses. This process is made more complicated for the girl when her father is absent or deviant. That this may be a significant factor in female delinquency is supported by data from Monohan's study of 44,000 children appearing in Philadelphia courts: only 29 percent of the girls had both parents at home, as opposed to 51 percent of the boys.[4]

However, it must also be understood that the male role of dominance is a desirable role, and one that includes no conflicting messages about sexual behavior. After the latency period, during which girls and boys both are encouraged to develop skills and expand their knowledge and control of their environments, the coming of puberty is stressed as a time when children must begin to learn traditional roles. Girls are suddenly told that they must be submissive, passive, and that they must be attractive to boys but not engage in sexual relations. Boys are encouraged and praised for their athletic, intellectual, and sexual victories. It is no wonder that some girls rebel upon reaching adolescence.

The psychoanalysts also point out that the acting-out behavior of the girl may differ according to the particular family constellation. Blos[5] and Robey[6] postulate four different patterns. In fatherless families, premature heterosexual involvement of a girl is often a reaction to a homosexual pull to the pre-Oedipal mother. Without a male figure to become the object of the girl's love, the transference to healthy heterosexual relationships is difficult. In other cases, the father is either absent, extremely weak, or criminally or mentally deviant. The girl blames the mother for "destroying" her father image, and continually acts out to find partners to fulfill the "good father" role. Another pattern is acting-out to deny something that has happened in the past, i.e., upon finding out that her father is not dead, but in jail, or being told she is adopted, a girl attempts to escape the truth through intense denial.

The fourth pattern of female acting-out, that of running away, is often an attempt to solve the problem of unconscious incest feelings incited by the mother. Robey[7] describes this pattern as stemming from the mother's push for the girl to engage in premature dating and close relationship with the father (so that the younger and prettier daughter can take her place where she has now grown older and unattractive). The father reacts by being restrictive and accusative of the girl since he projects his own fears of sexual involvement. The girl reacts by following through on his accusations by running away with inappropriate partners and engaging in sexual intercourse. Illustrative case studies of these four patterns can be found in works by Vedder and Kovar.[8]

These patterns can also be explained in terms of a struggle by the girl for dominance and independence. In a fatherless family, or one in which the father is weak or deviant, the girl may not see her mother acting in a traditonal manner of submission to a male. The mother may be the head of the family, the breadwinner and dominant personality. When the girl reaches puberty, however, both her mother and her peers expect her to follow traditional dating patterns and behave in a submissive manner towards males. Her family history has left her totally unprepared for this and quite naturally she may act out in denial of the traditional female role. In the case of restriction and accusation by a strong father, the girl may feel she is being treated in this manner only because of her sex and resents the intrusion by her father in her development of an independent personality. She acts out to demonstrate that she as an independent being can make decisions which her father, no matter how often he tells her are wrong, can do nothing about.

**The Unfulfilling Female Role.** Data from two different studies provide support for the idea that all girls are adversely affected by the focus on family, motherhood, and a life of service to a man, which inevitably means the lack of development of a strong individual identity. Frank et al. administered five projective tests to 100 young girls, ages 10-18, drawn from different SES levels in New York public schools. He found that "activities of girls arise from a strong desire to please, implying a lack or a denial of personal desires and interests. . . ."[9]

He found widespread fear of life, fear of growing up, fear of sex, and more frequent and severe emotional disturbance than expected. Further, he noted that there was confusion about the feminine role, especially in girls who had "high intellectual capacity or performance," because these are "generally considered masculine." He concludes:

There is noticeable absence of being happy or even satisfied to be feminine and little or no indication of positive expectations of becoming a woman. [p. 203]

Thus Frank illustrates clearly that the feminine role is one not looked upon favorably by girls, and one which causes a great deal of conflict and anxiety since it traditionally has meant denial of individual talents and strivings.

This culturally reinforced denial and avoidance of learning skills and achieving mastery on the part of girls is clearly shown by Horner's study of 178 college men and women. While it could be assumed that these women were actually able to fulfill some of their need for mastery and competence because they were in college, she found that they had a great deal more conflict and anxiety over their abilities than men: 65 percent of the women versus 10 percent of the men showing such anxiety. This anxiety is evident to the extent that Horner postulates a "motive to avoid success" among women:

consciously or unconsciously, the girl equates intellectual achievement with loss of femininity. . . . If she fails in an achievement oriented situation she is not living up to her own standards of performance; if she succeeds she is not living up to societal expectations about the female role.[10]

Thus the most able girls are most fearful of loss of love, loss of femininity, and loss of popularity if they express their skills and intellect to their greatest extent. Further, it can be seen how Horner's "motive to avoid success" has its roots in the early years of these girls' lives, as they are being conditioned to think of their future roles as wife and mother. Especially at puberty, when the search for an acceptable marriage partner begins, the anxiety of being better, smarter, and more able than a boy may become so great that all intellectual activity and exploration is repressed.

The effect of this emphasis on traditional roles can be more telling on delinquent girls because they less often, whether because of socioeconomic status or family patterns, have other outlets for gratification, aggression, or identity. Scott illustrates this point in a study where he asked groups of delinquent and nondelinquent girls to list the happiest moments of their lives.[11] The nondelinquent girls listed an achievement, election, or romance, in that order, while delinquent girls listed a family event, school attendance, or closeness to a parent. The delinquent girls remain more entirely focused on traditional female events, while nondelinquent girls also list aggressive and active events requiring development of mastery and skill. The absence of mention of a "romance" or a relationship with a boy by the delinquent girls further indicates their difficulty in forming positive heterosexual relationships. Their experiences with men are most often frightening and brutal—far from the usual "romantic" and mostly fantasy relationships of nondelinquent girls.

Evidence that delinquent girls in particular are caught in a confusing struggle for identity also comes from their responses to a questionnaire about attitudes toward female roles.[12] A group of eight adjudicated delinquent girls, in response to the question, "How do you feel about a girl who spends most of the time thinking and talking about boys," almost all answered that, "it should not be that important, a girl has to get herself together first." On the other hand, all but two of them failed to give the nonsexist answer to the question, "How do you feel about a woman becoming President of the United States?" The correct answer was, "she would make decisions and policies in the same way as a male President; she wouldn't necessarily be any better or any worse." Other answers circled were, "I wouldn't like it, she might be too emotional and not make good decisions," and, "being a woman might make it hard for her to relate to men who are Presidents of other countries—they might not listen to her."

When such girls make a conscious attempt to "get themselves together," i.e., find out what they really want out of life and begin to take action in that direction, they do not have the types of educational or vocational alternatives that are available to boys. Konopka, in her study of the *Adolescent Girl in Conflict*, cites that the availability to women of mostly the lower paying, boring and repetitive jobs and the lack of meaningful skill training are significant factors in continued acting-out behavior of girls. With only a boring job or an early, thus repressive, marriage to look forward to, a girl has little reason to want to cease her exciting, if destructive behavior. Konopka concludes that "the society's rejection of the status of equality is one of the significant factors in precipitating the adolescent girls into delinquent behavior."[13]

Delinquent girls are very clear in their understanding of the more interesting vocations being unavailable to them, the need for access to better training in order for them to get better jobs, and the contradictions of working for a week or more at a servile job to earn what they would in one evening of prostitution. One of the girls states: "Boys have it better. If they want to work hard, they can work on the roads and they get them decent pay. There is nothing like that for us" [p. 77]. The greatest wish of most of these girls is to be able to have a well paying job that lets them be financially independent of others, and have the freedom to travel and try out new things before marriage and a family. Why does this society make it so difficult for a woman to do this?

**Negative Reactions to Delinquent Girls.** Social attitudes are changing at a rapid pace, however, there still remains, among the majority of people, a limited view of what behavior is appropriate for adolescent girls. Those girls who step outside these limits are highly criticized and develop such low self-esteem as a result that suicide is frequently attempted. In the words of a girl from Konopka's study:

> I've traded love for agony,
> My joy has turned to fear.
> My friends are now my enemies
> My smiles now are tears . . .
> Tonight I'm going to kill myself—
> I'll be better dead!!![14]

That almost all persons are more critical of delinquent behavior on the part of girls than boys is pointed out by Ruth Morris' study of over 200 grade school youth in Michigan.[15] She found that both boys and girls, delinquent and nondelinquent were more condemning of the delinquent behavior of girls than boys. Further, those girls who had engaged in some delinquent behavior expressed more guilt and shame than delinquent boys who, in some cases, boasted of their exploits.

Another effect of sexist attitudes is pointed out by Reiss.[16] He states that especially in working-class neighborhoods, once a girl has engaged in sexual activities somewhat outside the norm, she may no longer have acceptable dating partners. The process begins when peers spread rumors of a girl's "loose" behavior. Peer dating patterns call for girl friends, as possible marriage partners, to be virginal or at the very least without a reputation of giving sexual favors. Thus a girl about whom rumors begin to spread is no longer "steady girl friend" material but rather one to whom a boy goes for sexual favors. This often puts the girl in a position in which she has to give favors in order to gain male companionship. This leads to more and more deviant dating partners and gradually engaging in other acting-out behavior. Once the process begins, it is hard to reverse if the girl stays within the same community, and it often leads to prostitution. Thus the double sex standard that overlooks and even condones early sexual behavior on the part of boys often condemns a girl to prostitution.

That the delinquent girl is the most alienated member of society is pointed out in Bertrand's study of hundreds of Canadian men and women, young and old, delinquent and nondelinquent.[17] She measured the extent to which persons felt as if they were objects, with little power to influence their own lives. She found, as predicted, that delinquent women and girls felt like objects, as opposed to agents (an agent is able to actively determine his or her own life), two to three times as often as nondelinquent men and almost twice as often as nondelinquent women. The reasons she gives are that delinquent women fulfill "latent and implicit" functions of society which are not allowed to become openly recognized. Thus the respect that a wife and mother obtains through her power in the child-rearing and household management roles is denied to the acting-out woman—the prostitute, the accomplice to a male burglary ring, the stripteaser.

Ironically, the behavior of a girl labeled "delinquent" and the behavior of other adolescent girls may not differ that much. However, the process of labeling a girl a "delinquent" has implications for her in this sexist society far beyond that for a boy with the same label. Attitudes toward women today have still not changed sufficiently to spare these girls years of negative experiences because of their past behavior.

*Implications for Service and Treatment for Delinquent Girls*

**The Training School.** The training school experience is the worst possible experience for a delinquent girl. She is isolated from normal peers, put in with other girls who may be older and more deviant, and generally treated with scorn and disgust by the matrons. The devastating effect on the self-image of the girl is described in the previous section—extreme guilt and shame, a feeling of being condemned for life, and serious attempts at suicide.

A common result of this isolation from normal adolescent behavior is to leave the girl without any friendships or ties to normal adolescents and their activities. The process of constant evaluation and exploration of new ideas which all adolescents engage in helps to shape future behavior for each member of a peer group. When all the peer relationships of a girl are deviant, she has little chance to discover meaningful alternatives to her acting-out or be reinforced for them. When she does try to break away from the pattern of her deviant peers, they try to bring her back so that they do not have to endure the comparison between their own behavior and that of a former peer group member who has been able to find new alternatives.

The factors of isolation from normal peers and forced association with other acting-out peers who will reinforce a girl for learning more deviant behavior remain as significant reasons for not institutionalizing a girl, regardless of whether there are good facilities or staff at a training school. However, most training schools have neither good staff nor facilities.

Typical staff members at institutions have no more than high school educations and very fixed and highly sexist views of what is appropriate behavior for an adolescent girl. They often are sadistic and even brutal in their relationships with the girls and in their extreme rejection of behavior that sometimes is identical to their own unconscious fantasies. For example, a discussion of past practices in a Massachusetts training school for girls,[18] now being phased out, reports of girls being locked into isolation rooms completely nude.

Facilities at girls' training schools generally show the same neglect as other services for delinquent girls, both in quantity and quality. The more negative attitudes of the society toward acting-out girls and less concern for their rehabilitation due to the nonserious type of crimes they commit, gets translated into fewer staff, less modern buildings, and poorer vocational, educational, and recreational programs than boys' institutions. This is clearly demonstrated in a report by the Center for Criminal Justice at the Harvard Law School on juvenile institutions in Massachusetts.[19] Eighty-six percent of the girls rated their institutional experience as poor or fair as compared to boy's ratings of five boys' institutions where only 21 percent to 41 percent rate their institution as poor or fair (other categories of response were good, excellent, or no response).

The potential for a girl gaining rehabilitative experiences at any training school, no matter how modern, is then very limited. Further, as this paper has indicated, the girl herself is not solely responsible for her behavior; "treating" the girl in isolation from her family and community where early disturbed family dynamics and the influence of sexist attitudes contribute to her acting-out, will not solve the problem in most cases.

In addition, the labeling process and records of commitment to a training school may be major blocks to a girl ever achieving a rewarding pattern of living. In the words of one girl: "I would like to be a nurse, but I am not sure that they take anybody who has been in a training school."[20]

**Community-Based Programs.** It is obvious from the above description of the training school that the answer to treatment of delinquent girls lies in community-based services which deal with the root problems of female acting-out, without the sexist overtones which lead to little else than a lower self-esteem on the part of the girl. The theory outlined in this paper points to four key components to successfully working with delinquent girls: family counseling, vocational and educational programs, sex education, and coeducational programs.

The limits of the success of these programs, however, will depend on the type of staff selected to work with girls. There must be both men and women, but staff of both sexes must fully understand the harm of imposing traditional views of women's roles on these girls and must be trained to aid the girls in developing strong self-images apart from marriage and motherhood.

*Family Counseling.* As pointed out above, one of the basic causal factors of delinquency in girls is disturbed family dynamics. Thus if a girl is to cease her acting-out, her family must be aided in understanding their role in precipitating the behavior, whether it be a mother who has destroyed the girl's father image, or a father who is overly strict and accusative for fear of his own sexual involvement.

Significant change in the girl's behavior can only come about through a program that includes change in the family's behavior and a mutual understanding between both parties as a goal. This kind of counseling is difficult to achieve when the girl is separated from the family and isolated in an institution.

*Vocational and Educational Programs.* The problem of sexual discrimination in areas of skilled, interesting, and higher paying jobs is compounded by the traditional de-emphasis of educational achievement and vocational training for girls. The very nature of the training available to girls has left them unprepared to take good jobs even when they have the motivation and intellectual level to do the work. Delinquent girls are at even more of a disadvantage because of their past behavior.

The sense that girls should follow the pattern of being a secretary or sales girl until such time as they marry and have children is hard to change. The era of forcing girls into taking sewing and typing courses, while only boys can take drafting, metal, and printing shops, however, must end. This again means inclusion of delinquent girls in community-based resources since the training school has neither staff nor facilities to provide adequate vocational or educational experiences such as on-the-job training.

*Sex Education and Woman's Role Education.* It is surprising how little many delinquent girls know about their own bodies, about sexual intercourse, about pregnancy and birth control. Their entrance into adolescence is often frightening and their sexual exploits brutal. They often use damaging practices to abort fetuses they are not sure they are carrying. They do not know what is normal and natural, but only what is deviant and manipulative about sex.

Thus sex education is a very needed part of any program for delinquent girls. They need to have access to information, medical care, and birth control devices so that they can make rational decisions about how to use their own bodies.

But sex education itself does not help resolve the guilt and shame over what they have done, nor does it provide a basis upon which to change future behavior. The more important ingredient of such education is information, discussion, and understanding about the sexist society in which they are more condemned for their behavior than boys, and how to overcome, in their own minds, the stigma that has been attached to them.

Such education must include an understanding of how they have been manipulated by sexist attitudes and how they can become more independent. Emphasis needs to be placed on each girl developing an identity of her own, built on skills and interests. Concrete ways to achieve individual goals must be provided to them so that they have real alternatives to acting-out. This in turn means that staff members working with the girls must work within the community to insure access by the girls to many opportunities now closed to them because of their sex and their past behavior.

*Coeducational Programs.* Coed programs are important for two reasons. First, they provide opportunities for developing normal heterosexual relationships and prevent the high incidence of homosexuality found in many institutional settings. The world is a bisexual place, and enforcing unisexual association limits the possibility of girls developing new behavior that can be carried over to their lives after they leave the auspices of a rehabilitation program. Further, the message that is given to both delinquent boys and girls is that they cannot be trusted to associate with members of the opposite sex for fear of wild sexual adventures occurring at or near the project site. In fact, the few coeducational group homes in Massachusetts have reported that they have had very little problem with sexual relations occurring between boys and girls in their centers. Rather, a positive brother-sister relationship is usually the pattern of behavior that occurs.

A second important reason for coeducational programs is that the tendency to serve mostly boys, who make up 75-80 percent of the juvenile court population, with the limited resources available in most states, generally means neglect of services for girls. An example is the funding patterns of seventeen new group homes in Massachusetts in 1971. Only one serves girls, with two being coed, providing for a ratio of 11 percent service for girls, 86 percent for boys, and resulting in about 50 percent of the girls needing group home placement remaining in undesirable programs. If an emphasis can be placed on coeducational program, it would guarantee that more services would become available to girls.

*Conclusion*

The view on delinquent girls presented here provides a concrete direction to take when talking about programs for prevention as well as rehabilitation. Clearly, delinquent girls do not benefit from being locked up in an institution where their poor self-image is confirmed and where the training programs consist of little else than housekeeping chores. Rather, they need to be encouraged and given the opportunity to develop mastery and skill in a number of different areas in an open, community-based setting, such as a group home, alternative schools, and vocational programs. They need to be made aware of acceptable, interesting, and high-paying alternatives to the wife and mother role, and they need to be reinforced for their interests and explorations into these nontraditional areas. They need to develop an identity around interests, skills, and achievement, as well as family life, in whatever area they choose, with their past behavior forgotten rather than constantly condemned. This type of approach will work, however, only to the extent that parents, friends, schools, and the community at large begin to understand and accept a wider variety of behavior from women in general.

### References

1. Sheldon and Eleanor Glueck, UNRAVELING JUVENILE DELIN-QUENCY (New York: The Commonwealth Fund, 1950).

2. William C. Kvaraceus, DYNAMICS OF DELINQUENCY (Columbus, Ohio: Charles Merrill, 1966).

3. Richard A. Cloward and Lloyd Ohlin, DELINQUENCY AND OPPOR-TUNITY (New York: Free Press of Glencoes, 1960).

4. T.P. Monohan, "Family Status and the Delinquent Child," SOCIAL FORCES 35: 250-258.

5. Peter Blos, in FAMILY DYNAMICS AND FEMALE SEXUAL DELIN-QUENCY, Pollack and Friedman, eds. (California: Science Behavior Books, 1969).

6. Robey et al., "The Runaway Girl," AMERICAN JOURNAL OF ORTHOPSYCHIATRY 34 (1964): 762-67.

7. Ibid.

8. Lillian Kovar, FACES OF THE ADOLESCENT GIRL (Englewood Cliffs, New Jersey: Prentice-Hall, 1968, p. 91). The case of Sally indicates the possibility of a homosexual pull towards her mother which was overcome by very early sexual relations. Clyde B. Vedder and Doris B. Somerville, THE DELINQUENT GIRL (Springfield, Ill.: Charles Thomas, 1969), pp. 103-108 and 75-77 describe the cases of Leslie, a girl in search of a father figure, and Jane running away as a result of incest anxiety.

9. Lawrence Frank et al., "Personality Development in Adolescent Girls," SOCIETY FOR RESEARCH IN CHILD DEVELOPMENT, no. 53 (1951): 180.

10. Matina Horner, "Fail Bright Women," PSYCHOLOGY TODAY (Nov. 1969), p. 37.

11. Edward M. Scott, "Happiness: A Comparison between Delinquent and Non-Delinquent Girls," PSYCHOTHERAPY 4 (1967): 78-80.

12. Carole Upshur, unpublished thesis data.

13. Gisela Konopka, THE ADOLESCENT GIRL IN CONFLICT (Englewood Cliffs, New Jersey: Prentice-Hall, 1966), p. 82.

14. Ibid., p. 96.

15. Ruth Morris, "Attitudes Toward Delinquency by Delinquents and Non-Delinquents," BRITISH JOURNAL OF CRIMINOLOGY, No. 5, (1965-66), pp. 249-65.

16. Albert Reiss, "Sex Offenses of Adolescents," in READINGS IN JUVENILE DELINQUENCY, Cavan, ed. (Philadelphia: Lippincott, 1964), pp. 268-272.

17. Marie Bertrand, "Self-Image and Delinquency," ACTA CRIMINO-LOGICA 2 (1969): 71-144.

18. Cecilia McGovern, "Visit to the Industrial School for Girls," unpublished paper, 1960.

19. Center for Criminal Justice, Harvard Law School, PROGRESS REPORT ON DEPARTMENT OF YOUTH SERVICES STUDY, Dec. 1971.

20. Konopka, ADOLESCENT GIRL, p. 79.

# 5

## Youth Service Systems: New Criteria

**Robert M. Foster**

Community services were being provided as an alternative to incarcerating delinquents in Boston more than 100 years ago by John Augustus, the man who is credited with "inventing" probation. He was the first man, not only in the United States, but in the world, who got court officials to let him try to rehabilitate delinquents whom they would otherwise have sent to jail. His 1852 report, entitled "The Labors of John Augustus for the Last Ten Years," describes a program of services—foster homes, job placement, use of volunteers— that is as modern as many a community has today.

The most dramatic evidence that Massachusetts' pioneering did not end with John Augustus is that it has taken the plunge no other state has yet dared to take. I refer, of course, to its decision to close all of its institutions for delinquent youth.

Present research and information indicates that locking youngsters up in institutions does more harm than good, that it is costly, and that the longer a youth stays in an institution the more likely he is to pursue a career of crime. But old ideas die slowly, and it may well be due to its long record of pioneering that Massachusetts was able to take this sensible step.

Everyone concerned is wondering what impact the release of these youngsters is having upon community programs—police departments, health, and various other treatment and rehabilitation services. Keeping youngsters out of institutions, even if the community is not geared to serve them, is all to the good. To take one further step and rescind the provision that the delinquent must be committed to the state—and thus labeled a delinquent—would be even better.

But both of these measures fall into the category of simply refraining from taking harmful actions. What about the positive measures of building up and maintaining the communities?

### Capacity to Provide Preventative and Treatment Services

Determining a strategy is one thing, but implementing it is even tougher. It is this nuts and bolts part of the job that I want to discuss here.

The mechanism the Youth Development and Delinquency Prevention Administration (YDDPA) would like to see adopted by every community in every state

33

is a youth services system that will divert youth from the juvenile justice system by providing comprehensive, integrated, community-based programs designed to meet the needs of all youth, regardless of who they are or what their problems may be. We envision a nationwide network of such systems, jointly planned and funded by local, state, and federal agencies. YDDPA is prepared to use its expertise, its relative neutrality among agencies that provide functional services—health, welfare, and so forth—and some of its leverage money to identify gaps and provide bridges between those service providers. It also minimizes the risk of further stigma to the target population because programs that meet their specific needs are integrated into services offered to the total youth population.

A youth services system has eight major characteristics, each one of which is designed to remedy a serious deficiency in programs as they now operate in most communities.

The first and foremost characteristic is integration of services. Services for youth are entirely too fragmented today. All too often the various agencies that may be serving a youngster do not know what the others are doing, and frequently they duplicate or even work at cross-purposes. Under a youth services system, contractual and other formal arrangements are required that will assure a genuinely integrated approach.

Another characteristic is adaptability. Too many agencies are not geared to make the rapid shifts in policies and programs demanded by today's rapidly changing social scene. The interaction among the agencies making up a youth services system stimulates them to work out viable programs. They are in a situation where it actually becomes easier to maintain a flexible, adaptive posture than to continue the traditional, static posture that many of them now find so comfortable.

A youth services system must also have scope. It must serve all youth in the area regardless of who they are or the nature of their problems. The youth who just walks in must get the same quality of service that is given to one who is referred by some prestigious agency. Long waiting lists, eligibility requirements, and other barriers to service have no place in a truly comprehensive program.

Two other characteristics of a youth services system indicate why we can be sure that the system will have scope, will be adaptable, and will offer integrated services. Those two characteristics are multigovernmental participation and joint funding.

Under a youth services system, appropriate state agencies and their federal counterparts at the regional level are convened formally and work with the local community to assure that the funds allocated for mental health, vocational rehabilitation or any other relevant service support are known for planning. Moreover, the commitments by these agencies are written right into their state plans, thus assuring that a definite portion of their formula grants will be allocated to the system year after year to maintain it, an assurance lacking when the decision to support a particular project is on a year-by-year basis.

A sixth characteristic of a youth services system has to do with the evaluation and transfer of knowledge. At present, most agencies do not have adequate capacity for evaluation, and what knowledge they do gain about the strengths and weaknesses of their program is not transmitted to others. Thus duplication of effort is often the rule, and one program's errors are repeated by programs throughout the country. Through a strong program of technical assistance at the state and federal levels, the local system's capacity for evaluation will be made available nationwide.

A related characteristic is the use of advanced technology so that positive results in one area can more easily be adopted by other states and communities. This is achieved not only by transmitting information about new approaches, but also by providing technical assistance to help communities adapt the new approaches to their own special needs.

Finally, and this is highly important, a youth services system is characterized by youth involvement. There is presently a great amount of justified criticism that youth themselves are rarely consulted and utilized in planning and carrying out programs that directly affect them. Under a youth services system, youth as the consumer is heavily involved in all phases of policy and program. Youth leadership training is made available, and youth are given important roles in program operation and in the policy-making bodies at all governmental levels.

There are at present twenty-three Youth Services Systems operating in different parts of the country. To visualize what they mean in human terms, I ask you to take an imaginary walk through one of them with a seventeen-year-old boy and contrast what actually happened to him under a youth services system with what you know would probably have happened under our traditional approaches.

This boy is a school dropout, with no job skills. He is estranged from his family and is experiencing the effects of an overdose of LSD. He refuses traditional professional help. However, he comes into the youth services system when he calls a youth-manned hot-line, which is part of the system, and asks to talk to someone about his LSD problem. A sympathetic youth talks him into visiting the hot-line's adjunct crisis center. An ex-addict at the center gets the youth to accept hospitalization. After a few days of intensive contact with the ex-addict, the boy also decides to accept professional help with his other problems.

A social worker at the center then works with the boy in developing a plan that includes counseling for him and his family, tutoring to prepare him for GED, prevocational training, and the removal of tattoos from his hands. The social worker at the center gives counseling service to the boy and a local private agency provides a counselor for his family. A teacher from the local school who has been assigned to the center tutors the boy and the local department of employment gives him prevocational training. A clinic of the local private hospital removes the boy's tattoo marks and this improvement in his appearance helps to build up his self-confidence. Although conseling is not successful in helping the boy and his family to become reconciled, it does help him to understand his problems better and to begin to do something about them. By agreement with the parent and youth a suitable living arrangement is made to a local boarding house.

He is eventually awarded a GED and through the Junior Chamber of Commerce, he obtains a job. Although he is now completely rehabilitated, he maintains his connection with the youth services system—giving volunteer service two nights a week, manning the hotline telephone and thus opening to others the opportunities that were opened to him when he was sick and desperate and called that line.

Behind the scenes, where it all got started in this case, the state vocational rehabilitation agency brought the community to the attention of YDDPA, reporting that it might be a good place to establish a youth services system because adults and youth were working well together on the hotline project. YDDPA's technical and financial assistance helped support the administration of the system and the development of an evaluation component. YDDPA also helped to work out the system of joint funding in the following ways:

1. For the hospital service, special tutoring and prevocational training, YDDPA worked out agreements with other units of the Department of Health, Education and Welfare, (namely the Health Services and Mental Health Administration and the Office of Education), and with the Department of Labor, which facilitated the local arrangements.
2. For the plastic surgery to remove the tattoos and for the family casework and Job Placement Services, YDDPA provided technical assistance to the United Way, to the Family Service Agency and to the private hospital, that maximize their participation in the system.
3. YDDPA, through the local agency which became its prime grantee—in this case, it was the Mayor's Office—made a big difference, not only in the life of this seventeen-year-old boy, but also in the way the community responds to its problems.

This is the kind of action that should occur in every community. In fact, the youth services system is such a logical and feasible approach that we at YDDPA consider it reasonable to expect that such systems will be operating nationwide by 1977.

To help achieve that goal, YDDPA is investing most of its resources in aiding local agencies—mayor's offices, welfare agencies, or any other appropriate organizations—that are prepared to serve as prime grantees. The responsibilities of a prime grantee include seeing that services are coordinated and integrated: monitoring the system to assure that the agencies in the system honor their agreements as to the services and funds they will provide; and performing advocacy functions—making certain that youth's interests and needs are considered in all community planning activities. We see our role as being a developmental one of using our financial resources to attract from $3 to $5 for every $1 that YDDPA provides.

Such systems will of course be costly, but perhaps no more so than the present, fragmented approaches. We estimate that the cost will probably average $1 million or more per system, with the YDDPA share averaging about $225,000. On the other hand, by diverting youth from the juvenile justice system, we estimate that there would be a cumulative saving, nationwide, of almost $1.5 billion by 1977. This estimate is based on the fact that, if present rates of juvenile court referrals continue, there will be 1.5 million juvenile court cases in 1977, whereas, if a substantial number of youth services systems are operating by then, the rates would go down each year so that by 1977 they would be down 25 percent.

The decision to adopt a nationwide strategy focused upon institutional change and to use youth services systems as the instrument for carrying out this strategy was based upon thoughtful analyses of the deficiencies of present efforts to curb delinquency and careful appraisals of the new approach.

However, the actual value of this new approach can only be determined by setting forth clear and specific objectives that the system must achieve if it is to be continued a success and by devising ways to measure the extent to which these objectives are being reached. The objectives decided upon and the methods to be used to measure their achievement are as follows:

1. *Divert youth away from the juvenile justice system into alternate programs.* The measure for this objective will be a statistical procedure reflecting a reduction in the annual rate of juvenile court referrals.
2. *Reduce youth-adult alienation.* Criterion measurements for this objective are in the process of assembly and development.
3. *Provide more socially acceptable and meaningful roles for youth.* Criterion measurements for this will include reduction of school dropout rates, the opening of job opportunities, and the extent of youth involvement and participation in community life.
4. *Reduce negative labeling.* The problem involved in measuring this objective is a field of conceptual exploration at present and is to be followed by formal research in the near future.

The merit of these four objectives is clear. Their achievement would remove the root causes of much of today's delinquency. With a new strategy and a practical mechanism for carrying it out, this nation is better prepared than ever before to mount programs that can reduce delinquency and open meaningful roles to youth who are now denied them. A nationwide network of youth services systems is a feasible goal, and one that would give genuine opportunities for useful, productive living to every American youth.

# 6

## From Institutions to Human Services

Herbert C. Schulberg

Although we clearly perceive the faults of the anachronistic institutional system which we wish to leave behind, the nature and merits of our ultimate destination in human services still remain obscured. Nevertheless, this policy of directed movement away from explicit, even rigidly defined, institutional services for juvenile offenders toward alternative programs in community-based settings is a development whose time has surely come. A review of program evolution for various populations at risk reveals a clear trend away from institutional services, and an increased emphasis upon decentralized, local care-giving arrangements. The tuberculous, the mentally ill, the retarded, the physically handicapped, and the adult offender are but some of the groups whom society, with varying degrees of ambivalence, is reaccepting into its midst.

Assuming the continuation of this trend, it well behooves us to consider the nature of emerging, community-based human services so that the planning and development of local programs for juvenile offenders can be undertaken within this broader context. My presentation, therefore, will review the current array of forces affecting human service activities, the professional's response to the growth of such programs, and the present efforts to establish human service systems which are conceptually sound, organizationally feasible, fiscally viable, and—above all—more effective in meeting people's needs.

There can be little doubt in the minds of even ardent skeptics that the rationale for, and the manner in which, human services are provided in 1972 differs significantly from the patterns of a decade ago. For example, the psychoanalytic precepts that guided the clinician's definition of problems and his assessment of treatment alternatives continue to be well regarded, but they no longer serve as the fundamental cornerstone upon which a mental health program is built. Sociological concepts that recognize environmental influences as well as the principles of learning theory have become equally relevant for structuring services and guiding personnel utilization. Along with the changes in conceptual rationales, we have witnessed related shifts in the professionals' armamentarium; as I have noted, community care rather than institutional services is now the treatment of choice for both acutely as well as chronically disturbed individuals. Furthermore, professionals have to come to accept the fact that they alone cannot resolve all behavioral problems and that the participation of other community care-givers, with varying degrees of sophistication, is essential to their mission. As a concomitant of the professional's growing community orientation, local citizens have gained increased opportunities to help determine program priorities, and we are coming to respect the value of this previously unfamiliar input. Finally, even traditionally intransigent academic training programs have been forced to alter their scope and emphasis to at least some degree, although many curricula continue to reflect anachronistic rather than future-oriented perceptions of where and how their students ultimately will function. In general, however, most indices of practice and training point to the fact that considerable change has occurred during the past decade, and it is clear that contemporary social welfare and correctional concepts and techniques have affected professional care-givers in many significant ways. Most professionals are now aware that American society has reached such a state of complexity, perhaps even chaos, that our usual highly specialized or piecemeal attempts to help clients are clearly outmoded. We increasingly are willing to acknowledge that the problems of the designated client often are as much rooted in his community's tumultuous social structure and fragmented care-giving system as in his personal psyche. Inevitably then, our contributions as individual practitioners will always be severely limited if they do not fit into a broader context.

*The Concept of Human Services*

It is the definition of this broader context which I submit is undergoing change. In the past decade our perspective and activities have expanded from the isolated clinic or agency to more encompassing social welfare and community mental health programs. During the 1970s we will be challenged to evolve our scope even further by designing far-flung human service systems that seek to provide comprehensive and coordinated assistance to clients. These new care-giving systems incorporate the following features: comprehensiveness of services; decentralized facilities located in areas of high population density; and integrated program administration which permits continuity of care from one service element to the next with a minimum of wasted time and duplication.

The increasing tendency to designate a community's variety of health and social welfare services as human service organizations reflects not only the desire to provide services more efficiently but also a growing societal as well as professional recognition of the common denominator inherent in the varied problems presented to us by clients. It also indicates an appreciation for the generic quality integral to the helping actions of professional and non-professional care-givers despite the multiple technologies utilized by them. The long adhered to distinctions between the problems germane to a psychiatric clinic and an alcoholism clinic, for example, or the traditional distinctions between the functions of different mental health professionals have become increasingly artificial, and many agencies have drastically revised their intake policies and clinical practices accordingly. Neighboring child guidance clinics and adult psychiatric clinics are being reorganized as combined family-oriented facilities, and agencies that previously excluded alcoholics, drug addicts, and other special problem cases now routinely accept individuals so troubled.

Furthermore, it is clear that genuinely effective, comprehensive services can be rendered only through the forging of systemic linkages which bring together the various care-giving agencies needed to provide a complex array of resources, technologies, and skills. Defenders of the *status quo* need only to follow a few clients through the present system in order to realize that it is poorly designed for meeting the needs of those it purports to serve. A working mother may easily obtain psychological consultation for her four-year-old child who is enrolled in a Head Start class but encounters severe difficulties in obtaining such services for her three-year-old who is too young for this special program. Similarly, families with multiple problems often receive help for only one of them because the initial agency to which they turn does not diagnose the other problems or is unsuccessful in referring the family to relevant resources. The parents of a developmentally disabled child might well have to negotiate individually with the Departments of Public Health, Mental Health, Public Welfare, and the Rehabilitation Commission to insure that he receives comprehensive services and fiscal assistance.

Despite the bleakness in much of the present situation, we are beginning to see examples of concerted meaningful effort to reorganize program components in such ways that they move beyond the currently fragmented care-giving network. At the heart of these efforts is an implicit, if not explicit, conceptual framework for helping people that recognizes human service programs operate as a system of organizations whose participants are interdependent and must be appropriately linked.

The application of systems concepts to these tasks represents an effort to optimize a rational, planned approach to the development of future care-giving arrangements. Planning has become increasingly sanctioned during the past decade within given categorical fields such as health or social welfare, but with change occurring at an exponential rate, the trend of the 1970s must be to broaden the planning base. Systems concepts are of singular value in providing the means to expand our grasp of a person's functioning and problems beyond the limited scope of a single categorical field, thus encompassing a greater array of human services.

*Operating Human Services Programs*

The characteristics of operating human services programs undoubtedly will assume many novel substantive and administrative features during the coming decade, and as a point of reference, let us assess the current state of program development. In those instances where human services programs are in operation or are being already planned, public health, mental health, and social welfare programs usually are included as key elements. More recently, correctional services are also being considered within this framework because of their heightened public visibility and the increased federal funding available for law enforcement activities. NIMH's effort during the past year to establish closer links with the Department of Justice's LEAA programs reflects an awareness of both the conceptual relations between the mental health and legal fields, as well as the recognition that scarce funds for the expansion of mental health-related activities can be readily obtained through other human service agencies.

Modified or evolving human services programs will develop a variety of structures for providing client services and the following four alternatives are arising at the community level.

**The Information and Referral Center.** This center is based upon a simple concept that has been utilized for over forty years. A small group of generalists receive inquiries regarding any type of problem from the defined community and make appropriate referrals and follow-up based upon their knowledge of available local services. More recently, these centers are emerging at the neighborhood level, perhaps in association with decentralized city halls, and thus are in even closer contact with their clients. Most requests for service are referred to those specialty agencies with which the information center is linked but, obviously, many problems lend themselves to immediate generic assistance, particularly by those staff members skilled in techniques of crisis intervention.

**The Diagnostic Center.** This center is more medically-oriented in conception and design; being based upon the premise that a careful analysis of the client's problems will lead to a more accurate intervention and treatment plan geared to his unique needs. In fact, the advocates of this approach urge that all clients be required to enter the community's organized care-giving network through the diagnostic center so that they can be helped in the most comprehensive and efficient manner possible. Although this model offers the benefit of careful problem analysis and subsequent referral to particularly relevant resources, it suffers from the fact that most clients dislike being referred after extensive diagnostic work-ups.

**Multi-Service Centers.** These centers received much of their impetus from federal legislation that provided funds to establish comprehensive programs meeting certain guidelines. These centers reflect the increasingly accepted rationale that human problems are multifaceted in nature and require multiple care-giving responses rather than a single categorical service. Approximately 200 such centers now exist throughout the country, and within them clients can obtain at a single physical location such diverse services as employment counseling, psychiatric consultation, legal assistance, and information on public welfare benefits. Even though these centers have not achieved an optimal level of comprehensiveness because of continuing categorical funding restrictions, they nevertheless have been instrumental in getting professionals to formally cooperate for the first time in providing high-quality services to inner-city residents.

**Human Services Networks.** These networks focus on building linkages between existing and planned organizations so as to facilitate client services, rather than seeking to incorporate all relevant services within a single agency. This approach recognizes that in most communities it will not be fiscally nor practically feasible for an individual facility to provide by itself all elements of a comprehensive program; in fact, some of the services may already be available elsewhere. The network approach is already evident in meeting the needs of such diverse populations as runaway youths and the elderly. After determining the basic needs of these groups and the essential services for meeting them, a consortium of agencies divided responsibilities according to their particular expertise. The leadership and coordinating tasks are assumed by a single agency and others participate in predetermined ways.

*Implications for Human Service Programs*

A variety of conceptual, political, and administrative forces affect human services programs, seeking to lead them in uncharted directions while simultaneously constraining them from moving too far from established patterns. Although these contradictory pressures create frustrating impasses and tenuous visions of the future, it still is possible to predict that during the coming decade human services programs may well be required to redesign their manpower utilization patterns, their training procedures, their operating practices, and their research foci in some of the following ways.

**Manpower Patterns.** Planners and administrators are assuming that the demand for additional human services personnel will be maintained during the coming years as society's value system evolves from its tradition of solving human problems by custodial welfare measures to a new emphasis upon community-based, service-oriented interventions. Although the additional personnel will successfully fulfill certain program purposes, it is unlikely that increasing the numbers of professionals alone will modify the problems created by maldistributed manpower. The maldistribution has resulted in inadequate services to the poor, minorities, rural folk, children and the aged, and this situation can be partially resolved by recruiting new indigenous manpower from these very same groups. Graduate schools have attracted and enrolled only a small portion of the young adult population possessing the potential for success in the human services, and the time has come to concentrate upon other manpower pools as well.

As training efforts are generated to attract new recruits to the human services field, it will be necessary to monitor and further these developments by emphasizing career growth and guarding against blocked mobility. The manpower challenge, then, is not merely that of generating a new breed of personnel but, more significantly, that of designing an overall training-service system within which individuals of varying ability can productively work toward common goals. The special skills of one group should complement voids in another.

Finally, future human services manpower patterns should emphasize that standards of practice are a function of the specific service to be rendered and not of the practitioner's larger identity. When possible, standards should be established so as to encourage controlled experiments in new modes of manpower use. Excessively high standards often are guises for discriminating against minorities, and in addition they are unheeded.

**Training Programs.** It is evident from the preceding analyses of future manpower patterns as well as from my description of human services trends that training programs will have to alter their scope and emphasis if they are to be aligned with societal demands and evolving job requirements. The need to proceed immediately with this process is highlighted by the fact that educators face a lag of at least five years between the time of their decision to renovate a curriculum and the appearance of graduates reflecting that change.

The urgency of providing contemporary training is made even more critical by considering that the careers of students now being trained for human services will extend into the twenty-first century. Most university programs have already taken steps in the direction of greater relevance to an era of human services, but it would not be excessively harsh to deem many of these measures as more euphemistic than substantive. In the field of community psychology, for example, several innovative graduate programs emphasize contemporary conceptual frameworks and appropriate technical skills, but these revised curricula are the exception rather than the rule.

Although I am stressing the need for human services training programs to expand their curricular foci so as to encompass a broader array of conceptual and programmatic concerns, I fully recognize the impossibility of producing graduates with in-depth expertise across the full continuum of this burgeoning field. With each addition to the professional's purview, the ensuing body of knowledge may coalesce as another subspecialty, or it can stimulate new careers coequal with older professions. The dilemmas which these developments can create for an existing discipline are strikingly evident in Albee's (1970) analysis of the uncertain future of the practicing psychologist. He contends that the problem of growing irrelevance in training and practice has remained largely unresolved, and in fact will become more critical with the passage of time so long as solutions are sought primarily within the intramural framework of psychology. One of the alternatives posed by Albee for the training of psychologists involves the creation of alliances with other professions possessing training facilities, e.g., medical schools, schools of social work, and schools of education. This option deserves support since it begins to recognize that human services increasingly will be provided within multidisciplinary settings.

Training must also proceed apace within live communities. Social workers have long utilized a variety of community-based facilities, but psychiatrists and psychologists have tended to restrict their trainees to affiliated teaching hospitals and counseling centers. The developing fields of community psychiatry and psychology are breaking this pattern, however, and experimenting with new training opportunities. Thus, neophyte professionals are being exposed in their training, for example, to the operations of satellite neighborhood service centers that community health and mental health centers increasingly are using for program decentralization. Although the trainee may experience considerable anxiety when assigned such ambiguous and unfamiliar tasks as coordinating his clinical activities with those of a self-help drug group or negotiating program policy with a nonprofessional citizen board, he ultimately will refine the skills and develop the orientation required to work in a setting where the human services role is determined more by expressed community needs than academic preconceptions.

**Practice.** In reviewing recent human services program trends, it becomes clear that their conceptual rationales and organizational structures are in the throes of change, away from categorical restrictedness and toward broader comprehensive concerns. As these developments proceed, a program's need for both generalist and specialist skills will generate incompatible demands upon human services personnel. This dilemma can be minimized by establishing teams which in their totality include the full range of requisite skills without requiring that any single individual possess all of these capabilities. Thus the team possesses a generalist sophistication in broad program areas while individual members contribute unique personal skills toward the comprehensive effort. Teams assigned the responsibility for human services to designated geographic areas can utilize this functional model of integrated generalists and specialists, and it has met with good success when proper supervisory links are established and maintained.

In addition to the new conceptual principles and technical skills that human services personnel will have to refine for working with unfamiliar client populations, they also will have to develop relationships with previously ignored or unknown colleagues. Bard's work in New York with police officers demonstrates that the staff of the law enforcement system, generally considered averse to contacts with human services professionals, can indeed collaborate as effective psychological intervention agents when supported by consultation. Human services professionals will also be required to negotiate policy issues and job functions with different types of administrators than the fellow professionals to whom they have customarily related. In many parts of the country, the persons assigned responsibility for administering local and statewide human services programs are management specialists and have not been trained in the social sciences or health fields. Being more often concerned with fiscal and bureaucratic considerations than professional prerogatives, these administrators may well demand a reassessment of previously defined professional roles in their quest for maximal client benefits and minimal personnel costs.

**Research.** A recent view by Williams (1971) of the Adult Manpower Training Program within the Office of Economic Opportunity led him to conclude that social science research studies seldom are relevant to the major policy decisions of federal human services agencies. Moreover, Williams contends, the social science research community as presently structured is unlikely to produce a consistent flow of studies relevant to social policy-making for the disadvantaged. Only undue optimism or excessive naiveté could lead one to disagree with Williams' conclusion.

I would like to suggest some contemporary human services research activities which might constitute small but meaningful contributions to the needs of policy-makers and program directors.

As an alternative to the myriad of methodologically sophisticated but barren studies emerging from research on the individual's psyche, greater attention should be paid to the implications of the ecological model that seems to understand and predict behavior within the person-environment system (Barker 1968). From the ecological perspective, most behavior represents a transaction in which a person is influenced by the environment, and the environment, in turn, is influenced by the person's response to it.

Kelly's (1968) study of adaption within high school environments, for example, illustrates the ways in which ecological analyses, considering both personality variables like exploration, and environmental variables like rate of population mobility, can lead to relevant programmatic decisions. The ecological model and its derivative research efforts hold considerable promise and warrant much more of our attention as we grope for recommendations pertinent to the resolution of pressing human problems.

### Conclusions

The finer features of human services programs during the 1970s can only be dimly perceived at present and yet enough of the general outline is evident to recognize that the major characteristics of these programs will include less segmented and more comprehensive approaches to client problems, decentralized facilities closer to population centers, and integrated program administration permitting community care. It is not premature to consider the impact of these developments upon participating personnel, and those issues germane to manpower patterns, training, practice, and research have been highlighted. If we respond appropriately, the human services will remain contemporary and vital; if we do not, our potential successes inevitably will turn to disillusionment and failure.

## References

1. Albee, G. "The Uncertain Future of Clinical Psychology." AMERICAN PSYCHOLOGIST 25 (1970): 1071-1080.

2. Barker, R. ECOLOGICAL PSYCHOLOGY. Stanford: Stanford University Press, 1968.

3. Kelly, J. "Towards an Ecological Conception of Preventive Interventions," in J. Carter, ed., RESEARCH CONTRIBUTIONS FROM PSYCHOLOGY TO COMMUNITY MENTAL HEALTH (New York: Behavioral Publications, 1968), pp. 76-99.

4. Williams, W. SOCIAL POLICY RESEARCH AND ANALYSIS. New York: American Elsevier Publishing Co., 1971.

# 7

## Alternative Models for the Rehabilitation of the Youthful Offender

### I. Ira Goldenberg

Today, as perhaps never before, there exists what might almost be described as a "national movement" aimed at phasing out the existing correctional institutions that house our adjudicated youthful offenders. In the Commonwealth of Massachusetts, for example, the Department of Youth Services, under the leadership of Dr. Jerome Miller, has committed itself and its resources to the single goal of "de-institutionalization"; that is to say, to closing down the state's archaic and often dehumanizing reformatories, and replacing them with smaller, more community-based facilities variously called "halfway houses" or "residential youth centers."

By and large, these efforts have been applauded, particularly by members of the mental health professions, and, despite the fact that de-institutionalization will proceed at an uneven rate (i.e., consistently marked by periodic setbacks and politically-motivated attempts to impede its progress), there is little doubt, at least from my perspective, that sooner or later it will be accomplished. In short, we are approaching that point in time when the youthful offender, even if tried and found guilty of a particular crime, will no longer automatically be sent to some large state facility where his continuing "education in crime" can proceed unencumbered, but will, instead, probably be remanded to a smaller, more personalized community setting where a host of concerned people, both professional and nonprofessional, will be available to help him deal with his "problems." Thus we finally seem to have moved away from a "punitive" model of corrections, toward one which will focus much greater attention on "rehabilitation," more than likely from a predominantly "clinical" perspective.

Let me state at the outset that the purpose of this paper is not to join with those who applaud the shift from a punitive to a clinical model of corrections. Neither, however, do I intend to unceremoniously downgrade nor belittle the change that is finally taking place. Rather, my intent is to both raise what are for me some serious questions about what is happening and to try to provide an alternative model for those of us engaged in the problems posed by juvenile delinquency. First, the serious questions.

### The Context of Change: Current Clinical Assumptions and Their Predictable Consequences

There is little doubt that the shift from punishment to rehabilitation is both warranted and necessary, not only because it is more humane but also because it represents an appropriate response, however long overdue, to the years of accumulated evidence indicating the failure of the punitive approach. Thus we join with others in welcoming this change, for we see it as indicative of some changed and raised consciousness on the part of our society as a whole.

There is also little doubt, however, that the change will result in the increased involvement of the mental health and mental health-related professions in the area of corrections. As was the case with the late-lamented war on poverty, money will almost assuredly soon be "coming down the Pike," and if history be our guide, we can say with some certainty that the mental health professions will be there to get their fair share of the new resources and accompanying power. It is exactly this state of affairs that worries me, for as was the case with the "human renewal programs of the 1960s," I am not at all convinced that the mental health professions currently possess either the conceptions for, or the approaches to, the problems of the youthful offender which do anything but continue to "blame the victim" however different and often dignified the rhetoric. I am, in short, concerned lest the mental health professions as a whole, and community psychology in particular, either wittingly or unwittingly, now come to replace the correctional system as our society's agents of deviance control. For that is exactly what will happen unless and until we examine our existing conceptions of the youthful offender and change the direction of the kinds of rehabilitation models that will invariably result from these conceptions. Let me try to be more specific.

Our current approach to the development of so-called alternative models in the area of juvenile delinquency is predicated on a view of the delinquent act as a particular and idiosyncratic response (variously labeled as "pathological," "anti-social," "maladaptive," etc.) by the adolescent to the universal needs and problems that characterize the transitional and conflict-ridden period of time between late childhood and early adulthood. And, given this perspective, the overall function and goals of whatever settings we develop to replace the larger prisons will still be directed toward *containing* (in a variety of different ways) the adolescent in the hope and belief that controlling and/or otherwise limiting his or her behavior will facilitate the process by which existing social institutions can effectively remedy previously unsuccessful or incomplete socialization and adjustment processes in the troubled adolescent. Thus, implicit in our current conception of the problems and needs confronting adolescents are the following assumptions:

1. Adolescence (presumably unlike either childhood or adulthood) is a particularly stressful period of time that is both universal in nature and predictable in onset.
2. Delinquent acts (especially those repetitive and/or serious in nature) are both the result and concrete symptom of inadequate, incomplete, or pathological socialization.

3. Existing societal values (particularly as embodied in the practices and orientations of the agencies and institutions charged with their protection, promulgation and perpetuation) are not only sound, but also conducive to, and supportive of, individual and collective self-determination and self-actualization.

The singular importance, of course, of the assumptions described above is that they provide what appears to be a consensually validated "theory" concerning the etiology of juvenile delinquency in general, and delinquent acts in particular. Similarly, the assumptions provide a context and framework for the development of programs designed to both perpetuate the segregation of a major part of the population (i.e., adolescents), while at the same time urging the population to lend itself to the ministrations of their "keepers" until such time as they are deemed "ready" for social, political, and economic inclusion. And finally the assumptions make crystal clear the belief that the adolescent and his society stand in unalterable opposition to each other, and that the adversary nature of this relationship can only be changed if and when the adolescent capitulates—the act of capitulation (variously labeled as "adjustment" or "growing maturity") taken as evidence that he has both identified with, and adopted as his own, the perspectives of the adult world.

Given the above, one can make certain predictions about the form, content and direction of the vast majority of "halfway houses," "residential youth centers" and "community-based treatment facilities" that will now spring up to replace the larger penal institutions. Among the most important predictions are the following:

1. While their only claim to fame may revolve around a demonstrated unwillingness and/or inability to work successfully with the juvenile offender (particularly the inner-city adolescent), most of the soon-to-be-available money will go to agencies and institutions with strong ties to the mental health power structure.
2. Whether or not they employ traditional jargon, the new settings will be clinical in nature; that is to say, places which deal with their charges (more than likely they will now be called "clients") as if their problems are primarily if not exclusively intrapsychic in origin and development.
3. The new settings will employ a variety of techniques ranging from the now faddish "rap," "encounter," or "sensitivity" approaches to more traditional kinds of one-to-one counseling, with a heavy dose of behavior modification thrown in somewhere in between. The particular approach notwithstanding, however, the overall focus of therapeutic interventions will be the individual—his head and his behavior.
4. While the new settings will employ nonprofessionals, they will usually be administered by professionals or professionally allied people and will, over

a period of time, seek to "upgrade" or "train" their neighborhood personnel by having them inculcate "clinically-appropriate" values and behaviors (e.g., objectivity, unimpassioned involvement, etc.) without the commensurate power or salary.

5. While the new settings will be physically located in the community, they will not choose to ally themselves with the muted aspirations of the people—preferring instead to join the existing agency network, a network by and large composed of the very institutions (e.g., the schools, welfare agencies, courts, police, industry, etc.) whose practices have "contributed" much to the problems that currently define life in most communities.

So much for existing assumptions and their predictable consequences. Let me summarize my concerns in the following manner. The shift from a punitive to a clinical orientation in the field of corrections, particularly with respect to the youthful offender, is a good and welcome one. It will, however, unless zealously guarded against, lead to the enfranchisement of the mental health professions as society's new agents of deviance control, result in the development of alternative models of rehabilitation that are dominated by clinical conceptions which, however rationalized, tend to continue to "blame the victim," and may, indeed, eventuate in the further separation of the "helping professions" from the very communities of which they become a part.

*An Alternative Model of Delinquency:*
*Implications for Rehabilitation*

Let me now turn to the development of an alternative model of the youthful offender by first examining critically the validity of the prevailing assumptions described previously.

To begin with, the assumption concerning the uniqueness, universality, and predictability of adolescence as a period of intense stress is certainly open to question. Cross-cultural and anthropological data gathered over the past thirty years have clearly indicated the "culture-bound" nature of the phenomenon (Benedict 1949; Hess and Goldblatt 1957; Friedenberg 1963). In essence, the data indicate that adolescence becomes a problem only in those cultures which, because of particular economic, social and/or sexual legacies, actively engage in developing specific practices aimed at excluding the adolescent from full societal participation. Thus, when Freidenberg refers to adolescents as "among the last social groups in the world to be given the full nineteenth-century colonial treatment," he is describing a situation not born of any social crises inherent in the developmental cycles surrounding puberty, but one in which a society, seeking to retain its traditional dominance and maintain some semblance of economic and political "stability" first develops and then acts to confirm a host of treasured myths concerning its heirs—its youth.

The second assumption, that of the implicitly pathological character of most if not all delinquent acts, is similarly difficult to defend. If one accepts (even partially) a "colonialist interpretation" of the relationship that currently exists between our society and its youth, one is then also forced to redefine "deviance" and "deviant acts" within a context which now focuses attention on the behavioral consequences of one or another form of systematic oppression. For the adolescent, oppression on a social level takes the form of legal exclusion and physical containment. On the psychological level it manifests itself in a variety of institutionally induced crises revolving around such issues as personal worth, identity, competence, and responsibility. And finally, added to this is the fact that within this matrix there currently do not exist any viable mechanisms for youth-initiated institutional change on the one hand, or even the simple redress of individual grievances on the other. It is, in short, a situation in which the "ruled" have little or no opportunities or options available to them through which they can in any significant and lawful way alter the conditions of their own captivity. Thus, whether we are talking about the delinquent act committed either by the "alienated middle-class suburban teenager" or the "disenfranchised poor youth" who lives in the inner-city, we are referring, almost by definition, to acts which if not directly political in nature, are certainly "adaptive" with respect to the conditions that spawned them.[a] This "adaptive" (rather than pathological) interpretation of many acts previously considered deviant or delinquent is well documented in the recent work of Brown (1965), Clark (1965), Gordon (1967), Liebow (1967), and the Kerner Commission (1968).

The final assumption—the assumption that existing institutions and agencies, especially those charged with the responsibility of socializing the youth, both represent and practice values consistent with an ideology predicated on concepts of self-determination and self-actualization—is, unfortunately, perhaps the easiest to refute. Simply put, the assumption is untrue, and the current nature of our society—divided and fractured by what often seem to be irreparable racial, sexual, and class antagonisms—is the clearest and most damning evidence available. More concretely, however, the assumption itself rests on two premises. The first is that there exists some discernible and positive correlation between the rhetoric and the operational reality of most socializing and social service agencies (e.g., schools, welfare agencies, etc.). Thus, for example, one would expect schools to focus their attention on the liberation of individuals and groups through the development of educational philosophies and processes stressing such fundamental values as trust, freedom, individuality and the intrinsic reward and excitement of the educational experience. Instead, as has been amply documented by the recent work of Goodman (1960), Kozol (1970),

---

[a]The above should not be interpreted to mean that *all* delinquent or deviant behavior on the part of adolescents is necessarily a response to "conditions of oppression." What we have sought to describe is an altered context within which it is no longer either necessary or valid to routinely apply the label of pathology to any and all behavior that violates existing "social norms."

and Levine (1970), both the learning experience and the social settings in which most formal learning currently takes place are by and large characterized by fear, the denial of individuality, and the affirmation of conformity, control, and coercion as appropriate mechanisms for shaping "responsible" behavior.[b] The second premise has to do with what might be called the "quality of life" within these social institutions, particularly those directly charged with the responsibility of "socializing others." Here, too, the situation is more than a little sad, for we now have data that clearly indicate just how poor and empty the quality of life really is for those (e.g., teachers, administrators, mental health professionals) who inhabit and work in these settings. Thus, for example, research by Sarason (1966), Argyris (1967), McIntyre (1969) and Goldenberg (1971) has raised some very fundamental questions concerning the ability of settings that are themselves "deviant" (i.e., racist, sexist, elitist, etc.) and "internally unhealthy" (i.e., characterized by reward systems which punish creativity; and/or the total absence of honest self-reflective dialogue, etc.) to foster health and productivity in others. It is, in short, a situation which suggests that our society's principal socializing institutions neither represent nor practice the very values that comprise either our own historical national rhetoric or their own immediate social mandates.

Now I want to develop an alternative conception of the youthful offender by offering the following definition of delinquency: *Juvenile delinquency, either as an isolated act or as a pattern of behavior, can often be defined as a condition of being in which the "offender" makes clear the marginality of his existence and serves notice on the world that he will no longer be contained or deluded by a social system which fails to take him or his needs seriously.* Even more, juvenile delinquency is a statement; a statement not only of the extremes to which the young have been pushed, but of the extremes to which a society has resorted in its efforts to keep from examining itself critically. And finally, the emergence of juvenile delinquency as a "national problem"—as a problem that cuts across traditional lines of race, class, and sex—should be evidence enough that youth are, in one form or another and through one institution or another, being alienated, isolated, and insulated from the possibilities of experiencing that sense of self, personal impact, and transcendence which when taken together define what it is about the human condition that makes living in a precarious world worthwhile.

Consequently, it should come as no surprise that more and more people are beginning to view juvenile delinquency as an increasingly alarming symptom of widespread social disorganization. For, indeed, juvenile delinquency is basically the product of inappropriate, malfunctioning and otherwise nonactualizing

---

[b]A colleague of mine, Murray Levine, once characterized the public schools as the "best single example of the complete fascist state." It is a situation characterized by the total absence of trust. Thus, according to Levine, it is a setting in which "the superintendent doesn't trust the principals, the principals don't trust the teachers, the teachers don't trust the students, and the parents don't trust anyone."

social institutions; it is related to broader issues of oppression; and it can only be approached from a perspective that defines the adolescent and his society as in a state of mutual and shared captivity. Thus, in a very real way, the liberation of our youth will do much to signify that the consciousness of our society as a whole has been raised.

If we take seriously the notion that juvenile delinquency can no longer be viewed, either solely or exclusively, in terms of individual pathology, that we can no longer accept the practices of our socializing and rehabilitating agencies with unquestioning faith, and that we cannot continue to divorce the problem of juvenile delinquency from the more general agonies through which our society is passing, then we have come to the point where the consideration of new directions in planning is dictated not by polemics but by necessity. Therefore, let me now list some of the characteristics of a setting that we might view as providing a truly alternative model for the "rehabilitation" of the youthful offender *and* ourselves.

1. The setting will view the problem of its own "internal moral credibility" as an issue of prime importance. Consequently, before addressing itself to the rehabilitation of others, it will seriously undertake an examination of itself—of the degree to which racism, sexism, professionalism, and power have molded people's thinking and behavior.
2. The setting will adopt a "treatment ethos" in which individual remediation is coupled with equal emphasis on institutional change, thus accomplishing two things: first, the de-mystification of mental health practice; and second, the forging of the kind of alliance between "staff" and "residents" in which problems are no longer viewed as residing solely "in the youngster's head," but are also identified (and confronted) in the institutions and subsystems that have already failed both the youthful offender, his family, and his community.
3. The setting will be governed (and its policies set) by the people (staff and youth) who inhabit it, with power, responsibility, and participation in the decision-making process being both shared and constantly up for review.
4. The setting will not only be in but also of the community. Thus it will lend and commit itself and its resources to community efforts to achieve self-determination, even if by taking that stance the setting places itself in conflict with its own source of funds and other existing agencies. In short, the setting's activities will not be guided by the goal of self-perpetuation at the expense of the aspirations of the community.

*Conclusion*

Let me state that I harbor no illusions about the probability of the model I have briefly outlined springing into existence at this particular time in our nation's life. Rarely does a society transcend its own historical consciousness. Rather, I offer it here for two reasons. First, because I should like to see as many of its aspects as possible incorporated into whatever community-based alternatives are now being developed to replace the institutions being closed down; and second, and most important, because one always hopes that prior knowledge of another distinct alternative will shorten the life span of the model currently holding sway.

It took us 100 years to replace a punitive model of corrections with the now-to-be implemented clinical one. I only hope it will not be another 100 years before the clinical model is replaced by the social action model outlined here.

### References

1. Argyris, C. "How Effective is the State Department?" YALE ALUMNI MAGAZINE (May 1967).

2. Benedict, Ruth. "Continuities and Discontinuities in Cultural Conditioning," in A STUDY OF INTERPERSONAL RELATIONS, ed. P. Mullahy (Hermitage Press, 1959).

3. Brown C. MANCHILD IN THE PROMISED LAND. New York: Macmillan, 1965.

4. Clark, K.B. DARK GHETTO: DILEMMAS OF SOCIAL POWER. New York: Harper & Row, 1965.

5. Friedenberg, E.Z. COMING OF AGE IN AMERICA. New York: Random House, 1963.

6. Goldenberg, I.I. BUILD ME A MOUNTAIN: YOUTH, POVERTY AND THE CREATION OF NEW SETTINGS. Cambridge, MIT Press, 1971.

7. Goodman, P. GROWING UP ABSURD. New York: Macmillan, 1960.

8. Gordon, J. "The Disadvantaged Boy: Implications for Counseling," in COUNSELING CULTURALLY DISADVANTAGED YOUTH, ed. A. Amos (Englewood Cliffs, N.J.: Prentice-Hall, 1967).

9. Hess, R.D., and Goldblatt, I. "The Status of Adolescents in American Society: A Problem in Social Identity," CHILD DEVELOPMENT 28 (1957): 459-468.

10. U.S. National Advisory Commission on Civil Disorders [Kerner Commission], REPORT. Washington, D.C.: U.S. Government Printing Office, 1968.

11. Kozol, J. DEATH AT AN EARLY AGE. New York: Bantam Books, 1970.

12. Levine, M. and Levine, A. A SOCIAL HISTORY OF HELPING SERVICES: CLINIC, COURT, SCHOOL AND COMMUNITY. New York: Appleton-Century-Croft, 1970.

13. Liebow, E. TALLY'S CORNER. Boston: Little, Brown, 1967.

14. McIntyre, D. "Two Schools, One Psychologist." THE PSYCHO-EDUCA-

TIONAL CLINIC: COLLECTED PAPERS AND RESEARCH, ed. Kaplan and S.B. Sarason. Boston: State of Massachusetts Press, 1969.

15. Sarason, S.B. et al. PSYCHOLOGY IN COMMUNITY SETTINGS: CLINICAL, EDUCATIONAL, SOCIAL, VOCATIONAL ASPECTS. New York: J. Wiley, 1966.

# 8

## Vision and Process: The Quality of Life in Community Group Homes

Howard W. Polsky

The transformation of large institutions for troubled youngsters into small community-based homes and programs offers us an unprecedented opportunity to think through anew the kind of community we ideally and realistically can create that best fulfills our individual and social needs.

The fact that the Commonwealth of Massachusetts is now committed to serving and caring for youngsters in the community means that designing a community culture in which individuals, staff, and youngsters can grow is no longer a frivolous or purely utopian venture. My own vision includes the basic premise that the single most important task of all the members of a community is to constantly explore together the meaning of living together, including the riddles of pursuing your own life and becoming a responsible member of a community. And my vision also includes the hope that a hundred or a thousand different Waldens will spring up.

It is in this spirit that I have created a personal vision of what the community group home can ideally become, a working paper if you please, as a basis for future dialogues about the kind of community life we can reach for, although perhaps never attain in practice. I am taking a stand on creating my ideal community to encourage you to take your stand, so that we can learn from each other not only how to deal with the practical necessities of everyday living but also to put at the top of our agendas the quality of life we are seeking for ourselves.

My second major premise is that the quality of shared life in the community group home is the single most important functional equivalent of the old custodial regimes that characterized former training centers. Either we can learn how to share and confront each other in tough and caring encounters or we will have to fall back on the older time-worn methods of manipulation and hierarchical power ladders. Ideals can take the place of dictatorial powers if we can deliberately plan together not only what we have to do in order to live together but what we want to become as a community.

The best way to begin is to restate values residential life should adhere to, to liberate the fullest potentialities of its residents. I believe people living together and identified as a social entity can build their own culture and transform themselves. The residential world is not a closed order nor a reality that must be statically accepted and adjusted to; it is capable of being looked at critically by its own residents who can be engaged in a dynamic encounter with each other and outsiders. Youngsters at every age perceive a personal and social reality and its contradictions, become more conscious of them, and create possibilities for being more liberated. I think residents have the right to name their world, to analyze and discuss their life together critically. People don't want to be, nor should they be forced to be, objects merely responding to changes occurring around them which submerge them in an imposed impenetrable reality. All residents should be encouraged to participate in building and consciously transforming their culture so that each person can become more spontaneous, caring, intimate, and competent—that is, more human.

A most important source of creative energy, I believe, is in the discontent (or dissonance) people have with themselves and their present situation. This should not be denied or programmed more rationally from above but should involve at every step all of the residents in dialogues and encounters appropriate to the units with which they are identified. The first task is to encourage everyone to share his discontent and his pictures of reality so that some kind of composite viewpoint emerges, to be sure with contradictions, that represents the collective outlook of the residents. We should take the time to understand fully the world as seen by the residents because important interacting elements that many may see only partially can be synthesized by a larger perspective. What they see then will be a synthesis of the reality in which they are now immersed and the contrasting perceptions by which they have been conditioned before.

Two dangers immediately present themselves: (1) to override, ignore, or deny the perceptions and feelings of the residents (they may appear naive, one-sided, or distorted but must be taken seriously as critical components in the present culture of the group); and (2) to work so exclusively with selected realities of living such as the routines of daily housekeeping and maintaining order that the residents as whole human beings come to be viewed as one-sided individuals compelled primarily to adjust to an imposed reality.

We have to learn how to enter into a dialogue with residents and stop considering ourselves as proprietors (often absentee) of living units who always know what is best.

I am fully aware that we live in a society in which power-holders use subordinates. Nowhere has this become more clear than in large total institutions that the "adjusted" created for the "rejects." The administrative bureaucracy is a pecking order with the residents at the base of the pyramid; and often residents use and exploit each other by adopting an attitude of "adhesion" to those who are using them in the stratified levels of power above them. After all, this is the most substantive fact of the culture. In identifying with this use of power, residents create an indigenous pecking order that locks user and used into a circle of manipulation. The tough resident who receives privileges does so often at the cost of exploiting, "keeping in order," the less stable elements within the living unit. The "trusty" in order to be sure of his job is often tougher than the custodian. In any case, those who have power at every level are prescribing, imposing their choices upon subordinates, and the subsequent behavior follows the guidelines laid down by those who have the authority and power to do so. Thus at every level we find those who have some edge of power internalizing this image of authoritarianism, ruling by prescription and limiting sharply the choices and decision-making by subordinates.

I do not see how this situation can be changed except by encouraging all residents to come forward with their mixed perceptions of what is going on, so that they can become the property of all to consider and to decide what they want to do about it. Not to do so is to perpetuate "pluralistic ignorance," a cultural condition where feelings of being exploited, used, and restricted remain the private suppressed property of residents not permitted to publicly surface, identify, and work through. The subordinates simply displace their anger and resentment on the most available and least powerful sub-subordinates.

We can either privately store up grievances, each in our own gunnysack, or more fully express ourselves; we can confront those whom we feel are using us or abide them; we can follow prescriptions laid down by those that have the power or expand the areas in which conscious decisions can be made about the way in which we want to live; we can be objects or spectators, or we can participate more fully as whole actors in the situation; we can speak out or be silent, and the most symptomatic sign of oppressiveness is the culture of silence.

Those of us who have the power will have to take a closer look at the constraints under which we operate and which we then tend to impose upon our own subordinates. As long as we live in this duality in which to exist is to exist like those who have power above us, then we cannot participate in the transformation of these residences into what the fullest human capacities of all their citizens can make them. And we cannot do this without each group at every level undergoing some kind of critical discovery of the uses of power to subordinate others and to use them.

Those of us who have privilege and authority and power will have to learn anew how to shed them so that we can be closer to those who feel the restraints and restrictions. No doubt, it is difficult for those of us who believe we have true knowledge of the whole situation to give up our power in an attempt to better understand the position of the subordinate and help him overcome his subordinate position and subordinate consciousness. Subordinates too will not easily relinquish domination over whom they in turn have power. It takes great humility and faith in a truly humanistic philosophy to help those who do not have a voice to speak and name the situation and the world in which they live rather than be adjustive and reactive all the time.

If we can enter the worlds of the residents and encourage a dialogue about the situation that everyone confronts, we can begin to shape a reality that will encourage more honest exchanges of feelings and perceptions. A central task remains to work in ways that can more truly reflect the needs of all of the group members. Reality constantly mediates, but it is mediated by the culture that arises out of dialogue and constant encountering among residents.

A distinction must be made between *encountering* and *problem-solving dialogues.* The latter is role bound and is based on intelligence, skill, and function regarding group goals and tasks. Encountering goes to members engaging each other as whole human beings with common needs and unique differences. My feeling is that groups exist not only to master the reality about them but to enable its members to grow through interpersonal encounters. Learning about oneself grows out of a group that can optimally blend trust and confrontation.

Trust in groups has various sources: (1) similar valves stemming from a common cultural, philosophical or ideological base; (2) achievement of group goals; (3) fun being together—sharing sports, music, conversation, and enjoying each other's wit, charm, intelligence, skill.

Still another kind of trust involves people sharing important personal concerns. For a long time it was believed that groups of individuals sharing personal problems were the exclusive province of professional therapists. The laboratory training movement exploded this myth and demonstrated that groups of strangers meeting for many hours during several weeks or a weekend can share important problems and receive significant feedback about themselves. Lab training raised the distinct possibility that individuals can band together to work on personal problems. This peculiar success was due to the ability of lab groups to foster trust, that is significant sharing of important concerns and constructively confronting each other about differences according to experience-tested feedback principles (see my "Notes on Personal Feedback in Sensitivity Training," SOCIOLOGICAL INQUIRY 41 [Spring 1971]).

Every trainer develops this group sense of members being ready to confront each other *after* the group has created a minimum culture of trust. And this came about by enough people in the group, including the trainer, being willing to personally disclose social and work problems. The group, particularly the trainer, guards zealously against pushing individuals who do not want to disclose themselves. These individuals have a right, indeed, an obligation not to reveal themselves in the face of group pressure. To be one's self takes precedence over conformity with T-group norms of sharing and revealing oneself. It is in this profound sense that members in training sessions get out of the group what they put into it. There appears to be a direct correlation between the individual's willingness to work on real problems and the *quality* of the feedback he subsequently receives about himself.

Once the minimum level of trust has been initially established by members sharing important parts of themselves, subsequent levels of trust are attained by individuals confronting each other within this original climate of trust. Trust is further thickened by individuals challenging that trust by sharing tough differences and negative feelings about each other, the trainer, and the group. It is incumbent upon a member giving feedback to document his perceptions by reference to transactions and events in the group and articulate his observations in such a way so that they make sense to the receiver and the other members. The other members are obliged to confirm, qualify, or negate these observations and feelings communicated by one member to another.

Confronting is liberation for giver and receiver when it is done in a climate of support and trust, that is, when members feel that others care, and are sharing their perceptions not to put others down and invidiously advance themselves but because they want to be helpful and because they too want to be helped. It is curious that in so many of the treatment modalities one side helps and the other is helped and the helper receives so much uncritical regard and authority to do so. In the laboratory training group the right to be listened to has to be earned.

In the delicate accelerating fusion of liking and helping, being liked and being helped, the laboratory training group works out the dialectic between confrontation and trust. Often this occurs at first between diads or triads and then is incorporated by the group as a whole. The ultimate aim is to build trust while sharply confronting each other. Group members vary greatly in their ability to tune in to other people, sustain concentrated interest and articulate perceptions. Learning how to absorb others' feedback in a constructive way enables the receiver to give more effective feedback to others. You get and you give, you give and you get in an emerging personal encounter-culture.

This is not to suggest that residential life become introverted and solely confined to interpersonal encountering. Reality is much too demanding and complex to be solved by better internal relationships. Encountering and group problem-solving cannot be separated from life. All the residents should be encouraged to reflect about themselves and the world that they have to live in and create. Such reflection can influence future actions as well as help understand the past. When actions and reflections are split, then the individuals either randomly "act-out" or lapse into apathy and silent resentment.

Needless to say, participatory democratic discussion and decision-making cannot arise all at once from the head of Minerva. It can only be worked at incrementally through delimited projects in which one critical area after another in the life space of the living unit can be selected for liberation.

On the first stage, selection of projects of various kinds involves the residents in discussions that air their views about vital issues in relation to their whole life situation. Then they discuss what they can do about it. The objective throughout all the projects is to afford residents opportunities to become more self-affirming and responsible to others in their collective living situation.

Two dangers emerge: (1) those who have been dominated all of their lives in subordinated positions come to believe that they cannot act freely; (2) it is of no worth to proclaim rhetorically that we want everybody's participation; the only way it can come about is by picking up concrete issues of importance to all of the residents and entering into a dialogue that takes their viewpoint into account, the actions proposed by everyone, as well as an ultimate decision about where to begin changing things. Only by constant reflection and discussion that includes everyone's attitudes and behavior, can the whole living group discover ways in which they can recreate their own reality.

One crucial change in the attitudes and behavior of the caretaker has to take place in order to implement the above program. The change is from regulating and prescribing to dialoguing and joint participation. It is from a ready-to-wear to an open-ended search that incorporates the viewpoints and activities of all of the residents in reflective discussions and actions. The custodian cannot think for the residents nor impose his ideas on them. The custodian preoccupied with the problem of control does not relinquish it, and he has little faith in the residents to control their own lives. The resident is not an empty vessel to be filled by the authorities. We have to move towards a joint undertaking of problem formulation and solving. Our goal is joint discovery rather than a transfer of information or the refined imposition of control upon those who have power over their subordinates. Reality is mediated by what has to be done rather than by the problem of controlling and being controlled. The residents are co-investigators in dialogue with the counselors. The problem is critical intervention into all areas of life so that all residents can more fully realize themselves. One area after another becomes problematic as all of the residents and counselors seek to find the best ways to live together.

The dialogue between and among residents and between them and the counselors is mediated by the living unit; a language has to be created so they can jointly construct the world and culture in which they want to dwell together. Everyone has the right to name that world. One side is not a consumer, and the other a producer; both sides are producers and consumers.

In order for this to take place two prerequisites are necessary: (1) trust, the feeling among all the members that others care in the sense that they want to help and not use each other. This trust emerges only by people sharing differences and important needs and aspirations; and (2) the belief that people can be active critical interveners into their life situations, that the cottage for example, is not a space merely to be filled in, but is a domain, a place of scope that takes shape as its residents choose to create their culture and way of life. The basic hope is that however confused any of the residents or counselors are, by sharing their ideas and needs, clarity can emerge about what exists and, in limited ways, goal priorities can be decided. I think those of us in power have to stop imposing our own view of the world upon people who are coming from somewhere else. We have to be more helpful in permitting the needs of all the residents to emerge, rather than what we think they need. We must help all of the residents make up their own minds about what they want to do instead of making up their minds for them. The worst kind of domination is not taking into account the particular views the residents hold about their situation. Any other program is merely an invasion from without and imposes the power holders' view upon the powerless.

To begin to share the limits of the situation means to begin to do something about them. The issues taken up by the residents contain, and are contained by, definite limited situations. They imply tasks requiring limited solutions. Discussions involving the residents and their own life ultimately lead to ideas about what can be done about their situations—that is, some kinds of untested feasibilities.

In order to work at problems growing out of their life situations and their description of them, the residents have to conduct each theme to the overall perspective and totality of the system in which they live and act. By tying up and relating the limited situation to the whole, they can assume a more critical attitude toward the specific situation they would like to see changed. These discussions deepen the comprehension of both overall and specific situations in which the residents are immersed. By taking up one project after another and acting upon particular issues, the participants gradually begin to overcome the sense of being overwhelmed powerless. Opening areas for discussion and decision-making leads to a more critical form of thinking about themselves and their world and their relationship to it. This occurs by the residents drawing a picture of the situation they confront, including their attitudes toward it; this codification and buildup of the picture must then lead to critical analysis of it—decoding, what is central, what periphery, determining the time sequence, the cause and effect, and so forth. This analysis is largely done in light of what must be changed in order to improve the situation.

Thus there is a constant buildup, putting together the parts of the situation into a full picture and then analyzing the whole by deeper study of its components' relationships. The discussants find themselves both objects and subjects discoursing upon themselves and their constructions of reality. So there is a constant movement from building up—abstracting from life to paint a picture—and then returning to the parts—critically decoding them to discover handles for change to overcome a heretofore overwhelming reality.

The difficulties in beginning these discussions—silence, helplessness, dependency, passivity, powerlessness, apathy—point up some of the underlying problems. That is why in the beginning it is important for everyone who lives together in a unit to act as co-investigators of their own situation. The more active they can become in exploring their own situation, the more deep the awareness of their reality and the more real the possibilities of taking action on their own behalf.

One of the dangers that we have to face as psychologists is the risk of shifting the focus of issues in the life situation from the system to treating only residents as objects of the investigation. Nor can we in our omniscience analyze the system for residents.

The initial step is to enter into an exploration with all the residents about what the issues are. I think here has to be explained the reason for this approach, how it is to be carried out and to what use it will be put. But most important of all, this whole way of work is only justified to the extent that all the residents feel that what they are talking about belongs to them; so it is not an attempt to learn more about the residents to "fix" them up as such, but to come to know with them the reality that is challenging everyone.

The counselors' attitude should be one of trying to understand the living culture of the cottage. Both the counselors and residents share their impressions and observations. When we settle upon a situation to get into in depth, everyone is encouraged first to talk about it. Anyone's attitude can challenge all the rest and others should also be encouraged to voice their thoughts. In this way the issue and group becomes alive as people strive together to understand different attitudes toward their own situation, its reality, and the potential for change. Differences and contradictions are food for further discussions. The contradictions shape the limits of the situation, involve new themes, and indicate new tasks to be done. Some may feel hopeless, a fatalism that implies lack of trust, power, or both. Some people will focus completely on the obstacles and reasons for not being able to do anything. Others may begin to explore openings and develop the potential awareness of what to do to change the situation.

In any case, the ultimate test is the "testing action" which reveals the possibilities for change. If the residents have been involved in building up a picture of their reality, then everyone is working on something that is familiar to them and is beginning to belong to them. Residents' perceptions of their previous perceptions may change. Discussions are real when they are related to felt needs of the residents. Abstractions initially will only produce silence and the old apathy. Alternatives to present life patterns may have to be brainstormed and contrasted so that people can begin to see other possibilities of how to live together. In this way they may, if they so choose, go beyond what they are embedded in to a closer approximation of reality that is responsive to their needs. It may be necessary to bring in outsiders, educators, and specialists who can help work through concrete programs to better fulfill their needs and aspirations. What is critical, however, is that counselors and residents become both thinkers and doers, that one doesn't do for the thinking other, and that the thinker doesn't think for the doer.

# Neutralization of Community Resistance to Group Homes

Robert B. Coates and
Alden D. Miller

In recent years the field of juvenile corrections has tried to alter its treatment of juvenile offenders. Part of this effort has focused on handling more youth within community residential centers or group homes in order to reduce the numbers of youth served by traditional reform schools and exposed to the degrading effects which are so often part of such institutional experiences. While the group-home concept for troubled youth is often philosophically accepted in both professional and nonprofessional circles, the actual establishment of group homes in local communities is often vehemently resisted by residents.[a] Thus a very pragmatic issue confronting both state and privately operated agencies is how to handle community resistance to group homes. How can community resistance be avoided or ameliorated when it arises?

This is a preliminary paper describing the first results of a continuing investigation into the dynamics of locating a group home in a community setting. We are concerned here with the politics of dealing with community resistance to the initial establishment of the group home. We will not, in this report, deal with community reaction to the program of the group home once it is in operation, nor with the effect of the program on the youth residing in the group home. We will deal with program only as it is represented as a proposal in the process of gaining entry into the community. Our analysis of resistance and strategies for neutralizing resistance will focus on the community level. Analysis at the state-wide and governmental levels is not included here.

The data supporting this study were gathered within the Massachusetts Department of Youth Services. Massachusetts is in the forefront of states seeking

This research was supported, in part, by grants from the Massachusetts Governors Committee on Law Enforcement and Administration of Criminal Justice. The authors wish to express appreciation to Lloyd E. Ohlin, director of the larger project of which this research is a part, and Elinor Halprin for helpful editorial assistance; thanks are also due Judy Caldwell, Robert Fitzgerald, and David Garwood who labored hard to gather the data for this analysis.

[a]For instance, a study conducted by Louis Harris and Associates for the Joint Commission on Correctional Manpower found 77 percent of a representative U.S. sample favored the idea of a halfway house, 50 percent would personally favor a halfway house in their neighborhood and only 22 percent believed that most people in the neighborhood would favor a halfway house in the area. Joint Commission on Correctional Manpower and Training, THE PUBLIC LOOKS AT CRIME AND CORRECTIONS (1968), pp. 16-17.

to discover viable community-based alternatives to the institutionalization of juvenile delinquents. As part of the deinstitutionalization process during the spring and summer of 1972, the DYS sought to establish several group homes throughout the state under a purchase of service arrangement. That is, the DYS proposed to buy group home services from private agencies. This arrangement was adopted for several reasons: (1) it was believed that the closer the "treatment" program to the community and the more involvement of private agencies and private citizens, the greater the likelihood of successful reintegration of program clients; (2) it was also believed that private agencies, particularly the more experienced agencies, were better prepared to handle group residential homes than most DYS line staff who had only worked with youth in an institutional context; (3) it was considered to be an easier task for existing or even newly created private agencies to work with communities in establishing group homes than it would be for DYS with its controversial image. The DYS had been strongly opposed by some interest groups in the state because they felt that the DYS deinstitutionalization effort was moving too quickly, and that the department's treatment approach was too permissive.

*Method*

In order to isolate those issues which are most sensitive to community resistance and to identify the various strategies for handling resistance, we looked at several planned group homes that failed primarily because of community resistance and at several homes which were able to neutralize resistance and establish ongoing residences. Three homes were selected within each of the two categories. Two of the agencies that failed had previously operated similar homes and had therefore been confronted with some of the same problems before, while one agency that failed had never before operated such a program. Two of the successful agencies had previously operated similar programs; the third agency had a parent structure with some prior experience, but the specific people involved in setting up the group home had had no prior experience.

The homes are located in six of the seven DYS regions. The seventh region was not studied because there was at the time considerable political turmoil within the region over other issues related to corrections. The selected group homes do not necessarily represent the full range of all probable conflict situations. They do represent a range sufficient to identify at least some of the key issues of strategy.

The data collection strategy focused on extensive interviewing of key actors. To learn most about the plans for each home, the first person contacted was either the executive director of the sponsoring agency or the director of the proposed home. During this initial discussion the interviewer identified other significant actors or interest groups to be interviewed at a later time. This snowball technique was followed until it became apparent that little additional, useful information could be gained by further interviewing. Typically the interviewing included agency representatives, police, clergy, neighbors, and city officials. In two cases the snowball technique was modified to accommodate the wishes of the group being studied. One involved an agency that failed and the other an agency that succeeded. The research team respected the intricacies of the ongoing political processes and tried not to endanger an operating program or the chances of any proposed home.

The interviews, while structured, were quite flexible. During the course of an interview with a representative of the social service agency, the interviewer obtained the following information: (1) the goals of the program and strategies for implementing the program; (2) the process of communication of goals to interest groups; (3) the kinds of people who agreed or disagreed with agency goals and strategies; (4) the communications from vested interest groups; (5) the strategies for handling opposition and support; and (6) the expected outcome. When interviewing representatives of interest groups outside the agency, the major blocks of information included: (1) perceptions of the private agency and DYS goals; (2) the source of information about the group home; (3) interest group goals for the home; (4) the strategies for attaining those goals; (5) the communication of goals and strategies—to whom, how, and why; (6) the kinds of people or groups that agreed or disagreed with goals and strategies; (7) the strategies for handling opposition and support, and (8) expected outcome. Three interviewers were involved in the data collection process. Each covered one group home that failed and one that succeeded.

In addition to interviewing the key actors, local newspaper accounts were analyzed as well as letters of support or opposition, and minutes of planning meetings and hearings where available. Together the data project a fairly good picture of the process and problems of placing a residential home in a community.

Throughout this paper we will refer to group homes and their communities by fictitious names. Many persons cooperated with us in our data collection efforts in order to contribute to the understanding of the process of establishing or resisting a group home, with the express understanding that we would respect certain confidentiality about the information and not identify our sources. Fortunately this need for confidentiality does not interfere with our purposes in this analysis, since the actual identity of the communities and group homes is not important for the kinds of inferences we are seeking to make and support.

*Results*

The major variables and strategies involved in the process of establishing the group homes in this study are summarized in Table 9-1. Data from the individual case studies will be compared and contrasted in order to derive at least tentative

**Table 9-1**
Successful and Unsuccessful Group Homes

| Characteristics of Group Homes | Failures | | | Successes | | |
|---|---|---|---|---|---|---|
| | Laurel | Palmyra | Whitewater | Eagle Grove | Sullivan | Hebron |
| Who established it? | An "established" agency with experience in group homes for drug cases | A sectarian religious group new to this sort of work | An established agency treating children with physical disabilities | "Ex-con" group new to this sort of work | An established agency with experience in group homes for welfare youth | An established agency with experience in group homes for delinquents |
| Selection of Community | Knew community but not with respect to reaction to delinquents | Did not know neighborhood community organization | Knew community but not with respect to reaction to delinquents | Knew community well | Knew community well | Learned community well *after* site selection |
| | Residential area working and middle class | Residential middle to upper class | Residential middle to upper class | Transient community, disorganized | Mixed transient but neighborly and "liberal" | Residential working and middle or upper class |
| Strategy for entering community | Talk to "significant few" and then campaign | Talk to "significant few" | Talk to "significant few" | Low profile ("quiet") | Low profile ("quiet") | Talk to "significant few" and then campaign |

| | | | | | | |
|---|---|---|---|---|---|---|
| Selection site | Across from school and no space for recreation | Fire trap, small yard | Busy road, small yard | Youth involved in improving house | Youth involved in improving house | Estate more than adequate, for expansion |
| Selection of name for program | Name designed to challenge youth | Name or label emphasized community's responsibility | Name or label emphasized community's responsibility | Name was de-emphasized | Name was de-emphasized | Name designed to challenge youth |
| Presentation of program-content | Presented as related to DYS-plan for a kind of problem-kid community did not have | No clear presentation or conception | Vague and too technical presentation | Presentation through kids' activity | Presentation through kids' and house parents' activity | Presentation in direct, informative style in meeting |
| Client and staff residence | Staff and supporters did not live in neighborhood | Staff and supporters did not live in neighborhood | Staff live in group home | Staff lived in group home | Staff lived in group home | Staff lived in group home |
| Serving the community | *Home* an unwanted service to community | *Home* an unwanted service to community | *Home* an unwanted service to community | *Kids* serve community | *Kids* serve community | *Kids* serve community |
| Resolution of conflict | Looking for middle ground | "Holy War" | "Righteousness"-getting community to meet problems | Avoidance of creating issues | Avoidance of creating issues | Straight-forward meeting of issues |

responses to a number of policy and strategy issues. The nine critical variables include such items as selection of community, strategy for entering community, and resolution of conflict. These nine variables provide the backbone of our analysis. Before proceeding with a detailed comparative analysis of the six homes in the study, it will be helpful for the reader to have an understanding of the general flow of the processes involved in setting up group homes and the kinds of opposition encountered. We will therefore present two brief hypothetical case studies, one representing failure, Clarion, and one representing success, Kimberly. The nine critical variables will emerge in these hypothetical case studies, as they did in the six real case studies, as the major steps in the flow of action, resistance, and effort to neutralize resistance.

**Clarion.** A long established social service agency, BURN (Boys United: Resources, Neighbors), attempted to set up a small group home for juvenile delinquents in the middle-sized city of Clarion. BURN had been operating a program designed to address learning disabilities in the city for six years. Its reputation was thought to be quite good, and on the basis of that reputation little opposition to the program's expansion was anticipated. The actual program was to consist of "free school" environment and provision of work experiences within the community. The group home would house eight to twelve boys ranging in age from thirteen to seventeen.

The initial strategy for setting up the home involved talking to a few key people in the community; people who were generally considered to be friendly toward the agency. These people included the mayor, two of the town's five selectmen, and other wealthy backers of the agency. Response from the mayor was noncommital; the two selectmen and the financial backers were quite supportive. After these initial conversations a site was selected. The selected neighborhood was primarily residential in character, with one gasoline station and a small store. Although unknown to the agency administrators, the neighborhood had in the recent past taken two actions to maintain its residential atmosphere. The residents had organized to prevent a light industrial plant from moving into the area, and it had also closed a teenage drop-in center that had operated for a brief period of time. This lack of knowledge about the neighborhood's capacity for organizing was to be a major factor in the failure of BURN.

Before the purchase arrangements were finalized, it was necessary for BURN to go before the town zoning committee to request modification of the zoning regulations in the case of the group home. Upon hearing of the group home for juveniles, abutters were incensed and alarmed. They were incensed because no one had told them about the plans previously, and they were alarmed because they believed that "gangsters were moving in next door." Over the next two-week period the abutters held a number of informal meetings to determine how the group home could be stopped. Neighbors indicated that their primary motivation for keeping the halfway house out of their neighborhood was to protect their own children. In addition it was pointed out that the neighborhood did not have any delinquency problem and did not want to be an "experimental lab for other neighborhoods who could not solve their own problems."

By the time of the zoning hearing, BURN was aware that it would encounter a little opposition. But it was believed that the support of various public officials would outweigh a few "strident antagonists." This did not prove to be the case. The hearing was underscored by a very well thought out confrontation on the part of the informal citizen group. They listed three reasons why the group home should not be allowed: (1) the site selected was inadequate for ten to twelve teenagers because of its small size and tiny yard (the lack of space would also cause an undue nuisance burden for nearby neighbors); (2) protection of children and elderly persons from the "criminal types" which would be associated with the halfway house; (3) the agency had no experience working with juvenile delinquents. One woman suggested that much of the fear expressed by residents was related to the acronym, "BURN." She said, "Why couldn't they simply call it AIDE or something like that."

Rather than attempting to deal with each of the specific reasons cited by the citizens' group, BURN administrators suggested that the citizens did not care about children, but only cared about property values. This righteous stance on the part of BURN only served to strengthen the bond among the citizens. Seeing the rift between the citizens and BURN the town selectmen had "no other choice" but to reject the home.

**Kimberly.** Several individuals who had previously worked with juvenile delinquents decided to set up a group home in the town of Kimberly. Eight to twelve boys would reside in the home; in addition another eight boys would participate in the program on a nonresidential basis. The program would focus on informal counseling and getting the youth into activities occurring in the community. These would include work, schools, and recreation. According to the staff the program was to project the image of a "large but concerned family," concerned about its members and the community. Youth would typically stay in the residential program for three to four months. After their residential stay, program staff would maintain contact in order to support the youth as they returned to their own or foster homes.

The program staff selected an area of Kimberly they believed best fitted their needs. The locality had a junior high school and a senior high school nearby; a number of small businesses were also within walking distance.

The strategy for setting up the home operated on two levels. Program staff were talking with various influential town officials about their proposal, and concurrently they were talking with local residents and leaders of civic organizations functioning in the target area. Initially some of the neighbors expressed fear and concern for their own welfare. However, the program staff handled this situation well. They explained that dangerous youth would not be participating in the group home and that if youth did seriously act out in the community they would be transferred elsewhere. At the same time it was said that the community could expect some minor incidents but these inconveniences would be balanced by the service to the community that the home offered. First, the home obviously offered a service to area youth who may be beginning a delinquent career, and second, youth would repair the house used for the group home and would hire out their services to improve and maintain the neighborhood. This concern for property values handled some of the more subtle opposition to the proposed home. Moreover, many residents were concerned about the occurrence of delinquent acts in their neighborhood and saw the group home as one means for dealing with the problem.

Town officials were for the most part supportive of the proposed home. This was particularly the case once it became apparent that the bulk of opposition had already been mollified. The police chief had been contacted by the program staff. He did not anticipate problems, but was taking a "wait and see" attitude.

A zoning hearing was called to pass on the proposed home. Three or four residents living in the area voiced opposition. They indicated fear for their children's safety and did not believe the program staff to be particularly qualified to work with troubled youth. The program staff responded very straightforwardly. They acknowledged that there were minimal risks but argued that the value of the home for the community outweighed the risks. They also described the program in detail, thereby answering any question about their competency to work with youth. In addition to the defense put forth by the program staff, other community residents spoke on the group home's behalf. Preparation of the community and cooperation with the community had paid off; the group home passed the zoning hearing and was established.

Having these two brief vignettes in hand and a feeling for the general flow of the processes involved in setting up community-based group homes, we can now turn to a more detailed analysis of the data summarized in Table 9-1.

*Discussion*

The real usefulness of studying the community resistance process comes from comparing those proposed homes that failed and those that were successfully established. This analysis should yield results which directly relate to policy and strategic considerations.

One of the initial questions administrators within the DYS raised as they closed the institutions and became involved in setting up community residences was whether the state should set up the homes, or whether it should contract this task to private agencies. DYS opted for the latter strategy for three reasons: (1) the DYS image was burdened by past controversy, and the private agencies were seen as potentially the easier way of obtaining the group homes; (2) privately run group homes appeared to offer better prospects for real community involvement in the youth corrections process; and (3) private agencies with a number of years of experience were expected to have a greater level of expertise about moving into communities and operating community-based programs than DYS had at that time.

Because there are no state-operated group homes within this study we cannot speak directly to this issue, but we can say something about the use of private agencies. There is no guarantee that the well-established private agency has the capacity to set up a new residence which a newly formed private agency, or for that matter the state itself, might face. And, the data within this study suggest that experience cannot be equated with finesse. Two of the proposed homes that failed (those in Laurel and Whitewater) were planned by agencies that had operated in those communities for a number of years. It may be that both agencies suffered from overconfidence, misreading of the community, and poor preparation for handling any resistance. In Hebron and Sullivan, we again have two agencies with years of experience, but each approached the communities very cautiously, with considerable preparation, and overall strategies for handling community resistance. As for the newly established private groups, one was a failure and one a success. The agency in Palmyra failed. And the agency in Eagle Grove, although it did have a nominal umbrella agency, was for all intents and purposes newly created and was quite successful.

Therefore we must beg the question for the moment; it is apparent that the answer to successful entry is not simply a longstanding privately established group or a newly created group. The answer is probably more directly related to the way the agency plans strategy and approaches the community. Some of the issues discussed seem likely to arise from use of a sectarian religious organization in a pluralistic community if the organization stresses religion as an issue. It is certainly reasonable for a Catholic church or any other to function well as a sponsor in a community where no other church exists or where the religious inclinations of the community are predominately in that direction, and for that church to use religious arguments. But where there is much religious diversity, religious groups may be more successful as sponsors if they are ecumenical or nonsectarian in nature, and do not emphasize religious differences. Any strictly sectarian operation in a religiously diverse community has a good probability of becoming embroiled in a "holy war." The effect of such a conflict is to focus debate on false issues related to other interests and to personalities rather than toward the issue of community responsibility for handling troubled youth.

*Selection and Survey of the Community.* Comprehensive understanding of the community and the particular neighborhood in which the proposed home will reside is requisite for the sort of planning that is demanded. It seems reasonable to anticipate some community resistance to any group home; the question is where will that resistance come from and how can it be neutralized. The form the resistance will take can be anticipated if enough is known about how the community has reacted in similar situations. Has the community recently organized to defeat a drug program or an alcoholism center? What sort of people live in the area—are they professionals or day laborers? Is the community an integrated area? Do people in the community recognize a crime or delinquency problem in their area? Who has power and how do they exercise it?

The lack of such knowledge was detrimental for agencies in Laurel and Palmyra. Particularly in Palmyra the proposed home ran into a very well organized community that had already gotten together to make a "passive park" and to object to college dormitories. This information perhaps should have suggested that the agency look elsewhere for the site or at least suggested potential problems which would have to be handled if the community were to be approached successfully in setting up the home. The agency in Hebron took ample preparatory time to study the area, the needs of the region, and the interests of the community. Here the primary problem involved the matter of timing. The agency took so long to complete the first phase of the preparation plan (that is, gaining support of regional professionals) that the second phase (talking with community leaders and abutters) was then made more difficult by news leaks. Information gleaned by surveying the community, its makeup and concerns, can be used for devising the appropriate strategy for entering the community. As we will see, some strategies are appropriate for some communities but not for others.

*Strategy for Entering the Community.* Once one knows something about the context of the community, the focus of power, and the way it organizes itself to serve the interests of its residents, one is in a position to consider alternative strategies for entering the community to establish a group home.[1] Three general strategies seem to have been put into operation by the group homes represented within this study: (1) maintaining a low profile; (2) focusing communication at a significant few; and (3) focusing communication both at the significant few and at the local resident. Some of these strategies seem to be appropriate for certain kinds of communities and very inappropriate for other kinds.

In general, the low profile entry into the community appears quite adequate for communities which are characterized by mobile populations, which have diverse groups in terms of age and race, and which have little experience in organizing to present a collective response to an issue. The purest type of low profile approach was discovered in the Eagle Grove community which could be described by each of the above characteristics. The agency sought a community with great diversity so that little attention would be attracted by a group of youth or by a staff made up of exoffenders. This low profile approach, which could be called the "quiet approach," has certain risks which are minimized in the transient community but which could be exacerbated in a residential community. That is, the danger of being discovered before the program has had a chance of proving itself is always a risk. It seems improbable that one could actually place a group home into a middle-class residential community without being discovered and then becoming involved in a bitter struggle to remain before having a chance to show what one's program can do.

The other community in which a low profile approach was used successfully was Sullivan. That community can also be characterized by having a diverse and mobile population, but it also had the capacity to organize itself to promote community interests. The approach of the group home was to win community support by functional approach. That is, the nondelinquent youth and staff became involved in the community on a personal level. They sold themselves as worthwhile persons and therefore sold the program. Then DYS youth were introduced into an existing group home, and were also urged to sell themselves. This approach probably works best where there is a sympathetic, widespread concern about community problems. In Sullivan, the residents recognized a crime and delinquency problem which had to be handled and furthermore believed that the program was in fact one way to deal with delinquency. However, it is problematic whether their approach would work in a relatively isolated suburb unwilling to acknowledge the existence of delinquency in the community or to accept any responsibility for coping with that delinquency. As long as delinquency is seen as another community's problem, the sympathetic support and understanding requisite for this low key functional approach would be missing.

The approach that places emphasis upon communication with a significant few persons in the community—the mayor, the selectmen, and key professionals—has had mixed success in the residential areas. Usually it has worked fairly well only where it has been expanded to include a fairly comprehensive communication flow with grass roots neighbors and abutters. In communities where there are upper-middle-class persons who recognize the value and use of collective power, elected town officials and professionals will be unable to force acceptance of a group home even if the officials are in favor. In most cases in a conflict, the officials, because of their desire to be reelected, will probably go with the majority or a very vocal minority of the residents. The proposed group homes for both Whitewater and Palmyra were very dependent on political and professional support. The agency in Whitewater had an international reputation among professionals but that reputation was not particularly useful when community residents resisted the idea of a group home in their neighborhood. In Palmyra, the power and influence of the Protestant Council with town officials was considerable, but it could not match the tenacity of the neighborhood residents. In both cases, the agencies were open to the rather serious charge that support came from the outside, or from suburban communities which would probably not themselves accept such a group residence in their own neighborhoods.

This approach has a rather glaring liability. The fears and emotions of a few are allowed to spread and to be voiced in group meetings where such feelings can easily be reinforced. One to one contact, with its greater likelihood of neutralizing the fear, was not employed sufficiently in these two cases.

The combined approach which incorporated both communication with the significant leaders and with the neighbors and abutters is perhaps more time-consuming than the above strategy. And it also has its risks. After all, the best-managed communication scheme may still be unconvincing, or perhaps the community is simply unwilling to accept the kind of responsibility that goes along with a group residence. However, for the organized, residential community, the combined approach seems the most workable. The strategy revolves around a desire for a community to assess its needs and to take an active cooperative role in meeting some of those needs. This strategy was backed into in Laurel, where it became a face-saving if not agency-saving strategy, and it was the planned approach in Hebron. The original approach in Laurel seemed to emphasize the professional, civic leader, and town official support. It depended a great deal on what was believed to be a good reputation in the community. This strategy blew up. Negative publicity was so rampant that one would wonder about the safety of the agency's existing programs. The program staff withdrew from direct confrontation with the residents of the community and began a massive education campaign directed at the press and at the local residents. This intensive communication with the grass roots seems to have stabilized the situation a great deal. Although the proposed site will be forgotten and the proposed home may be established in another community, the ongoing programs of the agency do not seem to be in immediate danger. In Hebron, the agency sponsoring the group home had developed a strategy which included emphasis on both the significant regional leaders and the community residents. There, however, the strategy was seen as sequential: first the significant leaders would be contacted and then the community residents. The time lag and the almost inevitable news leaks nearly proved to be the end of the proposed home. Again, a fairly concerted effort to communicate with concerned residents was instituted and the proposal was saved. Although initial groundwork may be necessary, requiring communication with the leadership of a community or a region, contact with the local residents cannot lag far behind or once again one will be open to the charge that the program does not care about the residents' concerns and that someone is trying to sneak a halfway house into the community.

This discussion suggests that specific approaches for entering a community with a group home can be tailored to the contextual makeup of the community. The "low profile" approach is most appropriate for the mobile, pluralistic community. The "significant few" approach may be adaptable in a residential community where the local residents are not particularly capable of organized opposition, but where the town and civic leaders are playing an active role in redirecting or shaping the image of the community. The combined approach, which stresses communication with both the significant leaders and the grass-roots residents, seems to be one of the few strategies with potential for gaining access to a community that has the ability to organize itself in support of, or in opposition to, issues.

A survey of the selected community should provide the information necessary for choosing the best entry strategy. However, well-laid strategies can be devastated if conflict cannot be avoided over such technical problems as appropriateness of the site, presentation of the program content, and intake procedures. We will now describe some of the more technical issues which could produce conflict and impede entry into the community; such conflict might result in focusing debate on what the agency would view as nonessential issues, and away from the basic issue of what a community is going to do to help its youthful offenders. After this discussion we will describe the third major step for neutralizing community resistance—how to resolve conflicts.

The *selection of the site* is of great importance. Care should be taken to avoid giving grounds for legitimate complaints about the suitability of the site for a group residence which will house, let us say, eight to ten youth and two houseparents. If structural questions are legitimate, the whole proposal can be scuttled simply because the agency did not do its homework well. Certain problems can be anticipated, such as the yard being too small, the traffic too heavy, or the house being inadequate. These are problems that any family thinking about buying a house must consider. The appeals board decisions in both Whitewater and Palmyra made specific reference to the shortcomings of the particular sites selected. One can debate such issues as maintaining the residential character of a community or the selection procedures to insure that only certain ages and certain offenders will be residing in the home, but it is most difficult to argue with these physical and structural issues which will inevitably be couched in terms of what is "good for kids."

*Selection of a name for the program* can also be strategically relevant. Program names are symbols that say something to the community as well as something to the clients. Some names may serve only to threaten and increase the anxiety of potential neighbors. In Hebron, one woman suggested that the name of the program caused as much concern within the community as any other factor. In many cases social service agencies try to put together acronyms that challenge the client but they may also raise red flags for community residents. Names such as BURN, SCARE, SMACK, BLOW-UP or JD may simply cause more problems with community relations than they are worth. Acronyms in the mental health field such as HELP and RECOVERY seem more neutral.

An issue related to selecting a name is deciding what generic label should be used to describe the program. Most of the agencies in this study did not refer to their proposals as halfway houses, even though many of the residents referred to them as such. Preferred labels were group homes, child-care centers, schools, or "family." Choice of a label has an effect not only on how the program will be perceived in the community, but also on whether a zoning variance will be required in residential areas. A residence with an educational program that will enable it to be called a school may find that in some areas the zoning question can be eased. In some communities the best strategy might be to set up a "family," which might avoid raising the issue of zoning regulations. This could be done by employing a couple, full time, to work with five to eight residents and who would bring into their home from time to time other persons with specialized skills to provide services for the youth. This could be seen as an expansion of the foster home model.[b]

*Presenting program content* carelessly can raise needless problems. It is ridiculous for a social service agency to lay itself open to the charge that it does not have a well-planned, well-articulated program for the residence. The proposed home in Palmyra was particularly susceptible to this charge, as was, initially the program in Laurel. In Laurel, an added complication arose because residents did not believe that a program which had been fairly successful with youthful drug abusers would necessarily be successful with juvenile delinquents. The program staff did not seem ready to handle this issue.

Issues involving selection criteria and procedures are included under program content. In Laurel and Whitewater residents were particularly upset over the possibility that tough older juveniles would be admitted to the program. The selection procedures must be worked out and articulated so that the community is assured the plan does not call for working with "dangerous youth" and that if such a youth does manage to make his way through the screening process and become unmanageable in the program, he can be rejected. The residents may still not believe the argument, but at least a straightforward program has been presented.

The importance of this presentation of program content can best be illustrated by the experience in Hebron. Because of a news leak and because of the name of the program, many residents were ready to organize opposition to the proposed home. At the Taxpayers' Association meeting, convened to discuss the group home proposal, however, the program staff presented a very honest, straightforward appraisal of their program. While they could not guarantee the community's safety, they did present the safeguards built into the program. Most of the participants agreed that the presentation neutralized any further efforts to prevent the establishment of the group residence.

In Sullivan, the program was actively presented to neighbors by both staff and the boys. They did not seek to dramatically publicize the program, but they

---

bThe Massachusetts Department of Mental Health has undertaken research concerning the definition of "family" in zoning ordinances. The department contends that "there is growing legal precedent in zoning cases in Massachusetts and other states to support the emerging definition of family [as] that of a group of people sleeping, cooking, or eating on a premises as a single housekeeping unit rather than as a group of people related by blood or marriage."

did quietly solicit the assistance of some neighbors, and the youth became involved in various work projects within the community. Again, the staff and youth knew what the program was about and could intelligently talk about it, if asked.

*Client and staff residence* can also materially affect acceptance of a group home. An issue that arose in the Laurel, Whitewater, Palmyra, and Hebron communities was the desire not to be dumping grounds for other communities' problems. This was particularly the case in Laurel where councilmen from other communities were kidding the Laurel councilmen about Laurel's being the leader in social service and saying that other communities would like to send their "tough kids" to Laurel. In Palmyra there was the complaint that the support for the group home came from the suburbs. And in Hebron, there was concern that the home would serve youth from Boston and Brockton. Residents in Laurel seemed willing to serve the needs of their own youth. And most residents in Hebron were willing to serve youth as long as the youth resided in the resort area.

A similar issue has been raised about staff. In Laurel, it was said that the program staff worked in the program during the day but then drove home to rather plush suburbs at night. And in Palmyra, it was said that the Protestant Council should set up their group home in their own neighborhood. Although these issues were not raised in Sullivan or Eagle Grove, in both cases some program staff resided within the home or the community.

The issue of community control is related to this question. If a community recognizes the need for a residential program for its troubled youth, such as the need to generate more community contact while the youth are in a "treatment" program and being reintegrated into that community, it also is reasonable for the community to make certain demands on the program. This may include a request that at least a specific portion of the staff reside within the community, that youth from the community have priority for entry into the program, and that residents have some influence on decisions about the nature of the program. A problem with community control arises when a community decides it has no delinquency and can therefore simply reject the notion of a group residence; at that point it seems the state must assume an *in loco parentis* role and provide services for troubled youth. Where there is community interest, however, one probably should not resist real "community-based corrections" by denying *shared control* over the program.

Finally, emphasizing that the *program will serve the community* can greatly ease entry. Obviously the home should have some impact on handling the community's delinquency situation. Successful integration of clients will prevent at least some crime. But the clients can also be used as resources while participating in the program. One woman in Hebron recognized this when she suggested that some of the youth could help her with a local historical society. Youth in the Sullivan residence became a resource for filling part-time jobs.

Youth in the Eagle Grove residence are becoming active in a prevention program.

*Resolution of Conflict.* We must reiterate that in most instances, with the possible exception of the very low profile approaches, any attempt to establish a group home in a community will incur some sort of resistance. Even if the issues discussed above have been well handled, some conflict will still probably arise over such issues as "we don't need a halfway house in this area," "this is not the kind of issue with which this organization should be involved," or "halfway houses are needed but in the next county." For successful entry into a community, it seems imperative for the social agency to develop strategies for resolving conflicts.[c] In general, an all-out fight will work against the interests of the social service agency and the youth whom the agency wants to serve. The administrators in Laurel recognized this when they said that it would be better for the youth to be located in a business-zoned area than to be in a residential community which simply did not want them. If all attempts to resolve conflict fail, this backing off may be one of the preferable alternative choices. Let us then turn our attention to ways of neutralizing conflict which may hold open the opportunity for establishing the proposed home, recognizing that conflict resolution strategies that make continued relationships of cooperation between the conflicting parties difficult or impossible are inappropriate in this case, although they may be helpful in other situations.

Any conflict will have at least two disagreeing parties. If each has a level of power sufficient to thwart the desires of the other, a situation where there can be no outright winner probably results. Even if the social agency can "beat" the opposition on a particular issue, if its tactics are unjust, the opposition may simply regroup and become an even more intense enemy.[d] It is desirable therefore to have available face-saving devices. The opposition should be given the sense that it has had some impact on the outcome. In Laurel, the agency sponsoring the group home, when it realized that its whole program could be lost, withdrew from direct confrontation to begin a massive education campaign. In a sense the education effort was a face-saving device; it provided a reason for avoiding direct confrontation and was a strategy which may reestablish the

---

[c]This is not to say that a certain level of conflict does not further efforts for establishing group homes. Conflict does clarify boundaries of interest groups for example. The function of social conflict has been discussed in numerous works, for example: Georg Simmel, CONFLICT AND THE WEB OF GROUP AFFILIATIONS, (New York: The Free Press, 1955), pp. 17-20; Ralf Dahrendorf, CLASS AND CLASS CONFLICT IN INDUSTRIAL SOCIETY, (Stanford, California: Stanford University Press, 1957), pp. 206-213; Lewis Coser, THE FUNCTIONS OF SOCIAL CONFLICT, (Glencoe, Illinois: The Free Press of Glencoe, 1956).

---

[d]It has nearly become a sociological dictum that conflict often tends to strengthen the opposition into an even more formidable opponent. See Kurt Wolff, THE SOCIOLOGY OF GEORG SIMMEL (New York: Free Press, 1950), p. 192; Lewis Coser, FUNCTIONS OF SOCIAL CONFLICT, p. 38.

agency in the minds of the residents as a viable, worthwhile organization. In Palmyra we had quite the opposite case. There, emotional invectives such as "unchristian" and "property-conscious" and "do-gooder" served to escalate the conflict and to make satisfactory resolution that much more difficult. In Hebron conflict was neutralized by confronting it, letting all the questions come, and dealing with them on the spot. There was no particular effort to "snow" the residents, but rather to be honest about the strengths and weaknesses of the program. The style that one uses to handle conflict can have considerable impact on its resolution.

A classic distinction in the study of conflict and conflict resolution is between realistic and nonrealistic conflict.[e] A basic principle that underlies this discussion, is that of generating and rising to only realistic conflict.[2] Realistic conflict is over an actual difference of interest clearly and accurately defined. Nonrealistic conflict is over something other than an actual difference of interest, and is therefore not susceptible to resolution. Nonrealistic conflicts often tend to be impersonal, couched in terms of ideas rather than actual personal interest. Such abstractly defined conflicts can be pursued with greater fury than can personal conflicts. This truth is represented in the common recognition that holy wars are more bloody than others, in the fact that "lynch law" has frequently been activated by couching a personal economic interest in terms of some widely held ideal, such as the saving of Southern white womanhood, and in the fact that when the federal government has been actively and successfully involved in solving racial problems, it has done so by focusing conflict on genuine economic and social interests, not on symbols such as Southern white womanhood. The role of the mediator in labor-management relations is also to focus the conflict on realistic issues and to get rid of nonrealistic issues.

The direct identification of the real issues and frank discussion of them by the group entering Hebron is a good example of focusing on realistic conflict with good results. So is the strategy of representing oneself to the neighbors in terms of what one is doing, and in terms of who the youth actually are, instead of as a halfway house, an abstract idea with nonrealistic connotations, or representing oneself by a highly symbolic name. The strategy of the Protestant Church Council in Palmyra is a good example of failure because of stubbornly generating and rising to nonrealistic conflict. Alinsky was fond of pointing out that when he approached church groups,[3] he did it on pragmatic grounds of economics, power, and the like, not on the grounds of religious belief. The conflict in Palmyra had clear realistic components, relating to property value, possible danger to residents, the intrusion of an outside group. The Protestant

---

[e]Ralf Dahrendorf, CLASS AND CLASS CONFLICT IN INDUSTRIAL SOCIETY. In order to regulate conflict "both parties to a conflict have to recognize the necessity and reality of the conflict situation, in this sense, the fundamental justice of the cause of the opponent," p. 225.

Council, instead of meeting these problems and resolving them, chose to generate a nonrealistic conflict over the practice of religious values, a conflict it could never win. Realistic conflict, probably susceptible to solution by compromise, since many of the objections of the community were probably quite valid, was escalated by the Protestant Council into a "holy war," perhaps either because of naiveté or because of a need for martyrdom. It was perhaps fortunate for DYS as well as for the community that the Protestant group was decisively defeated, because their tendency to make holy war would have had a generally alienating effect in the community.

To summarize, one must know the other side, its power and interests, be clear on the difference between one's own interests and the other side's, and do everything possible to focus the conflict on those realistic issues, avoiding nonrealistic conflict over loaded symbols. The voice of a group in determining the course of the community in which it lives should always be considered as one of the issues over which realistic conflict may arise. Thus one must consider the importance of face-saving. The possibility of escalating nonrealistic conflict by using a symbolic name, or by using a loaded shorthand description, such as halfway house, should also be considered, as should the danger of creating holy war. Also much of the conflict about technical issues such as the program name, selection procedures, and site selection can *simply be avoided* if one plans well and anticipates the consequences of decisions related to these technical issues. It is absurd as well as unfortunate to have a proposed home rejected because the sponsoring agency did not carefully do its own homework. Debates over technical problems and nonrealistic concerns allow for proponents and opponents to engage in conflict over petty issues while avoiding altogether discussion of the real issues. On the other hand, once the technical issues are out of the way, the possible value of forthrightly dealing with the real, unavoidable issues involved in differences of interest should not be underestimated, and meetings and educational campaigns designed to focus and resolve realistic conflict should be seriously considered.

## References

1. The importance of understanding the power structure and process of a community to facilitate community action is underscored by Roland I. Warner, THE COMMUNITY IN AMERICA (Chicago: Rand McNally, 1972), pp. 308-309; and Robert C. Wood, SUBURBIA (Boston: Houghton Mifflin, 1958).

2. Lewis Coser, THE FUNCTIONS OF SOCIAL CONFLICT, pp. 48-55; Georg Simmel, CONFLICT AND THE WEB OF GROUP AFFILIATIONS, pp. 27-28.

3. Saul D. Alinsky, RULES FOR RADICALS, A PRAGMATIC PRIMER FOR REALISTIC RADICALS (New York: Vintage Books, 1972), p. 88.

# Part III
## Strategies and Case Studies

# 10

## Effecting Changes in a Training School for Girls

Frederick Thacher

This chapter deals with the application of social change to the oldest reform school for girls in the country. Social change, a much discussed phenomenon on the theoretical level, was applied in practical terms to modernize and rehabilitate this institution. The girls school was in desperate need of rehabilitation. It had strayed from its designated function of training and rehabilitating young girls. After more than 115 years its function had become so distorted that even the cruelest deed against inmates was considered "for their own good." The government officials who knew how inhumane the situation was either ignored it or used it for patronage. No one seemed to know what to do about it. But it was clear that *something had to change*.

Recently there has been ample documentation of the horrors of punishment to delinquents. Any number of newspaper feature stories have been written; many film documentaries have been made. At this school a strategy for change was developed, and over a period of fourteen months that strategy was implemented. It proved successful in transforming an essentially inhumane prison into an open, human treatment and living center for young men and women.

*History*

In 1850 Mr. S.G. Howe responded to an inquiry concerning the need for a girls' reformatory in Massachusetts by stating:

It is an evil to shut up youth in houses of detention; and whether it be a necessary evil or not, depends upon whether the desirable ends, to wit, the reformation of those capable of reformation, and the safety of the community, can be secured in any other way or not; if they can, then such establishments are unnecessary evils.

Mr. Howe was also concerned with the consequences of labeling and went on to say:

A residence in the bosom of a private family, or in a community of vicious girls, though ever so well regulated, where she would be exposed to public gaze, and necessarily get for life the name and character of a 'House of Reformation Girl'? Surely not![1]

These and other arguments were well taken. A commission established by Governor Henry J. Gardner in 1850 began the necessary research and political maneuvering to establish an Industrial School for Girls. On April 12, 1854 a resolve of the legislature approved an appropriation of $20,000 for the establishment of such a school—provided an equal sum could be raised privately within six months. Within six months $20,300 was raised.[2] The Massachusetts Act of 1855 formally established the school[3] and on the 27th of August, 1856, the institution was inaugurated by religious services.[4]

For its day the ISG of 1855 was probably the most progressive girls institution in the country. There were no walls.[5] The emphasis was to be on reform with hopes of returning these girls back into society as good, God-fearing, productive members. It was "designed for those who are wayward, obstinate, or who from the poverty, ignorance, neglect or abuse of parents, are exposed to, or have become, vagrants, or have taken the initiatory steps in crime, and to save them from inevitable ruin, and from becoming a nuisance to society.... It is to be a home.... The government and discipline strictly parental."[6] Each cottage was administered by a supervisor and an assistant matron. These matrons were to be as mothers to the girls, giving love and discipline as it was called for.

By January of 1857 there were forty-four girls, six staff, one pair oxen, seven cows, eleven young cattle, three horses, and two dogs living on the grounds. Punishment was not harsh. The family style of living was stressed and early records indicate that all was progressing as Mr. Howe had wished.[7]

By 1877, some twenty years later, the school was overcrowded, a building had burned, and the nation was suffering a postwar depression. The reports from ISG focused on the need to build a separate structure where girls could be punished in "isolation or separate confinement, with or without work, as the case may require.... [Isolation] is conceded to be one of the most effective methods of bringing to a sense of duty the insubordinate."[8] The family philosophy of the ISG seemed to be breaking down. The warmth of the stories and genuine good feeling of the workers toward the girls seems to have been strained and greatly diminished by 1877.

By 1930 horror stories were coming from the school. Stories which—part fact, part fantasy—were being told as recently as 1971. Security men had been added to the staff, security rooms had been built into every cottage, the "hospital" was less a haven for the ill as it was a maximum security unit, every door was encumbered by steel locks and bolts (three per door), from the belt of every staff member hung heavy clanging keys.

What had happened to the family concept of the cottages? Why had runaways increased by nearly 5000 percent or more?!

*ISG 1970*

By 1970 the Industrial School for Girls had become a fortress without walls. Except for highly structured periods of sports or cleaning or walking escorted to the central school building, the girls were either locked in their rooms or confined to the cottage.

The superintendent controlled the school with an iron fist. She made every decision in the school. Subordinate staff were there to enforce policy, not to interpret or make policy. Their function was simply to carry out assigned tasks, watchdog policy, supervise routine operations and report to the superintendent.

The supply woman was the most powerful position next to the superintendent. She controlled staff schedules, including vacation schedules. It was her job to keep up staff discipline. As the person who distributed the supplies she came into intense and frequent contact with the line staff. If a matron complained too strongly about the quantity or quality of supplies she had better not expect to get her work or vacation schedule in order of preference. Women who towed the line and were willing to conform had their favors returned. Of all the staff, the supply woman wielded the sharpest axe. A simple request to purchase more eggs and less cold cereal had to first go to the supply lady, then to the superintendent, then to the clerks, and finally to the maintenance man who picked up supplies. The whole process was seldom completed.

**Maintenance and Security Men.** Maintenance staff consisted of two full-time painters, one full-time farmer, one full-time grounds keeper, and four assorted carpenters and handy men. Three maintenance men doubled as security men to augment the four full-time security staff. A maintenance foreman supervised all of the male staff and took his orders directly from the superintendent.

**The Hospital.** As a "hospital" it wasn't much. As a high security isolation unit it was superb. Nursing staff answered directly to the superintendent and had little or no contact with any other unit at the ISG. The rooms were colorless and barren with heavily screened windows and doors which were always locked. A girl who was being punished, or a girl who was at the bottom of the cottage pecking order, often ended up in the hospital in isolation. The infirmary section was used occasionally but girls who complained of being sick were often considered goldbrickers and thus discouraged from receiving medical treatment.

**School House.** A formal school system with grades six through nine was located in a central school building. Standard academic courses were taught by three full-time teachers; two arts and crafts teachers; two sewing teachers. These seven people were directly supervised by a principal. The principal was powerless. She had no control over the daily function of her school. She rarely met with the superintendent. Her main job was to teach typing, answer phones, discipline girls, and keep track of her school supplies.

Surprisingly, this school was completely isolated from the rest of ISG. There was no direct communication between cottage staff and teachers or between administrative staff and teachers. They were essentially ignored by all elements within the school. Even in the staff dining room teachers were segregated from other staff and seldom involved themselves in general conversation. Their primary source of contact with the rest of the ISG was through the girls.

**Clerical Staff.** As in most bureaucratic structures the clerks were highly influential at the ISG. The filing system presented a major obstacle for anyone wishing to collect data. Records were kept in several different places, files were highly personalized. When the superintendent was away, the senior clerk readily filled her place. The assistant superintendent was easily bypassed. The clerical staff were never allowed to offer opinions—they carried out orders and filled out forms.

**Matrons.** In each cottage (five cottages total) there were three workaday shifts, seven days per week. Each shift was comprised of two matrons—one supervisor and one assistant supervisor. During the 6:00 A.M. to 2 P.M. shift, the supervisor was responsible for waking the girls, getting them ready for the day, whether it be school or work assignment, attending to the daily housecleaning and discipline. Generally she was responsible for the day-to-day management of the cottage and the girls. At the end of her shift she reported in the log of the daily activities. She also reported any punishments given. These reports were then forwarded to the ISG superintendent.

The assistant supervisor was largely responsible for cooking and the kitchen. The supplies for the cottage were also her responsibility. In her daily charge were four girls who assisted in the cooking and who did most of the cleanup. With these four girls the matron had to prepare all three meals (the supper meal was prepared before 2 P.M. and kept warm) and clean up after two of them. She in turn reported directly to the supervisor matron.

During the early evening shift (2 P.M. to 10 P.M.) the supervisor's responsibilities varied only slightly. She saw to it that the girls returned to the cottage, cleaned up, and put the lights out at 9 P.M. The assistant supervisor cleaned the kitchen and assisted the supervisor. The 10 P.M. to 6 A.M. shift did mostly minor housekeeping chores: sewing, ironing, sorting of supplies, laundry, and so forth. At the end of each day the supervisor's reports that had been forwarded to the superintendent were returned with comments.

**Counselors.** The counseling staff were primarily young and fairly recent additions to the ISG staff. As counselors in a clinical sense they were ineffective and isolated from the girls and the other staff. Although counseling was given a great deal of lip service, very few people, including the counselors, understood what role it played. Their influence on the administration was practically nil. They were never allowed to make any real decisions regarding a girl. Their role was largely that of work time friend to the girls. (You will notice in Figure 10-1 that the counselors are not mentioned as contributing any degree of influence to the decision-making. Their role is so minor that it would be illegible on such a representation.)

**Overview.** The superintendent was the supreme commander of her staff. Those who showed the greatest loyalty were promoted fastest. Those who were least inclined to be creative were pulled into the inner circle of the main office. Staff had to relinquish their identities in order to carry out the ministrations and

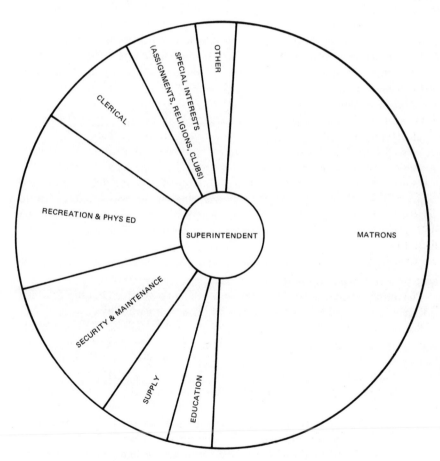

**Figure 10-1.** Direct Lines of Communication Between Institutional Elements and Their Influence on Superintendent in Decision-making Process.

dictates of the superintendent. Max Weber could describe well the process unfolding here: the leaders "glorified the loyal worker who did not seek acquisition, but lived according to the apostolic model, and was thus endowed with the charisma of the disciples."[9] This charisma was limited to a small group of people and as such found its limits only within their circle.[10] In this case the circle extended to a larger group, still extremely limited, the entire staff of the ISG.

The superintendent, in taking on the role of authoritarian leader takes "primary responsibility for assigning tasks and working indicating 'as the needs arise' the steps to be followed (rather than outlining the total plan ahead of time)."[11] This role was further reinforced by the staff. The staff was more than happy to be free of any real responsibility. It welcomed and fed on the dictates of the leader.

**Cottage Life.** In most instances the feelings between matrons were not good. The continual abasement of the assistant by the supervisor resulted in a great deal of anger and hostility. This anger could not be forthrightly manifested and often surfaced through the girls. The girls were set up by the assistant to act out against the supervisor.

Of all the matrons assigned to a cottage one always rose above the rest to dominate the entire cottage. She set the extreme limits and dictated the mood for all to follow. One cottage was known for strictness and control while another was known for its more democratic structure. These variations depended on the matron who "led" the cottage. Although the formal structure didn't allow for a "cottage director" there inevitably was one. She set the norms and they were adhered to by the rest of her work companions.[12] Anyone breaking into the cottage had to be ready to accept the group as it was. If not she was subject to a great deal of additional stress.[13]

In each cottage there were between twelve and twenty-four girls. These girls were further divided into subgroups, cliques,[14] and sometimes gangs.

The inmate cliques were established on a pecking order, membership of which is largely determined by cottage geography. Those girls who shared a hallway of rooms were more likely to form their own group than they were to join forces with girls at the other end of the building. One of the strongest influencing factors was the 13-hour per day lock-up. When these girls wanted to talk to one another they had to do so out the window. Since each was alone in her room, the nearest person within hearing distance was separated by locked doors and a wall. The window, even on cold winter evenings (there was no heat in the rooms), was opened and gossip and plans and fantasies and notes were passed. Friendships and alliances formed; a clique was born. Depending on the girls in the cottage, that clique might become the dominant one and govern the cottage.

Within each clique there was a pecking order. The lowest members served the leaders diligently. These were the retarded, brain damaged or most disturbed girls. The leaders often extracted stolen goods (usually cigarettes from the main office) or sexual favors from other clique members. Occasionally a clique formed around a matron who knew how to use it to help maintain order. On one such occasion two girls were struggling for cottage control; the matron sided with one and ordered the other to the hospital in isolation. The struggle was quietly settled with the matron in firm control.

Those who gained leadership positions were usually the ones who were the loudest and toughest. Most of them were urban kids. For their next-in-command they selected the girls who were capable manipulators and con artists. These girls had to also play the fall guy when need be. The lowest class of girls in the cliques were the passive-aggressive ones or the most obviously disturbed who were happy to do the punishable acting out.

For those girls who were at the bottom of the order there was continual harassment and threats. Their rooms were upset, their property stolen, their clothing dirtied. They were subject to physical punishment: on one occasion a retarded girl was attacked by the leader and her immediate lieutenant. They punched, kicked, and finally pushed her head in a sink basin filled with water. Other girls who were present did nothing to stop the obvious abuse this girl was receiving. Life became intolerable for the girl to the point where she would stay voluntarily *locked* in her room all day. Finally the clique leader (an unpopular girl with the matrons) was paroled home even though her behavior gave no indication she could return to her family.

**Homosexual Activity**. The extent of homosexual behavior was extremely difficult to determine accurately. It was one of the outwardly strongest forbiddens of the ISG, but it was tolerated. In many instances girls were found together by a matron. Usually it was during the late afternoon lock-up or the nightly baths that such actions took place. They were by no means isolated.

Hall girls were responsible for locking the other girls in their rooms during the afternoon. Usually the matron was "busy" in her office after giving the order for the girls to go to their rooms. The doors were not key locked but were bolted from the outside by the hall girls on duty. It was an easy matter for the hall girl to unbolt doors and let girls into each other's rooms, a practice quite common. Nearly 80 percent of the girls in one cottage admitted to homosexual behavior during a community meeting.

The average day for most of the girls consisted of thirteen hours of lock-up without bathroom privileges, possibly some school work (but not the rule), and always lots of farm work. To go into the complexities of the girls' subculture is not the intent here. For readers more interested in that aspect of a residential school, I would suggest reading *Cottage Six* by Howard Polsky.

The questions are endless. We know that the society we live in requires deviants for limit setting, for psychological comfort, for entertainment value, for the economic advantage of newspapers and their advertisers.[15] Limits must also be set on how far this society will go in encouraging deviant behavior.[16] There is an end point beyond which we can no longer force other human beings to take on a role and an identity we place on them.[17] The crime is not of persons against persons, it is society against the individual. Fortunately there is an end point—the institution. We cannot, in one sweep, alter the function of the society, but we can alter the function of the institution.

**A Plan for Change that Worked.** Many contemporary writers have warned of the dangers of institutionalization. They have dealt primarily with the consequences and the pitfalls of institutionalization,[18] without concerning themselves with the aspects and/or prospects of change. What I propose here is one plan, related to the institution, for social change.

*Plan: Phase I*

Keeping the above history of the institution in mind, along with Figure 10-1, a steady shift in function is observed. Originally it was rehabilitation. The family cottage unit, combined with heavy doses of God and country, was set up to deal with the manifest problem of "vicious or viciously disposed girls."[19] What a noble and honorable function, indeed. However, the function of the system, within less than three months, began to make its move. By the early twentieth century, that function was no longer the rehabilitation of "vicious or viciously disposed girls," but had become the maintenance of the institutional system itself. The comfort of the staff became paramount. The order of the system took precedence over all else. In order to assist in the maintenance of the system the structure was altered only slightly. The hospital, a legitimate part of the system, was partially redefined as the high security area. The farmer was partially redefined as the security man who would spank the girls. In later years security men were formally added to the structure and they became known for the severity of the beatings they inflicted upon the girls. (Recently a girl was pulled by the ankle from a truck, dragged across the seat onto the ground, and then kicked about the chest, stomach, legs and head by one of her "uncles.") But, essentially the structure was left untouched, the system was not disturbed. The function had become grossly distorted and inhumane. For the sake of order, girls were locked for weeks on a "light diet" in an unheated, unfurnished 4' x 10' room. Not only were they locked in, but they were stripped of their clothing and had no bathroom privileges. Things were hardly different in 1970. The duration was shorter and the girls still had to strip; however, they could now wear a johnnie.

The theory of reform had been internalized by the system. Those hired into it could not possibly see what was actually happening. Blinded by their own sicknesses and shrouded in some idealistic, moralistic theory, they could only think and say that the system, as it stood, was "best for the girls even though they may not appreciate it." The system and its structure had become the end of the means and *any* means necessary were employed to meet that end. No one was allowed to tamper with the system.

Sounds pretty formidable, but actually it wasn't. Remember the way the system was structured (Figure 10-1). What we had there was a series of autonomous elements. The laundry, the hospital, the bakery, the cottage, and so forth, all operated as separate units accountable only to themselves and unified at the hub by the superintendent. These autonomous elements had two implications for the analysis of social change; by their very nature they had a relatively thick, old insulation from the effects of change as a whole. However, these autonomous units were fairly susceptible to *autonomous* changes due to their insulation and meager links which held them together. Any attempts to change the entire system at once were doomed to failure because they would have been met with the unified effects of the insulation. However, an attempt to change each part would meet with a much higher probability of success. Each unit, because it was so isolated, would more readily accept change as an autonomous unit.

In our case, where each unit was strictly controlled by a central figure, we had to take our analysis one step further. That central figure, the superintendent, had it within her power to alert the system of impending changes. She could communicate her fears directly to each unit, for it was only here that the insulation was thin. Once this was accomplished the system would have effectively closed itself off and change would be possible.

Two things had to be accomplished: (1) the superintendent had to be isolated from the rest of the parts and (2) she could not be fully cognizant of the changes taking place.

The first of the above could be accomplished by redirecting the lines of communication from and to the autonomous units to and through another element. That element had to act as an insular mold around the superintendent. Yet that element had to be a legitimate part of the system as it stood.

From Figure 10-1, note the position of the counseling staff. They had little or no influence on the decision-making. Yet in theory (reform and rehabilitation), they were a vital part of the function of the ISG that everyone recognized. Also, in practice, I found them to be the youngest, least institutionalized staff with creative potential. They could become the collar around the office and the person of the superintendent. They had the energy necessary, and they had some semblance of an objective viewpoint.

With approval and sanction of the superintendent the counseling staff were reoriented within the decision-making process. To do this it was necessary to manipulate the theory of rehabilitation to the best advantage. All arguments had to be geared toward rehabilitation and the superintendent had to appear to be in control.

For this purpose the use of group techniques proved to be the best tool. Groups can be a dynamic force for the individual, helping that individual toward change,[20] and by extension they can become a dynamic force in helping an institution toward change. A group program at the ISG not only provided support for the counselors, it also had the effect of opening up each cottage and making them more susceptible to long-term changes. The initiation of a group program was not argued against because it was in the interest of the girls and their rehabilitation.

By supplying new strengths to the counselors through group process, they eventually developed the personal strength necessary to take on the added responsibilities required of them. At the same time each cottage began to feel the impact of the counselor. They increased their profile in the cottage and became a more vital part of the daily cottage life. The girls assigned to their caseload were moved to the cottage where the counselor had her office. The counselor was encouraged to eat and spend more time there. She was encouraged to intervene in a stronger and more consistent way in the daily routine. Increasingly she was able to take on the responsibility for more decisions. Fewer decisions were deferred to the superintendent, either concerning individual girls or cottage routine. A group setting was provided for these counselors to give them the comfort of numbers and the ego supports necessary to continue their work.

It is not important that each individual involved be aware of the process. In fact, I think it is vital that the process may not be fully known by too many of the people involved. They must be made aware of the fact that they are involved in social change, but at the conceptual level it is not necessary. The conceptual level thinking is the plan of strategy and once known it could easily be fought against by the system.

By turning more and more decisions over to the treatment unit, fewer decisions went through the superintendent. As the staff in the various autonomous units became more accustomed to turning toward the counselors, fewer decisions were made at the center and, in part, the insulation was thickened (see Figure 10-2). Only when that insulation around the center was well-established could we move on in our scheme of things toward change of the entire system.

The reference points of the cottage staff had to be safely and quietly reconstructed. The counselors were acting with more authority and confidence. The matrons could see them as acting with consent of the superintendent and had no reason to be alarmed at the drastic changes in authority figures. On the other hand, the superintendent was becoming increasingly isolated from the rest of the ISG. Presumably she would make an attempt to reestablish her old position of authority and reopen the old lines of communication. She had to be supported while these changes were being made. Sometimes the consequences of social change can be disastrous for the individual especially when the forces of change are beyond the individual's control.[21]

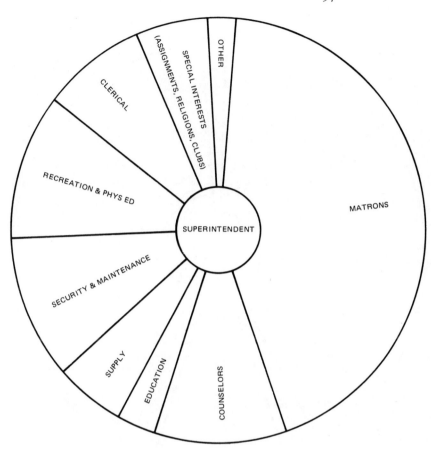

**Figure 10-2.** New Position of Counselors, Increase of Their Influence in Decision-making, and Decrease in Influence of Matrons, Recreation, and Other.

An attempt was made to alter the reference points on which she relied.[22] Since her former reference points were no longer able to assist her in a positive manner, they could only aid her in a negative manner[23]—and consequently act against the forces of change. This could have been an extremely delicate matter and could not have been undertaken by one person alone. The very real danger was that those negative referents might have been reactively strengthened by any attempt to change them.[24] A careful analysis of the situation was necessary. The best possible procedure was to control those referents, but this would have met with limited success. The establishment of new referents was the answer. For this purpose other authority figures had to establish trust relationships with the

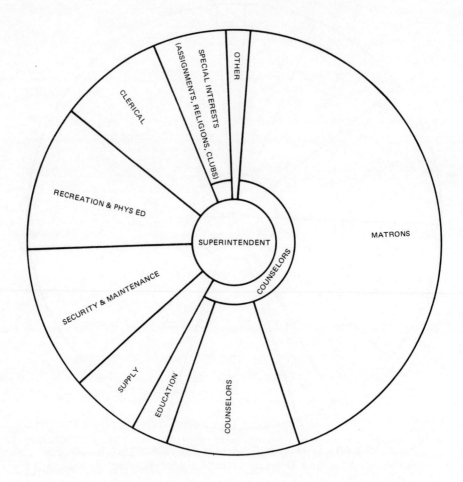

**Figure 10-3.** Increased Insulation of Superintendent Due to the Increased Activity of Counselors and Altered Lines of Communication.

superintendent. These people were representatives of the central administration and were fully aware of the changes taking place at the ISG. The old referents were isolated and allowed to sit quietly on the sidelines, where they could not influence the decisions of the superintendent.

Once this was accomplished (see Figure 10-2) we proceeded at an accelerated rate to change the autonomous units. With each part of the system effectively isolated from the others, the probability of success was greatly increased. Their own insulation which had previously shielded them from any changes for over 100 years was now used as a tool for social change. There was little opportunity for any one part of the system to come to the aid of another. And, with the central figure isolated there was little chance for all the units to come together. But, there was still an avenue—through outside social relationships—for opposition to form against change.

Any plan for social change of a system must be aware of, and take into consideration, the informal social relationships within the system. Whenever there is a shift in roles there is certain to be some role confusion.[25] This role confusion is likely to lead to reinforcement of other reference points. Possibly, reference points that were previously strictly social in function, but which under the stress of change, could be altered to provide additional support for the status quo and the system as it serves those people in it. The leadership of that social group must be co-opted and made to act in such a way as to support the changes. Their leadership must not be confronted. They must be allowed to continue as though their presence or their function were shrouded in secrecy. A confrontation would only force them to take a harder stand against the new elements.

*Phase I in Operation*

According to the plan outlined above, a group made up of counselors was initiated. That group, a training group, was able to provide the supports necessary for the counselors to assume the additional burdens required of them. By meeting on a weekly basis for nearly two hours, they were able to provide one another with encouragement so vital to their performance. Their individual strengths were reinforced and they drew on the strengths of their peers plus their leader. Problems and anxieties relating to their roles were aired and interpersonal relationships established. From this safe setting the counselors discharged frustration and confusion. They also took renewed energy back to their jobs.

Prior to bringing that part of the staff together it was necessary to convince the superintendent that their role was indeed vital to the rehabilitation of the girls, and that group meetings were part and parcel of that rehabilitation. Using the system's theory, that was a relatively easy task. It was also necessary to prepare the cottage staff for the increased involvement of the counselors. This was accomplished by direct intervention of the superintendent on their behalf and stress placed on the counselors to perform. After being assured of the important role they had to play, the superintendent used her powers of control to see that their profile was raised in the cottage. She met with each cottage and reassured them of her presence while telling them more decisions would be left to cottage staff, i.e., the counselors.

An important element not to be overlooked was the assistant superintendent. It was important to reestablish the strength of that position and to make it an influential part of the system. Equally important was the need to establish that strength and influence independent of controls placed on it by the superintendent.

By welcoming the assistant into the counselors' group, while at the same time giving him personal support, it was possible to help him establish such a role. The importance here was that in the official structure he held a position of strength, a strength the rest of the staff could relate to. This position was a positive reference point for both the superintendent and the staff. The liberal change-oriented person in that position needed strong ego support and through group and personal relationships he was able to get that ego support. As such, the position of assistant superintendent now acted as a source to increase the isolation of the superintendent (see Figure 10-4). It also acted as an additional source of strength for the counseling staff.

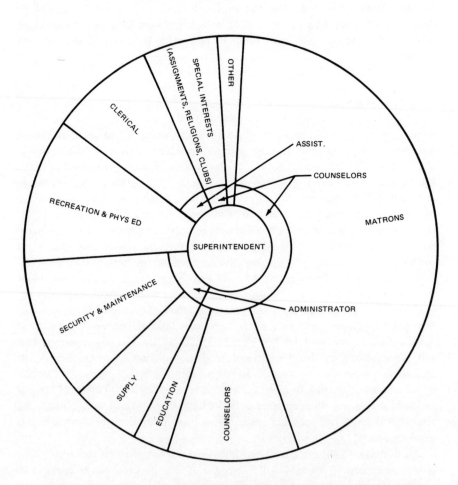

**Figure 10-4**. New Influence of Assistant Superintendent and Effect of Increasing Insulation of Superintendent.

Another point to consider is that in all of the sociological jargon about systems and systems function and structure is the patient; in this case the inmates of the ISG. They, too, had to be considered one of the most viable elements for social change. To bypass them in the process of isolating the superintendent would have been a major and probably fatal error. It was from the backs of the inmates that the system gets its energy. Without them it would have no need for existing. This additional source of energy can be transferred from support of the system to support of the social change by using groups and group process. The group can become a major dynamo of power. If the people who lead the group are the same people working for change, that energy can be easily and constructively guided by the forces for change.

In each cottage, once-a-week meetings were established. The matrons on duty were required to attend and the counselors for each cottage led the group. There were only two rules: (1) no one was to leave the room, and (2) no physical violence. Anyone could say anything he pleased and there were no sacred topics of discussion. At each meeting all of the girls living in that cottage could attend. Even those girls in lock-up were let out for the meeting.

Soon these groups established themselves as a major force for change within the cottages. The autonomy of each cottage was working in favor of new rules and new behavior. The matrons were being held accountable for their actions and were subject to the demands and criticisms of the girls. The smoking was increased by 100 percent (from two to four smokes per day), the afternoon lock-up was reduced by two hours, the girls could chew gum, use ballpoint pens and generally apply great amounts of pressure to the matrons. The matrons could only turn to the counselors with their complaints because the superintendent, having been partially isolated herself, would not respond in full to their cries. The new lines of communication had been established.

What about the informal social staff functions: alarmed by the changes taking place, a ladies sewing circle type club made up of staff members, rose to meet the challenge. They joined forces with the security and maintenance staff (a tenuous coalition at best). They wrote and talked with their state senators and representatives, they tried to sabotage the weekly cottage meetings, they even at one point physically threatened people who enforced the changes.

The political problems were handled from the executive level in central administration, but that still left the sewing circle opposition intact, and at the ISG. One of their members decided to confide in me of the happenings. Using this information, and information gathered from other sources, it was easy to determine who the leaders of this group were. Once their identity was established it was simply a matter of co-opting them. One leader was offered a promotion—out of the matron's ranks to become a supervisor (recall that few of these women really like each other). She faltered, but after much encouragement and support, she accepted. Effectively she had now joined the forces for change and in fact, she became a leader, on occasion, of one of the community cottage meetings. Her switch and then loss caused a serious division in the sewing circle group. The men, not having a serious connection with this women's group, broke away.

Had this faction not been known, and had it not been neutralized, it could have provided a major source of strength for the opposition. It could also have been instrumental in breaking down the isolation of the autonomous units.

*Plan: Phase II*

When the superintendent's position had become at least partially insulated from the rest of the system, it then became a matter of organizing change within the autonomous units within the system. During Phase I we saw where the position of the counselors along with the assistant superintendent was used to isolate the superintendent. The result was that fewer communications existed between various elements of the system and the hub. The situation as we found it in the beginning (Figure 10-1) had been sufficiently altered (Figures 10-2 and 10-4) so that the system could no longer rally and pose a unified front toward elements of change. The insular effect of the institution, that very strength within the structure which can ward off any change from the outside, is used to benefit change. The theoretical function of the system must be kept in mind at all times.

Recall that in Phase I we began using the inmate population as a force for change. This entire process was now speeded up. The weekly meetings were continued. Added to them were daily morning meetings. All staff had to attend at least several of these sessions each week. In this manner every person on the cottage level was held accountable for their actions. If they were imposing harsh and unfair punishments upon their charges they had to explain their actions. Their autocratic methods were under close scrutiny every day. No one was able to escape the group's judgments. The inmates did, through this democratic process, control much of their own treatment (treatment here is used to mean physical standards of living). The cottage became the focal point for the inmate from which she determined her treatment in the bakery, laundry, farm, and other noncottage areas.

The counselors, while maintaining their position within the structure, were also in a position to take on greater responsibility for daily life. The routine was no longer controlled by a matron. The punishments and rewards were not controlled by the matron. As their training increased, they became more competent professionals, and they began to develop more personal strengths.

The assistant superintendent was better able to assist the counselors in coordinating other elements outside of the cottage. He was able to subordinate the activities of these other elements. No longer, for example, was all of the bread for the institution provided by the bakery. No longer did all of the clothing, towels, sheets, pillow cases, and so on, for the institution come from power sewing assignment. These commodities were purchased from the commercial marketplace. Thus the function of assignment tasks for the girls was no longer cheap labor for the state and the ISG. More relevant training programs were provided, and slowly the laundry, bakery, farm, sewing, and so forth, took on the aspect of hobbies. For those who wanted them they were available, but their function no longer supported the school.

Toward the end of Phase II professionals in the field of child care began coming in to take over the directorship of the cottages. The power wrested from the matrons by the counselors was redistributed among the girls and all treatment staff (treatment here means redirection of impulses and establishment of better controls by the patient).

In order to reinforce the new policies of openness and democratic process a model program was developed. That program was drastically different from the other cottages. The girls wore regular street clothing, some worked off-grounds, several attended local schools. Girls were given responsible jobs within the institution and could also leave the ISG unattended and even have dates. Most old line staff predicted failure.

After this program had been operating for several months it was recognized as highly successful. Other cottages began to demand similar liberties. The intrusive changes demonstrated successfully in a new cottage began to generalize to other cottages. Had an existing cottage been rapidly and radically changed, it is certain there would have been a loud cry to stop. But a new cottage with no investment in the institution could be opened without the attending fear of "it's happening to me." Others could observe the difference, see that it wasn't destructive and slowly change themselves. Again the reference points had been altered successfully.

Within eight months only two cottages continued to operate in the old style. Even they had greatly changed. One cottage became a treatment center for preadolescent boys. Girls worked there on a volunteer basis and in paid positions as training child-care workers. In another cottage teenage boys moved in and it became the first coeducational halfway house ever operated by the state. Still another cottage was turned over to a private agency. At this writing only one cottage with only eight girls operates with any semblance of the old ISG. Considering that there were upwards of 120 girls incarcerated when the change process began, that's a good record.

It is important to note that most of the "old" staff stayed on and were happily retrained. Some of the older ones who couldn't tolerate the changes retired. All in all, it was a peaceful transition. There were no loud outcries of unfairness, no union disputes, no mass employee upset. There were many hairy moments to be sure—but none proved disastrous.

Many of the crisis situations were anticipated before they developed; all of the others were handled with ease. The usefulness and the strategy proved itself. An old inhumane institution was built into one that fostered democratic treatment principals. Locked cottages became homes and are noted for their openness and stability.

Institutional change is possible and should be encouraged. It isn't easy and it may not grab headlines for those responsible, but until all institutions can be closed it's a good alternative.

## References

1. S.G. Howe, A LETTER TO J.H. WILKINS, F.B. FAY, and H.G. ROGERS, COMMISSIONERS OF MASSACHUSETTS FOR THE STATE RE-FORM SCHOOL FOR GIRLS (Boston: Tichnor and Fields, 1850).

2. Francis B. Fay, MEMORANDUM AND FACTS, RELATING TO THE ESTABLISHMENT OF THE STATE INDUSTRIAL SCHOOL FOR GIRLS AT LANCASTER, MASS., private diary, 1862.

3. Massachusetts Act 1855, Chapter 442.

4. Fay, MEMORANDUM.

5. TELEGRAPH PIONEERS, Chelsea, Mass. February 9, 1861, vol 52, no. 6, p. 2.

6. First ANNUAL REPORT of the Trustees of the State Industrial School for Girls, January 1857.

7. Ibid.

8. Howe, LETTER.

9. Max Weber, THE PROTESTANT ETHIC AND THE SPIRIT OF CAPI-TALISM, by Talcott Parsons, trans., (New York: Charles Scribner's and Sons, 1958), p. 178.

10. Gerth and Mills, FROM MAX WEBER: ESSAYS IN SOCIOLOGY (New York: Oxford University Press, 1969).

11. Michael S. Olmsted, THE SMALL GROUP (New York: Random House, 1959).

12. Ibid.

13. B. Bohdan Wessell, M.D., GROUP ANALYSIS (New York: Citadel Press, 1966).

14. Howard Polsky, COTTAGE SIX (New York: Russell Sage Foundation, 1962).

15. James E. Teele, JUVENILE DELINQUENCY: A READER (F.E. Pea-cock, 1970); and Kurt H. Wolff, THE SOCIOLOGY OF GEORG SIMMEL (New York: The Free Press, 1964).

16. Erving Goffman, BEHAVIOR IN PUBLIC PLACES (New York: Free Press, 1969).

17. _____ , STIGMA (Englewood Cliffs, N.J.: Prentice-Hall, 1963).

18. Ibid.; and Goffman, BEHAVIOR.

19. Howe, LETTER.

20. Olmsted, SMALL GROUP; Phillip E. Slater, MICROCOSM (Boston: Beacon Press, 1970); Wessell, GROUP ANALYSIS.

21. Emile Durkheim, SUICIDE (New York: Free Press, 1964).

22. Milton Rokeach, THE THREE CHRISTS OF YPSILANTI, (New York: Random House, 1964).

23. Leon Festinger, WHEN PROPHECY FAILS (New York: Harper & Row, 1956).

24. Rokeach, THREE CHRISTS.

25. Erik H. Erikson, CHILDHOOD AND SOCIETY (2nd ed.; New York: W.W. Norton and Company, 1963); and C.S. Hall, and Lindzey, G., THEORIES OF PERSONALITY, 2nd ed. (New York: John Wiley and Sons, 1970).

# 11

## The Teaching-Family Model of Group Home Treatment

Dean L. Fixsen, Elery L. Phillips,
and Montrose M. Wolf

Achievement Place is a community-based, family-style, behavior modification, group home treatment program for delinquent youths in Lawrence, Kansas. The goals of Achievement Place are to teach the youths appropriate social skills such as manners and introductions, academic skills such as study and homework behaviors, self-help skills such as meal preparation and personal hygiene, and prevocational skills that are thought to be necessary for them to be successful in the community. The youths who come to Achievement Place have been in trouble with the law and have been court adjudicated. They are typically twelve to sixteen years old, in junior high school, and about three to four years below grade level on academic achievement tests.

When a youth enters Achievement Place he is introduced to the point system that is used to help motivate the youths to learn new, appropriate behavior. Each youth uses a point card to record his behavior and the number of points he earns and loses. When a youth first enters the program his points are exchanged for privileges each day. After the youth learns the connection between earning points and earning privileges, this daily-point-system is extended to a weekly-point-system where he exchanges points for privileges only once each week. Eventually, the point system is faded out to a merit system where no points are given or taken away and all privileges are free. The merit system is the last system a youth must progress through before returning to his natural home. However, almost all youths are on the weekly-point-system for most of their nine-to-twelve-month stay at Achievement Place. Because there are nearly unlimited opportunities to earn points, most of the youths earn all of the privileges most of the time.

The privileges that are available to the youths are *Basics*, which includes the use of the telephone, tools, and the yard, *Snacks* after school and before

The research and development of the Achievement Place program was made possible by grants MH 16609 and MH 20030 from the National Institute of Mental Health (Center for Studies of Crime and Delinquency) to the Bureau of Child Research and the Department of Human Development, University of Kansas. A film, ACHIEVEMENT PLACE, which describes this program can be obtained on loan from the Audio Visual Center, University of Kansas, 746 Massachusetts, Lawrence, Kansas, 66044. Further information on the program can be obtained from the authors, Bureau of Child Research, University of Kansas, Lawrence, Kansas, 66044.

bedtime, watching *TV*, and *Hometime* which permits the youths to return to their natural homes on the weekend or to go downtown. These privileges are naturally available in Achievement Place and add nothing to the cost of the treatment program. Other privileges that can be earned are one to three dollars *Allowance* each week and *Bonds* which can be accumulated to purchase clothing and other needed items.

A typical day at Achievement Place begins when the manager awakens the boys at about 6:30 in the morning. The boys then wash their faces, brush their teeth, and clean their bathroom and bedrooms. The manager, who is elected by his peers (see Phillips, Wolf, and Fixsen, 1972), supervises these morning chores by assigning specific cleaning tasks to his peers, by monitoring the completion of these tasks, and by providing point consequences for their performance. While some of the boys are cleaning their rooms and bathrooms, other boys are helping prepare breakfast.

After breakfast the boys check their appearance and pick up a daily school note (see Bailey, Wolf, and Phillips, 1970) before leaving Achievement Place to attend the local public schools. Since Achievement Place is a community-based facility, the boys continue to attend the same schools they had problems with before entering Achievement Place and the teaching-parents work closely with the teachers and school administrators to remediate each youth's problems in school. The feedback teachers provide for each youth is systematized by having each teacher fill out a daily report card each day. A teacher can quickly answer a series of questions about the youth's behavior by checking "yes" or "no" on the card. Some youths do not require daily feedback and they carry a weekly school note to class each Monday. In either case the youths return their completed report cards to the teaching-parents and they earn or lose points depending upon the teacher's judgment of their in-class performance.

When the boys return to Achievement Place, they have their after-school snacks before starting their homework or other point-earning activities. In the late afternoon one or two boys usually volunteer to help prepare dinner. During the meal or just after the meal, the teaching-parents and the youths hold a family conference (Fixsen, Phillips, and Wolf, 1972). During a family conference the teaching-parents and the youths discuss the events that occurred during the day, evaluate the manager's performance, establish or modify rules, and decide on consequences for any rule violations that were reported to the teaching-parents. These self-government behaviors are specifically taught to the youths, and they are encouraged to participate in discussions about any aspect of the program.

After the family conference the boys usually listen to records or watch TV before "figuring up" their point cards for the day and going to bed about 10:30. This brief description of a day at Achievement Place should give you an idea of the treatment program and how it operates. A complete description can be found in *The Teaching-Family Handbook* (Phillips, Phillips, Fixsen, and Wolf) and the *Achievement Place Novel* (Allen, Phillips, Phillips, Fixsen, and Wolf).

## Procedure Evaluation: An Example

The development and continued refinement of the Achievement Place program is the result of a commitment to evaluation of the program at all levels. There are at least three important levels of evaluation. First, a program can be evaluated in terms of the behavior of the youths five or ten or fifteen years after they graduated. If the youths become successful citizens who are an asset to their families and the community and if they are measurably better than other comparable groups of youths who received some other treatment, the program would be successful. This type of program evaluation is very important. Unfortunately, program evaluation does not provide the program staff with information about the effectiveness of specific treatment procedures, and it requires a long period of time between the application of the treatment and an evaluation of the effects of the treatment.

A second more immediate form of evaluation is progress evaluation. This method of evaluation is concerned with the progress of each individual youth toward his individual behavior goals. Since the goals of the program are spelled out in objective terms, it is possible for the teaching-parents to evaluate daily a boy's progress. When there is no progress the teaching-parents can try another procedure and again watch the boy's record for signs of progress. Thus progress evaluation allows the teaching-parents to adjust the program to the individual differences of the boys in a systematic manner.

Although progress evaluation allows a more immediate evaluation of the results of the application of a treatment procedure, it cannot provide the data necessary for evaluating the effectiveness of specific treatment procedures. Thus it is necessary to carry out a third level of evaluation, procedure evaluation. Procedure evaluations are concerned with the carefully measured effects of a specific, well described procedure on a specific, objectively defined behavior of a youth. To demonstrate the reliable effects of a procedure, reversal or multiple-baseline designs are used.

An example of procedure evaluation is the research we carried out recently on the self-government system (Fixsen, Phillips, and Wolf, 1972). The teaching-parents at Achievement Place spent about one year informally trying out and evaluating many possible self-government procedures to supplement the manager system (see Phillips, Wolf, and Fixsen, 1972, for a detailed description of the manager system). We then carried out a formal investigation to evaluate the effects of the system on one behavior, the participation on the youths in discussions of consequences for rule violations at the family conference.

*Definition of the Behavior.* "Participation in discussion" was defined as a youth suggesting alternatives, adding information, or making a statement that was directly related to the discussion taking place. In each case, a youth had to do more than agree with what had already been said.

*Observation of the Behavior.* Each family conference was video-taped. Each evening the boys would set up the video-taped equipment, tape the evening meal where the family conference was held, and dismantle the equipment after dinner. The next morning an observer would replay the video-tape and record the names of the boys who participated one or more times in discussions of guilt or consequences. The number of boys attending each trial varied from four to seven so these observations were converted to the percentage of boys participating in each discussion.

*Reliability of Observation.* For four trials during the experiment, interobserver agreement was measured by having a second observer simultaneously and independently record participation from the video-tapes. The two observers' records were compared for agreement of recording each boy's name for each trial and the percentage agreement was calculated by dividing the total number of agreements x 100 by the total number of agreements plus disagreements. Interobserver agreement for participation was 100, 92, 100, and 100 percent for the four trials. This high percentage of interobserver agreement indicates that the definition of participation was sufficiently objective to permit reliable observation by two independent observers.

*Experimental Conditions*

*Trial-Set Consequences.* In this condition the teaching-parents recorded any reported rule violation that would likely result in at least a 3,000 point fine. No consequences for the rule violation were actually delivered before the trial by the teaching-parents, however. At the family conference, the teaching-parents would call a trial on the boy accused of violating the rule and the boy's peers would decide his guilt or innocence and what consequence to deliver, if any.

*Preset Consequences.* In this condition the teaching-parents recorded each 3,000 point (or more) rule violation and delivered a consequence to the boy *at that time* (before the trial). At the family conference the teaching-parent would call a trial on the boy accused of violating the rule and the boy's peers would decide his guilt or innocence and what consequence to deliver, if any. The only change in the trial procedure in this condition was that the teaching-parents would tell the group how many points they had already fined the boys before asking for a discussion of the consequences. The boys were free to modify any preset consequence and the group decision on consequences took precedence over the teaching-parents' preset consequences.

*Unfair Consequence Probe.* The teaching-parents made every attempt to preset consequences that were fair and appropriate to the rule violation that occurred. For two trials, however, the teaching-parents set a consequence that was ten times greater than what they considered to be fair.

*Preference Probe.* Near the end of this experiment and after the formal data collection was terminated, the boys were asked on several trials whether they preferred to have the teaching-parents preset the consequences for rule violations or to have the consequences decided entirely by trial decision. The preference measure was taken for nine trials that had preset consequences and for three trials that had trial-set consequences. The preference question was asked sometimes before a trial and sometimes after a trial was completed. The boys would vote for the alternative of their choice by raising their hands.

**Results.** Figure 11-1 shows the percentage of boys who participated in each trial decision on consequences. During the first trial-set consequence condition where the teaching-parents did not preset consequences and the peers decided the consequence for rule violations in the trial, there was a median of 80 percent of the boys participating in each trial. When the teaching-parents began delivering consequences before each trial in the preset consequence condition, the percentage of participation dropped to a median of 40 percent. When the trial-set consequence condition was reinstated, the percentage of boys participating in the trial decision increased to a median of 83 percent and immediately decreased to a median of 0 percent when the teaching-parents once again began presetting consequences.

The unfair consequence probe (indicated by the two arrows in Figure 11-1) occurred during the second preset consequence condition. As shown in Figure 11-1, the percentage of participation increased sharply when the teaching-parents preset a consequence that was judged by them to be inappropriate to the rule violation that occurred.

On twelve occasions the boys were asked whether they preferred the trial-set consequence condition or the preset consequence condition. The boys' preference *after* four preset consequence trials was unanimously in favor of preset consequences. Their preference *before* five preset consequence trials was unanimously in favor of preset consequences on four trials and in favor of trial-set consequences on one trial. The boys' preference before and after all three trial-set consequence trials was in favor of trial-set consequences.

In the preset consequence condition there was an opportunity to compare the consequences preset by the teaching-parents with the consequences agreed upon by the boys. These data are shown in Table 11-1. Table 11-1 shows that out of

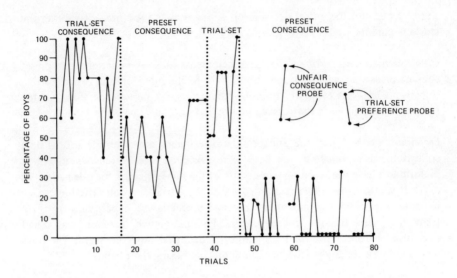

**Figure 11-1.** The Percentage of Boys Participating in Discussion of Consequences at Each "Trial" Under Each Experimental Condition. (Fixsen, Phillips, & Wolf, 1972).

fifty-three preset consequence trials the boys agreed with the teaching-parents on 62 percent of the trials, increased the consequences on 6 percent of the trials, and decreased the consequences on 32 percent of the trials. Table 11-1 also shows that the boys left the preset consequence the same most often for rule violations that were reported by school officials (83 percent) and least often for rule violations reported by the teaching-parents (31 percent).

Table 11-2 gives the types of rule violations reported by the peers, school personnel, teaching-parents, and parents. The rule violations are ranked in order of seriousness from stealing to not being prompt. Of the first four types of rule violations, the peers reported a majority of the rule violations in three of the four categories and reported as many as the school personnel in the fourth. Thus, of the twenty-seven rule violations reported for the four most serious rule violations in Table 11-2, the peers reported fifteen (52 percent), school personnel reported eight (29 percent), and the teaching-parents and parents each reported two (8 percent). The peers also reported rule violations in each of the seven categories.

**Table 11-1**

**The Location of Rule Violations Reported by the Peers, School Personnel, Teaching-Parents, and Parents**

| Reported by | | Location of Rule Violations | | | | |
| | | Ach. Place | School | Community | Nat. Home | Totals |
|---|---|---|---|---|---|---|
| Peers | No. | 17 | 7 | 6 | 0 | 38% |
| | % | 57% | 23% | 20% | 0% | |
| School Personnel | No. | 0 | 27 | 0 | 0 | 34% |
| | % | 0% | 100% | 0% | 0% | |
| Teaching-Parents | No. | 12 | 1 | 5 | 0 | 22% |
| | % | 67% | 5% | 28% | 0% | |
| Parents | No. | 0 | 0 | 0 | 5 | 6% |
| | % | 0% | 0% | 0% | 100% | |
| Totals | No. | 29 | 35 | 11 | 5 | 100% |
| | % | 36% | 44% | 15% | 6% | |

Source: Fixsen, Phillips, and Wolf, 1972 (see References).

**Table 11-2**

**Types of Rule Violations Reported by Peers, School Personnel, Teaching-Parents, and Parents**

| Type of Rule Violation | Rule Violation Reported by | | | | |
| | Peers | School | Teaching Parents | Parents | Totals |
|---|---|---|---|---|---|
| Stealing | 3 (75%) | 1 (25%) | – | – | 4 ( 5%) |
| Cheating | 2 (67%) | 1 (33%) | – | – | 3 ( 4%) |
| Physical agg. | 5 (38%) | 5 (38%) | 2 (15%) | 1 ( 9%) | 13 (16%) |
| Verbal agg. | 5 (72%) | 1 (14%) | – | 1 (14%) | 7 ( 9%) |
| School rules | 5 (20%) | 18 (72%) | 2 ( 8%) | – | 25 (31%) |
| Ach. pl. rules | 9 (47%) | – | 10 (53%) | – | 19 (24%) |
| Promptness | 1 (11%) | 1 (11%) | 4 (45%) | 3 (33%) | 9 (11%) |
| Totals | 30 (38%) | 27 (34%) | 18 (22%) | 5 ( 6%) | 80 (100%) |

Source: Fixsen, Phillips, and Wolf, 1972 (see References).

Four of the peer-reported rule violations were self-reports where a youth reported a rule violation he had committed. Of these four self-reported violations, one was for stealing, two were for physical aggression, and one was for violation of Achievement Place rules.

These data indicate that the youths participated in the self-government system to a much greater degree when they were given full responsibility for deciding the consequences for a peer who had violated a rule. This experiment also shows that procedures that are informally developed can be formally evaluated to determine their role in maintaining the behavior of interest. By evaluating the specific procedures that comprise a treatment program, the program can be continually refined and improved by discarding the aspects of the program that are ineffective or inefficient and retaining those aspects of the program that are effective. These procedure evaluations offer immediate feedback to the treatment staff concerning the effectiveness of their specific treatment procedures and can be conducted with very little cost to the overall program in terms of time or finances.

*Dissemination*

The teaching-family model is sufficiently developed to allow general application in other communities. Although there are still a number of refinements that need to be carried out, we feel the program is ready for further replication. To accommodate the expansion of the teaching-family model, we are developing an education program for teaching-parents to give them the skills to operate and evaluate professionally run group homes for antisocial youths. We are also training Ph.D. level personnel who will be able to start teaching-family group homes and education programs for teaching-parents outside of Kansas. The development of these training programs is critical to successful dissemination of the model since the professional teaching-parents are the key to the success of the program.

Our experience has shown that adequate sources of financing are currently not available for starting group home treatment programs. The cost of facilities in Kansas has ranged from $35,000 to $60,000 for purchase, renovation, and furnishings for a large, older home. For each group home we have been associated with, these costs were paid from donations contributed by civic groups and individuals in the community. For many medium to large-size communities, this has not been an insurmountable problem, but for smaller communities it is almost impossible to raise enough money even for a down payment on a house. Thus widespread dissemination of community-based group homes will require funding for facility costs from federal or state sources.

## References

1. J.D. Allen; Phillips, E.L.; Phillips, E.A.; Fixsen, D.L.; and Wolf, M.M. THE ACHIEVEMENT PLACE NOVEL. Champaign, Illinois: Research Press, in press.
2. Bailey, J.S.; Wolf, M.M.; and Phillips, E.L. "Home-Based Reinforcement

and the Modification of Pre-Delinquents' Classroom Behavior." JOURNAL OF APPLIED BEHAVIOR ANALYSIS 3 (1970):223-233.

3. Fixsen, D.L.; Phillips, E.L.; and Wolf, M.M. "Achievement Place: Experiments in Self-Government with Pre-Delinquents." JOURNAL OF APPLIED BEHAVIOR ANALYSIS, in press.

4. Phillips, E.L.; Phillips. E.A.; Fixsen, D.L.; and Wolf, M.M. THE TEACHING-FAMILY HANDBOOK. Champaign, Illinois: Research Press, in press.

5. Phillips, E.L.; Wolf, M.M.: and Fixsen, D.L. "An Experimental Analysis of Governmental Systems at Achievement Place." JOURNAL OF APPLIED BEHAVIOR ANALYSIS, in press.

# 12

## The University's Role in Public Service to the Department of Youth Services

Larry L. Dye

The University must loom large in any scheme to deal with the challenges to corrections. The University will be a potential source of support and innovation as the cry for 'law and order' places increased pressure on corrections. Both as a center for experimentation and a source of manpower and ideas for service and experimentation, the University must play the role of ally as corrections comes to grips with these challenges.[1]

The correctional community vitally needs the resources of the University of Massachusetts; but there have been very few cooperative or collaborative models that have been designed to merge the resources and the needs of corrections with those of the university. The university community can offer experiences that range from graduate and undergraduate training, in-service training workshops, or such radical approaches as facilitating the design of alternatives to institutionalization as presented later.

While correctional institutions have become aware of their dilemma, it has become increasingly clear that the university can no longer enjoy the "ivory tower" elitism disassociating itself from the social conditions prevailing in our society. In the last decade, numerous steps have been taken to make universities more responsible to the needs of the community.

The Carnegie Foundation for the Advancement of Teaching, at a conference on the University Campus at the Service of Society, defined public service as that which has to do

with the outreach of a University to society at large, with extending the resources of the campus to individuals and groups who are not part of the regular academic community, and with bringing an academic institution's special competence to bear on the solution of society's problems. It can take place on or off campus and can be related to either the governmental or private sectors of our national life. Lastly, the emphasis on public service is on converting knowledge into readily usable forms for immediate application.[2]

In December of 1970, Robert C. Wood was inaugurated as the sixteenth president of the University of Massachusetts. During his first year of office, President Wood commissioned a major study entitled "The Future of the University of Massachusetts" as an effort to conceptualize the future growth of state-supported higher education. One of the major recommendations of that report was that "the University should develop a coherent public service policy, including efforts to insure that public service activities serve a University purpose as well as a public purpose."[3]

This statement was further emphasized by the Faculty Senate Ad Hoc Committee on Community Outreach and Course Related Field Work when they stated, "The Committee is in unanimous agreement that the emphasis on community outreach and public service activities on the Amherst campus must be increased."[4]

This thrust for a public service policy on the University campus was developing simultaneously with the changes that were taking place in the Department of Youth Services, making the climate ideal for collaboration between the Department of Youth Services and the University of Massachusetts.

Something is amiss in this country. We have become a nation that cannot deal with its young. Not only is it the case that delinquency rates continue to soar, but even more problematic, the institutions that have been created to prevent and control juvenile delinquency are, apparently, overwhelmed and unable to deal effectively with the problem.[5]

### Department of Youth Services (DYS)

Under the commissionership of Dr. Jerome Miller, the Department of Youth Services started in 1970 to implement child-care services which moved from large, long-term, institutional-based programs to small, short-term, community-based programs. It was argued that the best way to bring about the change from a punitive modality to a rehabilitative one was to deinstitutionalize the department.

The department felt that the more community involvement, the higher the chance of success for both the youth and the program. Since the department considered juvenile delinquency a social problem, not a criminal one, the communities would be required to assist in its solution and sought active community involvement. DYS assisted in the setting-up of community treatment centers and encouraged private groups to do so, providing the technical assistance needed by the communities.

In the transition from institutional-based programs to community-based programs, the university presented the Department of Youth Services a number of models. This chapter will briefly outline some of the programs which are presently in operation, examine the implications for the various groups served, and review some of the social forces which create a climate conducive to the development of these programs.

Community service programs are not new to the University of Massachusetts. Close to 1,000 students participated in community service projects during the academic year of 1971. All of these projects were supported by the University's

Recognized Student Organization (RSO), which coordinates volunteer service groups and provides funding through the student activities levied and budgeted by the Student Senate and approved by the Board of Trustees.

The Juvenile Opportunities Extension (JOE) program is a Recognized Student Organization established to provide voluntary student services to youth incarcerated at Westfield Detention Center.[a] Four graduate students began the initial volunteer effort in July 1971. After the tragic incidents of Attica, these students were invited to speak at a teach-in focusing on the concept of prison reform, the philosophy of the Department of Youth Services, and efforts to cut off the flow of juveniles to adult prisons. At that time, interested students were invited to organize and assist in the efforts with the Department of Youth Services.

The subsequent organization of the university's undergraduate students evolved into the Juvenile Opportunities Extension, or JOE program. After incorporation in accordance with the Student Senate by-laws, JOE solicited Student Senate funds and its members were awarded a $700 grant to begin working with the youth at the Detention Center. By December of 1971, there were over 150 undergraduate students contributing up to 700 man hours per week at the Detention Center. The students were involved with program activities such as: developing arts and crafts programs, macrame, sewing, tie-dying, painting, etc.; organizing indoor and outdoor recreational activities, including weekend camping trips; offering specialized courses in guitar and music appreciation, human sexuality, and drug abuse; and providing tutoring and counseling on an individual basis working with the educational coordinator at the Detention Center.

The involvement of the undergraduate students helped to counteract some of the boredom inherent in such an institution and allowed, because of increased manpower, the opportunity for the staff to undertake new rules at the center to further the goals of the Department of Youth Services.

*Juvenile Opportunities Extention II (JOE II)*

While the JOE program was developing at the university, Dr. Miller began phasing out the Shirley Industrial School for Boys. The closing of this institution created a number of problems. Anxieties and frustrations over job security and role definition by the staff were transmitted to the youth which resulted in

---

[a]Westfield Detention Center is a state operated, maximum security facility that is ten years old and has a capacity of servicing twenty-five boys and girls from the four western Massachusetts counties. It services youth between the ages of seven and seventeen who are on both detention status (detained for courts pending adjudication) and youth who have been adjudicated delinquent in the Commonwealth. During 1971, it received 1500 youths from twenty different courts in Western Massachusetts.

acting out behavior on the part of the youth. This behavior was manifested in fights, riots, the burning of buildings and escapes. As a result, community members became upset and espoused the reopening of the industrial school, creating the potential of a repetitious cycle that could have resulted in larger and more secure institutions.

In December, Dr. Miller announced the closing of the Lyman Industrial School for Boys, the first and oldest industrial school in the United States. On the day of the announcement, representatives of the university were discussing strategies of collaboration between the department and the university in western Massachusetts. Out of that meeting came the strategy of conducting the JOE II Conference.

The basic premise of the conference was that rather than winding down the Lyman Industrial School for Boys and catalyzing incidents similar to those at Shirley, it would be far more expedient to remove all youth at Lyman in one day and place them in alternative care.

The program was undertaken to demonstrate that traditional institutions can be closed rapidly and in a positive way by using an alternative environment. All youth at Lyman were screened, and those that could be immediately placed or sent home were done so from the institution. The youth that did not have options for going home at that time were brought to the university. The program was designed to be a one-month experience establishing a one-to-one living relationship with student volunteers called "advocates" on or near the UMass campus.

The program had four basic but very critical factors in it. These were: (1) placement; (2) advocates; (3) group leaders; and (4) a national conference on delinquency prevention and treatment programs.

**Placement.** One of the primary emphases of the overall conference was to phase the youth back into their own community or an alternative living situation as quickly and as effectively as possible from the UMass campus. The campus served only as a buffer zone helping to alleviate some of the difficulties in making the transition from the institution to an open community environment. The established goal was to provide a number of placement opportunities or alternatives to each youth. And secondary to that goal were three basic components to the placement of each youth: (1) a viable living situation, (2) employment and/or educational opportunities, and (3) a mechanism for follow-up procedures on the youth in the community.

**Advocacy.** The most critical part of the JOE II Conference was the establishment of a one-to-one relationship between the youth and the student. Each youth who came to the campus was housed with one student called an "advocate." The primary responsibility of that student was to supervise the activities of the youth twenty-four hours a day, seven days a week; and secondarily, to assist in the placement of the youth back into his or her own home community, helping to facilitate the transition from the institution to the university and ultimately to the community.

**Group Leaders**. Critical to the central administration of the overall program were the group leaders. The group leaders were selected from the staff of the Westfield Detention Center. Each of the group leaders coordinated a group of between ten and fifteen youth. It was the primary responsibility of the group leaders to conduct small discussion groups with their youth and students to counsel the interpersonal behavior problems which arise out of such an intensive living situation and to work out the ultimate placement of the youth back into their home communities.

**National Conference**. This conference was seen as a mechanism to provide a series of ongoing activities for the youth while they were on campus. Each week of the month long sessions were devoted to one of the following four themes: (1) social problems, (2) education and employment, (3) family and, (4) alternative placement models. Each day of the week was then devoted to a specific subtopic. For example, during the week of social issues, one day was devoted to drug abuse, another day to prisons, another to sexuality, and so forth. All activities revolved around the topic of the day and were planned to be both educational and practical for the youth. There would be a group meeting in the morning, afternoon, and evening. Each day incorporated a presentation made by a nationally-known figure, small discussion groups among the youth, the advocates and the group leaders, and social activities ranging from movies and plays to dinners and dances. The rest of the day the youth and advocates had the opportunity to utilize the recreational and educational programs functioning on the university campus. This was coupled with an extensive outdoor program and the opportunity to travel.

The program started on January 17, 1972 and terminated on February 13, 1972; overall it served ninety-nine youth. The JOE II Program allowed the population of Lyman School to be significantly reduced in one day and had a minimal negative effect on the department and the youth involved. It served to break down the resistance to the reforms of Dr. Miller and was useful in further implementing his philosophy.

*The Massachusetts Association for the*
*Reintegration of Youth (MARY)*

The MARY program is another Recognized Student Organization and is one of the residential treatment centers being funded by the Department of Youth Services.

MARY is an outgrowth of a group of ex-convicts from Soledad prison coming to talk to students at the university. In November of 1971 a group of concerned students in the Lewis dormitory on campus became interested in trying to help resolve some of the problems confronting our prison system. These students, with faculty support, drafted a proposal which established the MARY program on campus. The spring semester of 1972 was spent in a planning and training program for the students of the MARY project, and finally in September a number of youth from the department were selected to participate.

The program is based in two dormitories—Lewis House and Webster House. In each of the dorms there are six student advocates who share their rooms with youth who traditionally would have been committed to an institution. Also living in the dorm is a residential counselor dealing specifically with the interpersonal relationships of the DYS youth and students. Coordinating the entire program is the project director who has the primary responsibility of developing resources on a campus-wide level for individualized programs for each youth. As in the JOE program the student advocate has the primary responsibility of working with the youth on a twenty-four hour a day, seven days a week basis. For this program, individualized credit is negotiated with faculty members for their experiences in the dormitory. The average length of stay at the university is approximately three months. This allows the youth the opportunity to be exposed to a number of various educational and vocational oriented activities under the guidance of an individual student, leading to the development of an individualized program to assist the youth in readjustment to his own community. The program is designed to deal with approximately fifty youth annually.

*Implications*

**University Resources.** Major universities are developed for the purpose of providing educational, social, and recreational activities for the population that they serve. The resources that are available on the university campus are wholly underutilized and untapped. These range from the human resources of the student, faculty, and staff including but not limited to the knowledge and skill that could be applied toward dealing with a social problem to the physical resources of the gymnasium, audio-visual technology, theater, and social activities. Rather than developing a model within a correctional institution to provide for social, recreational, educational, and vocational activities, the university model utilizes existing resources and applies those resources to a social problem.

**Students.** University students are looking for more and more involvement in community and social action programs. Programs like JOE and MARY provide them the opportunity to become directly involved with social action while simultaneously pursuing their degrees. These programs utilize the idealism and activism of students in working with other human beings. Student interest was exemplified when the residents of Lewis House voted on whether or not they would allow "delinquent" youth into their community. With one hundred and thirty students registered in the dorm, there were four students absent for the vote and six students who voted negatively. A vote of 97 percent was in favor of bringing the delinquent youth into the dorm.

**Youth.** The obvious implication for the youth in developing an individualized program on a university campus is that the negative self-concept which results from incarceration is changed and a more positive self-image and self-identity can be developed with each individual youth. With the resources that are available on the campus, various programs can be worked out tailored to satisfy the needs of each youth. These may be educational, vocational, or counseling-oriented in nature and can be coupled with social and recreational programs. With one student working with each youth, there is an opportunity to more clearly conceptualize an overall goal and program for the youth in their own community. The goal is to take a very negative experience and turn it into a very positive situation that will hopefully have impact on the future of that youth.

**Community.** The implications for the community are not as socially-oriented as those of the student. However, they are economically-oriented. The University of Massachusetts program has demonstrated that we can place a youth through a program at half the cost of institutionalization. So the main benefit for the community is a reduction in taxes, and as the program proves successful, a reduction in the recidivism rate of individual youth in those communities.

**Higher Education.** The implication for the university community is the opportunity for involvement with social action programs located on campus without an interruption in their traditional intellectual pursuits. Developing this kind of lab on campus also provides students who are interested in community action and youth in trouble the opportunity for a new kind of educational experience. That educational experience can be very much integrated into the overall academic program for the student. This assists higher education in making the transition from an "ivory tower" institution to an institution that serves public needs.

**The Department of Youth Services.** The university provides a number of different kinds of opportunities for the department. We have already discussed a number of benefits for youth in the department. However, still another program provides graduate training for correctional personnel allowing them the opportunity for upward mobility. A model in operation on campus at this time, called the Advocates for the Development of Human Potential, has admitted fifteen

Department of Youth Services personnel into graduate school. By program design each staff will take on the responsibility of one youth in the department. The youth will reside with the graduate student and his or her family. The program is one year in length and is designed to serve the hard-to-reach youth. Staff in the Department of Youth Services have experience in working with thirty or forty youth at one time. Here we are utilizing their skills and the resources of the university as we pair them to work individually with one youth while pursuing a graduate degree.

*Summary*

In practical terms every University will realize that it can no longer adopt the simple course of rejecting public service altogether. Interdependence between the University and society has become too great for that. The University *must* have society's support. Society *must* have access to the University's resources. Were the University to turn its back on society's needs, it would be tantamount to self-destruction.[6]

There are numerous implications and benefits derived from a collaborative model between a university and a major state agency. This report tried to briefly outline a number of programs in operation at the University of Massachusetts. The most significant part of the university's involvement is that it was student initiated and student funded, although, the university administration provided the atmosphere conducive to the growth of the program.

If the MARY program alone, serving 12 youth, was replicated in the 5,956 four-year colleges and universities throughout the United States,[7] it would open new opportunities for 71,472 of the youth presently incarcerated in juvenile institutions at approximately half the cost of our present programs.

**References**

1. Polk, Kenneth, THE UNIVERSITY AND CORRECTIONS, POTENTIAL FOR COLLABORATIVE RELATIONSHIPS, January 1969, p. 2.
2. THE UNIVERSITY AT THE SERVICE OF SOCIETY. Summary of a discussion by the trustees of the Carnegie Foundation for the Advancement of Teaching. Annual Report, 1966-67, pp. 4-5.
3. "Report of the President's Committee on the Future University of Massachusetts," Boston, Mass., December 1971, p. 90.
4. "Report of the Faculty Senate Ad Hoc Committee on Community Outreach and Course Related Fieldwork." Mimeo, June 1972, p. 1.
5. Polk, Kenneth, DELINQUENCY PREVENTION AND THE YOUTH SERVICE BUREAUS, ... AN ASSESSMENT OF THE JUVENILE DELIN-

QUENCY PREVENTION AND CONTROL ACT OF 1968. December 1970, p. 87.

6. The Carnegie Foundation for the Advancement of Teaching, THE UNIVERSITY AT THE SERVICE OF SOCIETY, 1967, p. 9.

7. Figure obtained from U.S. Bureau of the Census, STATISTICAL AB-STRACT OF THE UNITED STATES: 1972 (93rd edition); Washington, D.C., 1972), p. 128.

# 13

## A Strategic Innovation in the Process of Deinstitutionalization: The University of Massachusetts Conference

Robert B. Coates, Alden D. Miller,
and Lloyd E. Ohlin

The idea of using university resources to protect and aid young offenders while institutions are being closed is a new one.

Since November of 1969, the Department of Youth Services, under the direction of Commissioner Jerome Miller, has been moving steadily toward its overall objective—to provide a diversified range of community-based services for troubled youth within the Commonwealth of Massachusetts. The department is moving away from just locking up delinquents in training schools, and toward the construction of community-based alternatives. Some of these, such as group homes and foster care, are administered by the department and other private agencies under contract to DYS.

To facilitate this change, DYS has regionalized its services and administration. Seven regional offices now exist. Each region tries to handle the youth within its geographical territory. Detention and reception centers, group homes, foster-care placements, and after-care programs are increasingly being administered from within these regions.

During the month of January 15-February 15, 1972, the DYS conducted an innovative experiment as part of the effort to bring about the closing of these traditional youth training schools. After an abortive attempt during February 1971 to close the Shirley Industrial School for Boys gradually, it was realized that to close an institution efficiently and with minimum stress, quick and decisive movement of the committed youth is essential. Gradual withdrawal of youth creates an environment in which both staff and youth act out their anxieties about their changing situation on each other—leading to runaways and other serious disturbances. In order to alleviate the possibility of such a development, alternatives were sought which would permit the removal of large numbers of youth quickly.

When Shirley was finally closed in December of 1971 those youth who could not be paroled or quickly placed were moved to other institutions to avoid a slow winding down process. The next step in departmental deinstitutionaliza-

This research effort was sponsored in part by grants from the Massachusetts Governor's Committee on Law Enforcement and Administration of Criminal Justice. The authors would like to acknowledge the efforts of the field research team consisting of John Albach, Judy Caldwell, Robert Fitzgerald, David Garwood, and Arlette Klein.

tion, the closing of the Lyman School for Boys, was more complicated because it was not possible simply to transfer all difficult-to-place youth to another institution.

The solution which evolved was to send 100 youth from various DYS institutions to the University of Massachusetts to participate in a month-long youth conference entitled National Conference on Juvenile Delinquency Prevention and Treatment Programs. The conference was seen by DYS as a prerelease experience which would prepare the incarcerated youth for reintegration into the community upon their release.

The Juvenile Opportunities Extension (JOE), an established university student organization consisting of about 125 college students with previous experience working as volunteers at the nearby Westfield Detention Center, had responsibility for administration of the daily affairs of the conference. JOE was strongly supported in its efforts by the School of Education at the University of Massachusetts. Each youth was to be matched with a college student advocate; the advocate would be paid $40.00 a week and the youth $12.00 a week. Ten youth and ten advocates were to form a group directed by a group leader. The group leaders were to be drawn from the full-time professional staff at the DYS Westfield Detention Center on leave from their usual work. Together each advocate and youth were to work out a satisfactory placement for the youth with the group leader acting as coordinator and resource person.

An important difference should be noted between this advocacy model and the more typical volunteer model for working with youth. In the latter case, the volunteer is expected simply to provide some skill and/or comradeship; in the former, the advocate is expected to provide skills and comradeship, but, of equal importance, he is expected to speak in behalf of the youth during the placement process in the community, so that the best interests of the youth are served both by DYS and the community.

Serious consideration of the idea of such a conference began about three to four weeks prior to the actual beginning of the conference. The final decision to go ahead took place only days before the conference began. DYS concluded that the use of University of Massachusetts facilities during the period between semesters provided the best opportunity to effect the closing of Lyman. It was necessary to move quickly to take advantage of these propitious conditions.

However, the lead time for planning was so short that many necessary preparatory tasks simply could not be completed in time. For example, in order for the placement process to operate smoothly it would have been necessary to bring together Boston office and regional representatives who had responsibilities for placement to explain placement alternatives and procedures to the group leaders and advocates; lines of authority and responsibility for the routine of the conference needed to be clarified; and coordination procedures between the Boston office, the regional offices, and the conference needed to be settled. The lack of time for such planning resulted in uncertainty about the conference and placement procedures within DYS and probably impaired the efficiency with which youth were placed. However, even with these difficulties, the conference demonstrated an interesting and effective alternative for handling youth outside of large institutions and for involving the community in the youth corrections process.

## Method of Study

The conference was seen by the Harvard Center for Criminal Justice staff as innovative and as central to the overall plans of the DYS. Therefore, as part of the center's larger study of change with DYS, it was decided to devote staff resources for the evaluation of the conference.

The overall strategy for monitoring and evaluating the conference included observation of daily events, extensive informal interviewing with conference participants while the conference was in progress, structured interviewing of participants after the conference was concluded, and outcome data such as placements and recidivism rates. Group leaders and JOE staff were interviewed at the early stages of the conference and at its conclusion; a number of university and community leaders were interviewed shortly after the end of the conference; several Boston office staff members were interviewed at the beginning of the conference and again at its conclusion; and many advocates and their assigned charges were interviewed while at the conference. In addition, a sample of advocates were interviewed following the conference. This interviewing effort was hampered by the difficulties of finding and interviewing youth in the open community and by the fact that a large number of advocates simply departed to distant and/or unknown destinations. Still, as can be seen in Table 13-1, the samples appear to be quite representative of the population in each case. We were able to interview sixty-one of the ninety-nine participating youth or 62 percent and of the ninety-seven advocates, fifty-four, or 56 percent.

The available data permit us: (1) to portray the activities of the conference; (2) to reflect views of the conference from the perspective of the major participating groups; (3) to consider the impact of the conference on youth by looking at outcome data, and (4) to make some preliminary judgments about the viability of the youth advocacy model as reflected by the University of Massachusetts experience.

## Goals of the Participating Groups

A number of groups actively participated in the conference and each group's evaluation of the conference sheds some light on its value. In order to put the groups' evaluation in perspective, it should be seen in relation to the set of goals expressed by each group. While there was general consensus that such a youth

**Table 13-1**
**Comparison of Population and Sample Characteristics**

| Characteristic | Youth | | Advocate | |
|---|---|---|---|---|
| | Population | Sample | Population | Sample |
| Sex | | | | |
| Female | 25 | 21 | 29 | 38 |
| Male | 75 | 79 | 71 | 62 |
| Total | 100 | 100 | 100 | 100 |
| N | 99 | 61 | 97 | 53 |
| Race | | | | |
| Black | 29 | 27 | 32 | 32 |
| White | 62 | 70 | 63 | 57 |
| Other | 8 | 3 | 5 | 2 |
| Undetermined | 0 | 0 | 0 | 9 |
| Total | 100 | 100 | 100 | 100 |
| N | 96 | 60 | 97 | 54 |
| Type of Placement Received | | | | |
| Home | 48 | 49 | | |
| Foster Home | 10 | 16 | | |
| Group Home | 8 | 7 | | |
| Institution | 11 | 11 | | |
| Run | 11 | 16 | | |
| Pending | 12 | — | | |
| Total | 100 | 100 | | |
| N | 99 | 61 | | |
| Institutional Origin | | | | |
| Lyman | 39 | 35 | | |
| Westfield | 32 | 37 | | |
| Lancaster | 17 | 12 | | |
| Roslindale | 8 | 8 | | |
| From the Run | 3 | 2 | | |
| Other | — | 4 | | |
| Total | 100 | 100 | | |
| N | 99 | 49 | | |

Note: Data on total populations were made available by the JOE staff.

conference was a good idea, the several groups were sometimes pursuing quite diverse objectives through the medium of the conference.

The Boston office had four major objectives for the conference. First, the conference was seen as an emergency means of enabling removal of a large number of boys and girls from institutions within a matter of hours. Second, the conference was viewed as an experiment for creating new forms of community placement for youth. Third, the conference provided a means for looking at the viability of the youth advocacy model. And, fourth, the conference provided a backdrop to dramatize for the public the direction and scope of DYS reform efforts.

The group leaders emphasized as their primary goal placement of youth in the community; they often referred to the conference as a "placement conference." It was expected that the advocate would expose the youth to a wide number of placement possibilities, and the actual placement would be worked out between the advocate and the youth with a group leader supervising the process. The group leaders were also ideologically committed to the closing of institutions and saw this as a significant objective of the conference. Last, the group leaders saw the conference as a framework within which to develop a new professional role of community resources coordinator, one upon which a community-based DYS would depend greatly in the future.

The JOE staff was principally interested in two objectives: (1) to involve the university in social action, and (2) to illustrate that college youth could function as valuable correctional resources by helping to place youthful offenders in the community. Because of their previous experience in providing volunteers to work at the Westfield Detention Center, JOE staff were convinced that the university and college students could play an important role in juvenile corrections.

Of all the participants in the conference, the advocates as a group probably had the least clearly defined objectives and expectations. Their major objectives were to do something which would be helpful for youthful offenders, to learn about delinquency problems and corrections, and to gain experience by working with youth. With the exception of those advocates who had worked at Westfield, few advocates knew what to expect of youth who had been committed to institutions or what was really meant by "placement." And many of the advocates were rather anxious about suddenly becoming responsible twenty-four hours a day for another human being.

The DYS boys and girls as a group were also anxious about going to the conference, but seemed to have more clearly perceived goals than the advocates. First, and foremost, they wanted to get out of the institution. Second, the conference was seen as a place to have fun. Third, a point, slightly different from the first, they saw the conference as a means for facilitating their return home. For example, it is *not* clear that the boys and girls expected to be placed in group homes or foster homes. Most instead seemed to feel that they would go directly home from the conference.

*Selection and Training Processes*

Because a major objective for the conference was to support the closing of Lyman, thirty-nine boys from that instituion were selected to participate. In addition, boys and girls from other institutions were selected to reduce institutional populations and to provide for a coeducational conference. In the closing of Lyman, most youth who could be paroled directly home were paroled; youth who posed potentially grave risks to the community were transferred to secure treatment facilities. The remainder of the population participated in the conference.

The brief amount of lead time meant that JOE staff had to select the advocates during a two-week period. Many JOE members who had been volunteers at Westfield had already left or had made other plans for the semester break and were not available to take part in the conference. The JOE staff thus had the difficult task of bringing together on short notice a hundred volunteers who would be able to make a twenty-four hour a day commitment to youth.

According to one staff member the selection process was as follows:

Initially we sent out letters to many of the dorms and called for volunteers to come to a meeting—anyone who might be interested in going to bat for a kid, working with a kid twenty-four hours a day for a month. And we got an initial response and passed out applications at that point which listed vital information. We then gave personal interviews. [Actual selection of advocates] was an intuitive thing, based on experience in working with the volunteers [JOE volunteers at the Westfield Detention Center]. Some people were rejected because they were too nebulous, too idealistic or too young.

Most of the advocates came from the University of Massachusetts. However, some were students from Hampshire College and a very small number were community volunteers. Eighteen advocates were shortly dismissed because they were not able or willing to cope with the one-to-one relationship.

A two-day training period was conducted for the advocates just prior to the conference. Responsibility for training rested for the most part on the group leaders and other Westfield Detention Center staff along with some residents. The advocates had two principal questions which were not adequately answered during the training period. They wanted to know more about the characteristics of the boys and girls with whom they would be working and how they, as advocates, were supposed to help them. Because the training staff was from Region I, they could not inform the advocates about formal placement procedures operative in other regions, and they dismissed the need to know about the boys and girls by suggesting that advocates could best discover all they needed to know by talking with the youth and further indicated that delinquent youth are not peculiarly different from other youth.

As a consequence most of the advocates in later interviews expressed the belief that they were not adequately trained for their role. They suggested that the training period should have been longer, with more structured presentation by professionals on how one can handle interpersonal problems as an advocate. Moreover, according to the advocates, the training should have involved representatives from DYS better prepared to answer questions about the characteristics of youthful offenders and of life in an institution. They also felt the need for a clearer statement of the objectives of the conference. Some also suggested that they perhaps should have been taken to visit the institutions and even to visit "their kids" while they were still in the institution. Others thought that a week's experience at Westfield would have offered the best preparation. The old adage "learn by doing," although possibly meaningful advice for persons who work daily with youth, was not viewed as adequate preparation for college students who were being asked to work intensively with youth for just a short period of time. The advocates suggested that the training and orientation period should have provided the opportunity to define clearly the parameters of the group leader-advocate-youth relationship, and the lack of clear understanding subsequently created problems in the placement of youth.

*A Typical Day at the Conference*

Prior to the conference it was envisioned that approximately ten advocates and ten youth would form a group under the leadership of one of the Westfield staff. There would be ten such groups. These groups were to meet regularly to handle behavioral and placement problems. The group process was considered important in handling problems of juveniles which would emerge from their inability to cope adequately with the groups or other social relationships. The groups were expected to attend daily conference-wide lectures given by persons with some expertise in such areas as juvenile problems, race relations, criminal justice, and education. These lectures were to take place in the morning; the group meetings were to occur in the afternoon using the morning's lecture as a starting point for discussion. This planned schedule was never fully operationalized. A number of advocates stated they were "turned off" by these expectations and therefore did not encourage "their kids" to attend. This lack of commitment to the schedule may be traced back to the selection and training processes. Many advocates simply did not see the schedule as a means of "helping kids." They did not see themselves as having had a role in setting up the schedule, and felt it interfered with their assigned responsibility to provide support for the boys and girls in a one-to-one relationship.

It appears that two expectations were in conflict. The group leaders and JOE staff had expected the group process to be a focal point of the conference, yet the most attractive feature to the advocates had been the prospect of forming one-to-one relationships with "their kids." The latter feature had also been stressed by the training personnel, JOE staff, and representatives of the Boston office. Also the expected relationship of advocate and youth to the group leaders was never clearly defined—or at least never clearly perceived by the advocates. However, because the group leaders became the chief source of information on placement, the relationship with the group leaders had to be nurtured for the advocates to become successfully involved in the placement process. Many advocates did nurture and maintain this relationship but many others did not, and the group leaders frequently found themselves actually developing placements for youth instead of simply coordinating the activities of advocates and youth in the placement process.

Because of these various conflicting role expectations on the part of some of the conference participants, the schedule did not proceed as planned. The JOE Office area became the focal point of much activity other than simply administrative coordination. Group leaders were on hand to assist individual advocates and youth but the group meetings for the most part had been abandoned as unproductive by the middle of the second week. When the guest lecturers spoke, only a small number of advocates, youth, and group leaders ordinarily were present. The entire structure of the conference became much less formal than had originally been planned. Problems were handled individually rather than in regular group meetings. Advocates and "their kids" did their own thing and for the most part this appeared to work out rather well.

*Participants' Evaluation of the Conference*

**Evaluation by Group Leaders.** Although the group leaders, with few exceptions, were not selected until a few days prior to the conference, and were therefore not involved extensively in planning for the conference, they occupied a focal position in the conference which placed them in contact with all the other participants.

To a large extent, the group leaders considered their problems with the advocates to be the result of the advocate selection and training procedures. Group leaders believed the advocates did not receive clear instructions that the primary goal of the conference was placement and therefore advocates for the most part were not sufficiently committed to helping youth find placement in the community. The group leaders suggested that at least a week of intensive training was needed and the training probably should have included first-hand experience at the Westfield Detention Center. Since many of the group leaders were very much involved in the actual training in contrast to the selection process, it is apparent that *after* the conference, more than before, the group leaders realized the need for more organized and systematic education of the advocates about the nature of delinquency, institutionalization, and interpersonal relations than could be acquired while doing the work of advocacy itself.

One group leader expressed his evaluation of the advocate as defender this way:

I think that the advocate as a defender is fine, and it was a good idea, and I think that by and large that is what happened but I think that if someone is going to fight a bureaucracy, they have to know what they are fighting. You can't fight a bureaucracy you don't know anything about . . . and when you sit down, and I can say, to the advocate, listen we both know that this kid is not going to go home . . . he is either going to go to this placement or that placement or the conference is going to end and he is going back into the same cycle. I agree that this number one placement isn't the idealistic best way but it is a hell of a lot better than anything else that we can offer the kid. And that is the bureaucracy, and maybe I can't see it because I am in it. But even so, you have to know what your odds are and your alternatives are before you can do a good job as a defender.

Because of lack of knowledge on the part of the advocates of how the placement system works and because of the unclear priority of placement in the minds of the advocates, group leaders believed that the major responsibility for placement had become theirs by default. In the beginning, the advocate, the youth, and the group leader were to work the placement out together. By the close of the conference, many of the placements were arranged by the group leaders while the advocates were "taking care of the kids."

When asked about the quality of placements, the group leaders indicated that they thought the placements were fairly good given the quality and availability of placement possibilities. One of the liabilities of having all the group leaders from the same region was exacerbated by the fact that they knew placement possibilities in their own region very well, but were not particularly aware of resources elsewhere in the state, where many of the youth were from. Consequently, group leaders felt placements could have been improved, particularly for the youth from the Boston area, if there had been more consistent coordination and support from the Boston office.

Many of the youth participating in the conference, according to the group leaders, expected just to have a lot of fun. One group leader noted, "Many kids thought it was just an interim period before something else happened to them. 'Always, something is happening to me—not I make it happen,' that was always the attitude."

Group leaders also expressed mixed feelings about the viability of having such a conference at a university. They stated that it was very helpful to have good health and recreational facilities which could be utilized by the youth, and most university personnel cooperated fully to assist whenever needed. However, several group leaders pointed out that the university is so spacious that it proved difficult at time to assemble all the youth and advocates. The group leaders also felt that they lacked leverage to encourage some youth to accept a placement since almost any placement would seem less desirable than the free environment of the university.

**Evaluation by JOE Staff.** The JOE staff also occupied a central position at the conference since they worked with members of all the other participating groups.

On selection and training of advocates, it was suggested that selection procedures might have been more carefully carried out, but that it proved difficult really to discover the various motivations of the volunteers to become youth advocates.

When asked about the role of the advocates, JOE staff indicated that most advocates had developed a fairly meaningful relationship with the youth, but that a number were either not willing or felt they were not permitted to perform in a real advocacy role. Some of the advocates had complained to JOE staff members that they felt like baby-sitters. However, this was attributed by JOE staff to the fact that the advocates' lack of knowledge about community placements and the relative unavailability of community placements forced group leaders to become increasingly responsible for placement.

The experience of the conference indicated for JOE staff that for the youth advocacy role to be successful, the youth advocate must have available a number of external supports, for example, knowledge about the background of the boys and girls, generation of community resource alternatives by DYS, and encouragement when good decisions are made. Reflecting on the conference experience, JOE staff members believe that the university offers a most desirable resource for youth advocacy. In response to the charge that the university is too free an environment and has too many of its own problems, such as drug use, JOE staff members maintain that the university is no more free or perverse than the home communities of these juvenile offenders.

According to the JOE staff who were responsible for the relations between the university and the conference, university representatives were very cooperative and helpful. For the most part incidents were not blown out of proportion and conference personnel were generally permitted to handle these crises. For example, during the first week of the conference a number of youth were involved in pilfering at the campus book store. The incident was made known to the conference and the group leaders arranged for monitors to be placed in the store. This served to handle the problem. JOE staff felt that it would be naive not to expect such crises with a conference of this dimension, but that they could probably be handled with the cooperation of the university.

Although the relationship between the JOE staff and the university was very good, some of the JOE staff indicated that coordination between DYS and the university could have been improved if a top Boston official had worked full time at the conference. The lack of interest in taking any firsthand responsibility in coordination suggested to the JOE staff that top Boston office administrators were only interested in publicity: "They handled the press; they were here the first day when all the press was here and again when the governor came."

Finally, for JOE staff, one of the important by-products of the conference was encouraging students to become involved in social action and, in particular, in youth corrections. They noted that the relative lack of major problems created by the conference for the university should also make it easier for the university to support similar kinds of social action in the future.

**Evaluations by Advocates.** Sixty-nine percent of the advocates contacted concluded that youth advocacy was a useful and helpful program. When asked what
they did for youth which best described their role as advocate, 37 percent of the
advocates responded first by indicating that they tried to be the "youth's best
friend," 23 percent indicated that they "tried to talk with the youth," and 12
percent indicated that they "tried to intervene in the placement process." One
female advocate described her attempt to convince a girl's parents that
placement outside the home would be best. It took two trips to the parents'
home, but she finally gained their confidence and their consent for the
placement.

Several advocates suggested that the screening process should be more tightly
controlled in order to have only advocates who have a sufficient commitment to
helping the youth through any kind of problem. Sixty-five percent of the
advocates believed that they had not been adequately trained. According to our
sample of advocates, training could have been improved by providing some
personal experiences with youth, by providing information on institutions, by
providing more lead time for planning, and by arranging for the advocate to
meet the youth before he arrived at the conference.

It is clear that some advocates felt that they developed a very good working
relationship with the group leaders while others saw their relationship with
"their kid" as a very personal thing and did not want to involve the group
leaders in that relationship. Typical responses that indicated an effective working
relationship with the group leaders included:

The group leaders tried to help during the program despite little organization.
They gave us a lot of help and support. They were available when problems came
up, and took the responsibility for crises.

Yet another advocate indicated little desire for help from group leaders or other
staff: "The program turned me off, but I ignored that. It was just between me
and my kid. I was his friend, unconditionally."

Almost all the advocates indicated that they regularly met with other
advocates to discuss mutual problems in handling behavioral and placement
problems that they had to face. They found such informal groups helped more
than the formal groups originally planned to serve this function. These informal
groups were also utilized to reduce the pressure of being responsible for the boys
and girls twenty-four hours a day and to allow time off when classes resumed.
Another example of group involvement among advocates occurred when several
advocates rented several rooms in the campus Center Hotel to be shared by them
and "their kids."

Although these informal group activities emerged, they were for the most part
obscured by the general flow of activities so that other conference participants
were not fully aware that such processes were playing a significant problem-solving role.

Another criticism of the conference came from advocates who were concerned about the planned program. One person indicated that much of the conference, particularly the speakers, was directed to the advocates and not to the youth. Others cited again that the lack of coordination within the conference diminished the likelihood of the program's having any positive effects on the youth.

A striking 89 percent of the advocate sample believed that the university should continue cooperating with DYS in programs for youth in trouble. Some of the dissenters questioned the suitability of the university campus for such a program. They felt that the university was perhaps too unstructured for these young boys and girls. They pointed to the difficulty of having to impose a double standard which permitted college students to do things DYS youth were not allowed to do.

Many of the advocates talked to us during the conference about continuing their relationships with "their kids." Afterward, 78 percent of the sample indicated that they planned to continue contact. One advocate stated: "I see my kid once a week, and he can call me at any time if anything should go wrong." Another noted that he tries to stay in contact "through correspondence and when I travel to Boston, I will look him up and talk for a while or maybe go out to a show or something."

As a concluding evaluative question we asked our sample of advocates what they liked best about the conference. Thirty-one percent gave as their first response the one-to-one relationship with youth, while 23 percent gave as their first response the chance to help DYS youth outside of institutions, and 17 percent cited as their first response the learning experience afforded by the conference. When asked about their strongest dislikes about the conference, the most frequent response was the lack of planning (fifty-six percent).

**Evaluations by Youth.** In general, the youth responses are rather favorable. When asked whether the conference had helped them, 66 percent of the sample responded affirmatively, 25 percent responded negatively while the remainder were unsure. In order to discover what about the conference was helpful the youth were asked to specify their answers. Thirty-eight percent indicated that the most helpful fact of the conference was that it helped to change the youth's behavior. For example, "It helped make me more responsible; I learned to be more structured in my use of time." Twenty-nine percent of the youth believed the most helpful element to be the one-to-one relationships with advocates who were trying to look out for the youth and "who cared." Twelve percent felt that the most helpful factor was simply being in an alternative environment to the institution, while 10 percent cited good placements. Sixteen youth believed that the conference was harmful; these youth stated that there was too much freedom and that parole and placement procedures were bad. One might expect considerable response variation by age. Youth sixteen and over were a little more favorably disposed toward the conference than youth fifteen and under—73 percent compared to 58 percent. Boys were a little more favorably disposed toward the conference than girls (70 and 54 percent respectively) and whites were a little more favorably disposed than blacks (68 and 53 percent respectively).

Youth were also asked how they got along with their advocate. Eighty-three percent responded "good," 12 percent "alright," and 10 percent "poor." When asked to specify, over 60 percent of the youth gave responses focused on the fact that an advocate was taking the time to do something with the youth. Typical responses included: "My advocate talked to me about going outside in the community to live without getting in trouble," and "It taught me to respect myself and to do what I feel like without getting in trouble." Many of the youth expressed appreciation of the advocates' willingness to provide new experiences and interesting recreational opportunities. Bowling, movies, and cross-country skiing were mentioned. One youth related how three pairs of advocates and "their kids" toured Vermont. Others expressed amazement that their advocate was so willing to help them. One pointed out that his advocate had taken him "250 miles just to get a drum head." Another youth said that his advocate showed him "different halfway houses in case I couldn't go home." Youth who had good relationships with their advocates were more likely than those who had poor relationships with their advocates to believe that the conference had been helpful (Gamma = 0.61).

One of the critical outcomes of the conference was the placements and their quality. Sixty-three percent of the youth indicated that they like their placements, 14 percent said that they were alright, while 24 percent disliked them. Not too surprisingly youth who like their placements were the ones most likely to believe the conference to have been helpful (Gamma = 0.71). Over 75 percent of the youth placed in group homes, foster homes, or returned directly home believed that the conference program had been helpful. One-half of the youth who ran from the conference and only 17 percent of the youth who were returned to institutional settings believed the program to be helpful.

One of the last questions we asked the youth sample focused on the youth advocacy conference idea as a means for handling youth, regardless of whether the youth believed that the University of Massachusetts Conference had been a good experience. Eighty-two percent responded favorably—that it was a good idea—while 7 percent indicated "no," with the remainder saying "don't know." As with the advocate sample, the major reasons given for the favorable responses were the one-to-one relationship between advocates and youth and freedom from institutional environment.

To summarize, while many youth went to the conference expecting to go directly home, it is evident that the measure of success of the program finally used by youth was the quality of placement received. Whether or not the youth perceived the conference to be a "placement conference" in the same sense that it was perceived as such by the group leaders and whether or not the youth recognized that the major outcome of the conference for them took the form of some kind of placement, it was the successfully placed youth who predominately thought the conference a success.

**Evaluations by the University Community.** Interviews with several key university personnel (including the campus police, deans, and the Campus Center staff) were conducted to obtain their assessment of the conference. These individuals were very positive about the conference and the role the university had played. One source indicated that he believed it had been "a great learning experience for all of us at the university." The major value was that it exposed the university community to the DYS youth and their problems and focused attention on the entire problem of juvenile corrections.

The major criticism from the university community was the short lead time available for the key figures to communicate the objectives of the conference to others in the university and surrounding community. They felt that this prevented more adequate planning as to how the university could best serve the conference.

Each of the interviewees estimated as minimal the impact of the incidents that occurred. One official expressed the view that these incidents were rather "miniscule when compared to the normal number of incidents our 17,000 students cause in any given month. If they had not been JOE kids we never would have had a second thought about these incidents."

Most of these sources expressed a desire to involve the university in similar programs in the future. Only one person suggested that the university might be a poor place for DYS youth on the grounds that college students might be a bad influence on an impressionable teenager.

**Evaluations by Boston Office.** During and following the conference we have been in contact with Boston office personnel and regional directors to obtain their assessments of the conference. Boston office staff in general believed that placements were quite good relative to the placements the youth would have received if they had been placed more gradually through the normal parole process from Lyman. One person stated that the placements were "a little more productive than if the placements had been done out of "Lyman" because the advocates were more motivated than staff."

Regional directors, however, were not as favorably impressed with the placement procedures as Boston office staff. Several of these directors told of youth who had been placed in their regions without their knowledge. They noted that this type of problem could have been prevented by better coordination of the conference placement plans with the regional offices.

The value of advocacy was well supported by the conference according to the Boston office staff. However, the Boston office staff members did express concern over the selection and training of the advocates. They felt that some of the advocates offered alternatives and options to the boys and girls that were not realistic. Furthermore, they noted that in some cases the advocates' supervision broke down so that youth were left with a lot of "idle time" just like in the institutions. Yet they still believed that the university environment was a good thing for the youth, because it allowed them to merge with the student body. The youth did not stand out as being different since "very often one could not distinguish between the student and the kid."

Two comments probably best sum up the Boston office assessment of the conference. It was "a good mechanism to get out of Lyman." And, "public relations-wise it was a good thing, because it showed that the kids could be taken away from large institutions and placed successfully with very few incidents."

**Outcome Data on the Conference**. The effectiveness of the youth advocate model and of the conference as a prerelease placement procedure can be measured in terms of the types of placements made and in terms of the number of youth who remain in their placements, that is, who are not on the run and have not recidivated to the DYS or adult correctional system. The center has obtained data on the number of youth placed in the various available alternatives. It should be noted that such facts remain at best only approximate, indirect measures of effectiveness of the youth advocacy model because a number of alternative explanations can be made to explain why youth either did not receive "good placements" or failed to remain in placements. Good placements may simply not have existed, particularly for the more difficult youth. Structural or legal constraints may have prohibited appropriate placement, for example, lack of agreement between advocate and group leader on placement or lack of agreement with the parole officer who had to approve the home or lack of preconference planning and coordinating of resources.

In Figure 13-1 the disposition at the end of the conference (February 16, 1972) of the ninety-nine youth who participated in the conference is shown. Because the major objective of the conference was to remove youth from institutions, we may for this purpose classify any placement which removed the youth from an institutionalized lifestyle as a successful placement. Using this yardstick, we discover that sixty-five youth were put in placements other than institutional settings. Eleven youth were placed in the major existing institutions, and another eleven youth ran from the conference during the month. (Parenthetically, it should be noted that being on the run does not necessarily mean that the conference did not have a positive impact upon a boy or girl—it may be that the youth "got his head together" and will stay out of trouble.)

Twelve youth remained unplaced at the end of the conference. Of these twelve some continued to remain with their advocates while others were held at institutions in a "pending placement" status.

While approximately two-thirds of both boys and girls were successfully

NO. OF YOUTHS

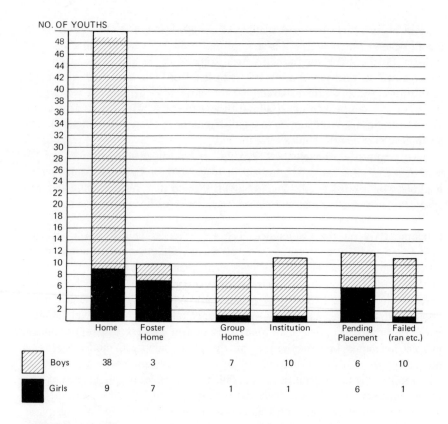

|  | Home | Foster Home | Group Home | Institution | Pending Placement | Failed (ran etc.) |
|---|---|---|---|---|---|---|
| Boys | 38 | 3 | 7 | 10 | 6 | 10 |
| Girls | 9 | 7 | 1 | 1 | 6 | 1 |

**Figure 13-1.** Placement of Youth from the University of Massachusetts. Source: Table constructed from data provided by JOE staff.

placed, the kinds of placement vary considerably by sex. The largest number of boys were returned directly home. However, seven were placed in group homes, compared with only one girl who was successfully placed in a group home. In contrast, seven girls were placed in foster homes while only three boys were placed in foster homes. The lack of group home placements for girls is probably indicative of the lack of available group homes for girls within the DYS and within the community at large. The disproportionate number of available foster homes for girls may suggest that this placement strategy is appropriate for girls but may be more difficult to arrange for boys. It may be the case that the girl is seen as less threatening by potential foster parents, particularly if the husband works away from home during the day.

The second outcome measure used here to assess the U. Mass experience is a recidivism index based on presence or absence of youth appearing in court after participating in the conference. Data from the Massachusetts Department of Probation were used to determine whether youth had appeared in court. The follow-up effort involved an eleven-month period. Court appearance is used as an index of recidivism because it is the most reliable follow-up data available to the Center. It is acknowledged that such an index is a very stringent estimate of recidivism. However since the department is handling many more youth through informal referral measures, commitment rates are no longer accurate reflections of youth getting into trouble with social control agencies.

The overall recidivism rate for all youth participating in the conference was 48 percent, that is, slightly less than one-half of the youth appeared in court at least once during the eleven-month follow-up period. Fifty-seven percent of the boys and 20 percent of the girls recidivated. It can be seen in Table 13-2 that most of the initial court appearances occurred within the first four months (69 percent of the boys and 40 percent of the girls) after the youth took part in the conference. No initial court appearances were recorded during the tenth and eleventh months of the follow-up period. It would appear that the 52 percent which were free of trouble during the first eleven months have a fairly good chance of remaining free of trouble.

**Table 13-2**

**Length of Time Until First Court Appearance Controlled for Sex for Those who Recidivated**

| Length of time until first court appearance: | Sex | |
|---|---|---|
| | Males % | Females % |
| less than one month | 21 | 40 |
| 1-2 months | 24 | 0 |
| 2-3 months | 24 | 0 |
| 3-4 months | 10 | 0 |
| 4-5 months | 2 | 0 |
| 5-6 months | 7 | 0 |
| 6-7 months | 5 | 20 |
| 7-8 months | 2 | 0 |
| 8-9 months | 5 | 40 |
| 9-10 months | 0 | 0 |
| 10-11 months | 0 | 0 |
| Total | 100 | 100 |
| N | 42 | 5 |

Note: Recidivism data for our sample of youth is quite comparable to that of the entire population. The overall rate for the sample was 49%.

Although the number of youth in each type of placement is somewhat small, comparing recidivism rates by type of placement yields some interesting results. Foster home placement is the most successful placement alternative with no boys failing and only one girl failing. Less than half (47 percent) of the boys placed directly home recidivated; only 22 percent of the girls placed directly home recidivated. On the other hand, 71 percent of the boys and the only girl placed in group homes recidivated. This finding should not be construed as an indictment of group homes because the conference marks one of the department's first experiences with the use of such facilities. Assessment of the relative adequacy of group homes must await further study which is presently being undertaken. As one might expect, 80 percent of the boys and the only girl placed back into institutional settings recidivated, making the institutions the least auspicious placement. Seventy percent of the boys and the one girl who ran from the conference also recidivated. Sixty-seven percent of the boys whose placements were pending at the conference's end recidivated. None of the girls whose placements were pending returned to court.

Because the group leaders came from Region I only, it was believed by some conference participants, including the group leaders themselves, that youth coming from Region I or the Westfield area were probably being better served than youth from other regions of the state. Results in Table 13-3 that depict recidivism rates by institutional origin of youth are mixed. Fifty-four percent of the Lyman boys and 54 percent of the Westfield boys recidivated; therefore no difference in recidivism patterns between the two largest sources of boys.

**Table 13-3**

**Recidivism by Type of Placement and Institutional Origin Controlled for Sex**

|  | Sex | | | |
|  | Males | | Females | |
|  | % | N | % | N |
|---|---|---|---|---|
| Type of Placement: | | | | |
| Home | 47 | (38) | 22 | (9) |
| Foster home | 0 | (3) | 14 | (7) |
| Group home | 71 | (7) | 100 | (1) |
| Institution | 80 | (10) | 0 | (1) |
| Run from conf. | 70 | (10) | 100 | (1) |
| Pending | 67 | (6) | 0 | (6) |
| Institutional Origin: | | | | |
| Lyman | 54 | (39) | – | – |
| Westfield | 54 | (24) | 0 | (8) |
| Lancaster | – | – | 29 | (17) |
| Roslindale | 75 | (8) | – | – |
| From the Run | 67 | (3) | – | – |

However, it is apparent that girls who came from Westfield were more successful than girls who came from Lancaster, 0 percent compared to 29 percent.

The type of charge that youth receive can indicate whether the relatively low recidivism rate is a function of having a population which is biased toward youth who exhibit nondescript, minor kinds of acting-out behavior. Charge data indicates that this bias is not present; in fact, only one of the forty-two boys recidivating was charged with a "delinquent act." The others were charged with crimes that would be punishable if adults had committed them. Two of the five recidivating girls were charged with "delinquent acts."

While calculations on court-appearance recidivism rates in the past are not yet completed, it is thought that the recidivism rates reported here for youth in the conference are probably somewhat lower than court appearance recidivism rates characterizing youth from the institutions in years past. The recidivism data on the conference taken as a whole would suggest that using something like the U. Mass conference as a tool for deinstitutionalization does not pose greater risks to the youth or to the community than the routine risks involved with incarceration. In fact, the role of the youth advocate has been supported as a viable conduit for reintegration of youth into the community.

### Conclusions and Recommendations

Given all of the information obtained thus far, what can one conclude about the University of Massachusetts experience? First, the conference certainly facilitated the rapid and relatively painless closing of Lyman School. From what we have observed, the University of Massachusetts experience was quite positive for most youth, and compared to what one might expect from a more gradual process of removal of youth from an institution, the youth probably fared much better by being at the University of Massachusetts. Second, it would appear that the youth advocacy model is as effective a placement technique as other modes of placement presently being used within the department. Although a number of youth either were not adequately placed or did not remain in their placements, there was no immediate wholesale return of the youth to the DYS, as some observers had predicted. From the viewpoint of many conference participants, and from our own perspective, if more appropriate screening and training processes were employed in the future, one could strengthen this model and improve its effectiveness. Third, the university remains a significant reservoir of resources for youth correctional services. It would appear that if such a conference with 100 youth can be carried out on a university campus without major crises, smaller scale conferences could be employed with perhaps even greater success.

In addition to these summary conclusions, a number of recommendations emerge for policy consideration if such conferences are to be repeated.

**Planning and Lead Time.** Persistent criticisms voiced by most of the persons involved with the conference concerned the lack of preconference planning, the shortness of lead time, and the failure of continued coordination. It seems that the Boston office by design or inadvertence did not clearly define its own role either for administering the conference or for providing placement support. This lack of clear-cut and accepted responsibility resulted in feelings on the part of conference participants that various parties were not living up to their obligations.

However, despite frequent criticism by conference participants of the lack of preconference planning, the dangers of overstructuring and overplanning should also be considered. The two principal dangers are: (1) reduction of an organization's flexibility for choosing alternative strategies while the program is in midstream; and (2) structuring roles so rigidly that the creativity of persons filling those roles is discouraged.

Another aspect of planning and the allowing of lead time about which there were complaints was the lack of advance notice given to the community. The issue is complicated. After the fact, university and community officials were favorable to the conference. However one result of early publicity can be a premature confrontation between opponents and proponents before the value of a program can be demonstrated, we have no way of knowing whether university and community officials would have been favorable in the face of advanced publicity. Certainly key figures within the community need to be a part of the advance planning. In the case of the University of Massachusetts Conference, for example, it was essential to involve the university president, certain deans, and the police department.

Once a conference is in progress, information should be presented straight-forwardly to the public. Knowledge of the facts concerning incidents will do much to dispel fears and anxieties. The press may be used to accomplish this task, but, in still another way, the strategy may have its costs as well as its rewards. If program staff perceive the use of media as simply a play for publicity or indulging in self-aggrandizement, the staff may become easily alienated because they believe that their objective to serve youth has been subjugated to less idealistic goals. It is important then for those who speak to the press also to explain clearly to program staff their objectives to educate and to encourage public support, and to show how such objectives can complement, rather than detract from, the major goal of helping troubled boys and girls.

Given these pros and cons of planning, we are led to suggest that such a conference should be well organized in the sense that all participants are clear on what is expected of them and on what ways a corrections agency can support them in efforts to achieve those expectations, but the actual means, "how to advocate for a kid," should be loosely defined to allow for creativity and judgment in the specific situation or relationship.

**Selection of Advocates and Youth.** Selection of advocates should be based on the advocates' commitment to helping youth and on their sense of realities. Advocates should be persons who can be trained in a short time to relate to real youth (as opposed to an idealization of youth in trouble) over prolonged periods in sometimes difficult circumstances. They should have some sense of what they are getting into and what they are themselves capable of. During the process of screening, the goals of the advocacy program should be clearly spelled out, including the boundaries of the advocates' responsibility. This is particularly important if the advocate is expected to work within a group under the direction of a group leader.

Participating youth should be selected by obtaining as much information on their background as possible, and assessing the potential risks for the community, for the youth, and for DYS if they should run from the conference. All available information on the youth should be made available to the advocate or the group leader to facilitate placement.

**Training of Advocates.** Training of advocates should include both the didactic and the experiential approaches. In a week's training, the advocate could be made aware of some of the causes of juvenile delinquency, the process of juvenile corrections, and the specific objectives of a correctional agency.

Training should be designed to enhance creative handling of behavioral and placement problems. In other words, potential advocates should be made aware of the kinds of problems they will confront and, perhaps via role-playing or some similar technique, to work out solutions. A disservice might be done however if the advocate left the training session with the idea that problem A should always be solved by using solution X.

**Location and Size of Conference or Advocacy Program.** For a number of reasons the university remains a suitable setting for youth advocacy programs. First, a wealth of willing manpower exists in most universities. Many students and faculty seek out the kind of social action represented by such a program. While individual students and faculty may come and go, the university itself can provide the lasting framework needed for a continued flow of social action involvement in youth advocacy. Second, both students and faculty share skills that are most appropriate for handling troubled youth. These skills may include special tutoring, psychological counseling, social work, or recreational techniques. Third, the university also has the necessary administrative skills and resources to coordinate an advocacy program, that is, funding facilities and matching of advocates and youth. Fourth, advocacy programs should be well received on most university campuses because they do provide students and faculty with an opportunity to develop and refine action and treatment strategies. While the university poses some hazards for youthful offenders, the benefits of the one-to-one relationship with concerned, sensitive, and capable persons seems to outweigh the potential problems.

Finally, as there are many university campuses scattered across the state, youth advocacy programs could be scaled down in size and run concurrently in several universities at once. Scaling down the programs to a smaller number of advocates and youth and instituting more programs on more campuses should produce some favorable effects such as: (1) reducing the management and coordination problems; (2) diminishing the possibility for negative subcultures to emerge; (3) allowing each program to be flexible with respect to the length of time it runs (some programs could run for an extended or indefinite period); and (4) permitting a more nearly maximal use of available resources throughout the state.

**Placement.** As part of his training, the advocate should be fully informed about the availability of placement alternatives. Persons who organize and administer youth advocacy programs should be very knowledgeable about resources located in the areas where participating youth reside. The sponsoring agency must recognize its responsibility to provide effective support for the advocates as they attempt to place youth. The advocacy model augments, and does not take away, the placement responsibility from the agency. The agency must continue to generate placement alternatives, provide advice on the quality of specific placements, and, wherever possible, reduce the bureaucratic red tape which hinders the placement process.

In the final analysis, the University of Massachusetts Conference, despite its planning and coordination problems, shows that the Massachusetts Department of Youth Services has put together a most unique and effective means of handling certain youth needs without relying on the crutch of institutionalization. Adopted on a smaller scale this youth advocacy model would appear to have much merit for tapping new resources of support for troubled youth.

## Part IV
## The Massachusetts Experience

# 14 Closing Massachusetts' Institutions: A Case Study

Yitzhak Bakal

Among the several states attempting new approaches to juvenile corrections, without doubt the most rapid and dramatic reorganization has occurred in Massachusetts. Under the leadership of Commissioner Jerome G. Miller, between 1969 and 1973 the Department of Youth Services (DYS) closed all the state reform schools and replaced them with a regionalized system of community-based group homes and other treatment programs, largely operated by private groups. As the most comprehensive demonstration to date of a "deinstitution-alized" approach to the care of delinquent and troubled youth, the Massachu-setts experience has excited praise, criticism, and above all curiosity among human services professionals across the country. It has been hailed as the harbinger of a new and better day for youthful offenders, attacked as a threat to society, and dismissed as a well-intentioned but superficial liberal reform.

The Massachusetts experiment *does* represent an important breakthrough in juvenile corrections, and may well emerge as a new model for state human service agencies. While Commissioner Miller has left Massachusetts to head the Illinois Family and Children Services, the reorganization he began is still very much in progress. In the group homes and halfway houses, the keystone of the new system, staff and youth together are working out their individual programs. The same may be said of the many nonresidential programs—parole, foster homes, court liaison, youth advocacy—sponsored by DYS. In the department's central and regional offices, staff are adjusting to new management roles and responsibilities, including systematic collection and analysis of data on costs, recidivism, educational and vocational achievement, and other measures needed to monitor and evaluate the effectiveness of a noninstitutional system.

Yet a preliminary case study of the reorganization of the Massachusetts Department of Youth Services can serve three useful functions. First, both within and outside the human services professions—among legislators, for example—there is a demand for information about the virtually unique bureau-cratic and administrative changes that occurred in Massachusetts. Second, under Commissioner Miller the DYS leadership demonstrated an unusual set of change strategies that resulted in impressive successes, as well as some near-disastrous failures. Their strategies for institutional change included a developing set of political tactics by which issues and opponents could be isolated, understood, and overcome. For state personnel in similar positions these strategies may prove replicable, and the mistakes avoidable, since many of the issues, and the sources of Miller's support and opposition, are essentially the same in social service agencies in other states.

Finally, an analysis of the formative results of the changes themselves may provide some clue to the range of impacts achieved in DYS and other Massachusetts agencies, even though final judgments must be withheld. Certainly the costs to DYS staff and leadership were enormous. For human services professionals in other states, the key issue is the degree to which those costs were matched by benefits to the agencies and institutions involved, to the state and its taxpayers, but most of all to the children in the care of the department.

A major concern of this case study is the amount and type of planning that went into the changes brought about by Commissioner Miller and his staff. For in Massachusetts, the shift from custodial state institutions to state-managed or state-purchased services, from old and inadequate facilities to a broad range of group homes, preventive programs, intensive therapeutic environments, and humane treatment centers, was not merely a matter of managing the dynamics of planned change. The process also involved many ad hoc decisions, based on intuition, good luck, manipulation of information, and the ability to learn from mistakes and to capitalize quickly on new developments. Flexibility was perhaps the most important element involved, and also responsible for many of the department's achievements and not a few of its setbacks.

This narrative, then, is organized around planned and unplanned change strategies employed by DYS leadership, and their interim impacts. To establish the context for change and to introduce the major themes in the change process, it begins with a historical review of the department. Following sections discuss in detail the successive phases of the department's development: the pressure to change; Commissioner Miller's first attempts to prepare the system for change; the restructuring of the department; the impacts of the changes on DYS and other Massachusetts human service agencies, and their legislative and bureaucratic institutionalization. A concluding section summarizes those aspects of the Massachusetts experience that are most pertinent to the theory and practice of organizational change.

*Historical Review*

For the past ten or twelve years the nature and dimension of the juvenile delinquency problem in the United States and around the world has been changing rapidly. The crime rate is definitely on the rise, and with it the public's concern. The President's Commission on Law Enforcement and the Administration of Justice pointed out in 1967 that young people are committing a disproportionate amount of crimes for the number of youths in the general population; and their recidivism rates are higher than those for adults. This position was reiterated at the end of 1969 by the Eisenhower Commission.

However, these findings and the increased public concern have resulted in very few new and innovative programs in the field of delinquency prevention and control. Instead, the prevailing response to these problems had been to commit more money and more resources to existing and traditional youth service operations.

The Massachusetts Department of Youth Services represents a unique experiment because it has radically departed from traditional approaches in two significant ways. It was the first state in the nation to close its institutions for youths, without any major repercussions; and secondly, it has developed many innovative and promising programs for its troubled youth without a major increase in its budget or in its personnel.

If this department can survive the test of time and prove to be effective in delinquency control, there is no doubt that the example of Massachusetts will bring an immense amount of pressure on other states to follow in its path.

**Agency Profile Prior to the Reorganization Act.** The Youth Service Board was created in 1948 by a legislative act, as a quasi-judicial tribunal with responsibilities of classifying, placing, training, and supervising adjudicated delinquents committed to the board by the courts. This act removed the authority for sentencing a youth from the presiding judge and placed the case in the hands of the board. In 1952 another legislative act changed the board into the Division of Youth Services, under the direction of the State Department of Education but not subject to its control. The director of the division, Dr. Coughlin, was responsible for making all decisions pertaining to the treatment, custody, and parole of youthful offenders. While these legislative acts provided a mandate for change, no reform followed. Instead, the different studies and investigative commissions that reviewed division's operation described the agency as stultified by the rigid enforcement of outmoded practices, and one which lagged far behind other states in establishing progressive programs for the youth in its care.

Three studies were conducted during 1966-1967 that gave a detailed analysis of DYS's operation. These studies criticized the administrative structure of the division for investing too much authority and responsibility in one man. The previous director had failed to delegate responsibility to his staff in the central office, yet at the same time, had allowed the different institutions and detention centers to become relatively autonomous. They were free to do their own hiring and firing, and to develop their own programs without the direct supervision of the central administration. Even budget appropriations were made on an institution-by-institution basis.

In 1969 the division operated five large training schools: the Lyman School for Boys (ages 12-15), the Shirley Industrial School for Boys (ages 15-17), the Oakdale Residential Treatment Unit for boys (ages 9-11), the Lancaster Industrial School for Girls (all ages), and the Bridgewater Guidance Center, a maximum-security unit. The division also operated four regional detention centers: two in the Boston area, one for girls at South Huntington Avenue and one for boys in Roslindale; the third was a co-educational center in Worcester and a fourth in the western part of the state, Westfield.

These facilities, with the exception of two detention centers, Worcester and Westfield, operated on a custodial, training-school model for the treatment of the children in their custody. They were mostly outmoded, uncoordinated with idiosyncratic management and sporadic links to other social services, and the department in general. Their communication with the division at large was almost nonexistent. The institutions themselves were hidden either in suburban or rural locations and were isolated from outsiders, and very often were subject to local patronage influences.

Programs in the institutions were poor. There were no certified academic or educational programs, and vocational training was limited, offering youths outmoded skills, which would provide little opportunity for future employment. Clinical services were almost nonexistent because of the lack of professional staff. Those who were hired as clinicians spent their time producing reports at the reception centers, which were unlikely to be used for classification or treatment, since the children were assigned to the different institutions according to age rather than their needs. In addition, staff members were untrained, unskilled, and unlikely to learn newer treatment methods because they ranged in age between forty and sixty years old.

The treatment of youths inside the institutions was at best custodial, and at worst punitive and repressive. Marching, shaved heads, and enforced periods of long silences were regular occurrences. Punitive staff used force; made recalcitrant children drink water from toilets, or scrub floors on their hands and knees for hours on end. Solitary confinement was also used extensively and rationalized as a mode of treatment for those who needed it. It must be noted that the children who happened to be sent to the Worcester or Westfield Detention Centers were treated more humanely and were involved in much richer programs.

The communication between the different offices of the division was almost nil. The offices of parole, after-care, clinical services, educational services, etc., each operated autonomously, with no coordination and with little knowledge of what was going on in other parts of the system. The most disjointed and incoherent part was the parole system, which lacked accountability and supervision and, by and large, operated as a police model rather than as an advocate for the youths.

This system, with its retributive and custodial orientation, produced many angry youngsters whose attempts to strike back at the system through stealing cars, theft, or running away brought them further trouble with the law. A high percentage of the division's children who started their career as truants, runaways, or "stubborn child," were later diagnosed and labeled as "habitual runners," "assaultive," "violent," or "hard-core." They thus became the victims of a vicious spiral ending up in adult correctional institutions.

The department's image in the eyes of professionals, judges, the press, and the youths in its care was associated with repression and punishment. This image was most vividly described in a cartoon by SZEP in the *Boston Globe* (April 21, 1967) showing the previous director, holding chains and handcuffs complaining, "they're breaking up that old gang of mine," referring to Mr. Buryl Cohen's critical report following an investigation of the Division of Youth Services.

**Pressure for Change**. From the mid-1960s on, the Department of Youth Services was subjected to increasing pressure for change by the legislature, the public, the media, and professional and civic associations. This external pressure led directly to the legislative reorganization of the department and to Jerome Miller's appointment as commissioner, and contributed in no small measure to the accomplishments of his administration. Since widespread support for reform, and Miller's skillful use of that support, played so important a role in the DYS change process, this section is devoted to an examination of its sources, forms, and influence.

In Massachusetts as elsewhere, the training schools have been a deservedly popular target of the reform-minded since the mid-nineteenth century. But they have also demonstrated bureaucracy's renowned ability to close ranks and weather passing storms of criticism. What seems to have made the difference in Massachusetts was that by the sixties, conditions in the system had deteriorated to an almost *pathological* state. Once a leader in youth services, Massachusetts had evolved one of the worst systems in the country.

The most telling measure of effectiveness, recidivism, had reached 80 percent. Annual costs per child ranged as high as $11,500, twice the national average; corruption was widely suspected and frequently proven. In the state's three large training schools and other facilities, academic, vocational and even recreational programs were moribund or nonexistent. Discipline was the watchword at the institutions. Punishment for offenses against discipline ranged from denial of privileges, to solitary confinement in the "lock-up," to brutal beatings by guards. The ratio of custodial to professional staff in the department was 22 to 1, most of whom were protected from review, promotion, or demotion by civil service or political cronyism. The institutions had almost universally hostile relations with surrounding communities, in part because they were obvious "warehouses" for the children of the poor, generally blacks. Of the inmates, 89 percent came from homes where parents were on, or eligible for, public assistance; 60 percent had parents with alcoholism or drug-addiction problems.

These and other weaknesses of the system were documented by a series of reports, investigations, and exposes, coming with increasing frequency and effectiveness. The first was the 1965 report of the Governor's Management Engineering Task Force, followed by a 1966 report from the Attorney General's Advisory Committee on Juvenile Crime. In 1965 Governor John Volpe asked the Children's Bureau of the U.S. Department of Health, Education, and Welfare to conduct a comprehensive evaluation of the division for the governor's office.

The scathing findings and recommendations of the HEW study were withheld for almost a year until discovered and exposed by a major Boston newspaper in 1967. The disclosure of the HEW report prompted a new wave of studies both by public bodies—e.g., the Massachusetts Committee on Crime and Youth—and by private groups such as the Friends of Youth Association and the Parent Teachers Association. The Massachusetts Legislature conducted hearings to review the policies of the division and to consider new legislation. The governor appointed a blue-ribbon panel to review all aspects of the HEW report and to conduct a definitive investigation of the division.

During this period the press also lent its support to the campaign for change, through numerous editorials and reports, including several "under-cover" stories written by reporters who had gained positions in various institutions. The keynote of the media case for reform was the simple and dramatic issue of humane treatment. "Simply 'caging children,' as Governor Sargent so aptly put it, 'is not the way of an enlightened society.' " Less visible but certainly present in the popularization of the reform movement were the various other charges of the division's critics, such as civil service formalization and protection of political appointees; centralized and undelegated power in the hands of the director; poor coordination among institutions and a developing autonomy and lack of control within institutions; lack of effective therapeutic and educational programs at the institutions and very few qualified professionals to staff them.

Naturally the division's senior staff defended the system against the growing pressure for change, but the division's critics were apparently correct in citing a breakdown in leadership as a serious problem. While it is difficult to single out a particular event as that which catalyzed the reform movement into legislative action, certainly the most likely candidate was an internal division dispute. Institutional superintendents enjoyed considerable authority over their own staff and autonomy from other institutions and the central office. For each institution had its own state-appropriated budget and personnel, and did its own hiring and purchasing. Few institutional decisions were beyond the personal control of a superintendent. At the Bridgewater Juvenile Guidance Institute, a conflict developed between the superintendent and assistant superintendent, which involved the reform of the installation's maximum-security practices. Supported by the director of the division, Dr. John Coughlin, the superintendent brought charges against the assistant, who appealed to the Civil Service Board. In a much-publicized hearing, the assistant successfully defended his case and was reinstated. Responding to the public outcry against the division's leadership, Governor Sargent pressured Coughlin to resign. Coughlin submitted his resignation in March 1969, effective in May.

While the political battle over reorganization did not end with Coughlin's resignation, the Bridgewater incident and its aftermath did seem to mark a turning point for the reform cause. In May a panel established by the Massachusetts Conference on Social Welfare called for still more resignations of senior staff members and the closing of several facilities. Governor Sargent appointed a former professor of the Boston University School of Social Work, Frank Maloney, as acting director of the division, and lent his support to a reorganization bill pending in the legislature. While reorganization had been debated in legislature since the 1967 HEW report and a succeeding Senate committee investigation, the bill now moved easily through the Senate and House.

Opposition was based principally on the argument that "decision-making powers" would be taken "away from a trained and experienced board and given to 'clinicians.' " A preliminary House vote of 221 to 5 in early July, however, demonstrated the weakness of the opposition. Throughout July Boston newspapers maintained the momentum of the reform movement. For example, the *Globe* described the institutions as "a mess," "antiquated," "old," and "dreary," all under the headline "There's No Lobby for the Outcasts." When the governor signed the Reorganization Act in August, it was in much the same form as presented by the Massachusetts Committee on Crime and Youth several months before.

The Reorganization Act had several impacts, some of them subtle and not foreseen at the time of its enactment. First of all, the bill's very passage increased the credibility and visibility of the reform movement. The Act elevated the division to the status of a department, and moved it from the Department of Education to a super-agency consisting of Welfare, Health, Mental Health, and Corrections. The new department was to be headed by a commissioner and four assistant commissioners of his choosing. Third, the Act set a new professional tone for the agency, using key words such as therapy, prevention, community services, purchase of services, and research. Finally, the Act broadly empowered the new department to "establish necessary facilities for detention, diagnosis, treatment and training of its charges including post-release care." While these powers in themselves did not mark a major new thrust, the language of the Act later proved sufficient grounds for Commissioner Miller and his assistant to implement a noninstitutional system.

The intent of the Act was clearly reflected in the search for a director. The search panel consisted chiefly of professionals such as Dr. Lloyd Ohlin, Head of the Harvard Center for Criminal Justice. They in turn looked for a fellow professional capable of upgrading the department. While the panel officially did not rule out the possibility of choosing a new director from within the ranks of the department, it was expected that an outsider would be selected. Three months after the reorganization bill had passed, Dr. Jerome Miller was the leading candidate. His training at the Ohio State University School of Social Work and his experience in the military, developing a youth services agency for Air Force dependents, met both academic and pragmatic criteria. Governor Sargent confirmed Dr. Miller as the first commissioner of the Department of Youth Services on October 28, 1969.

To sum up, the movement for reform of Massachusetts youth services was prompted by outrage at the high human and financial costs of operating an almost pathologically ineffective system. The movement was external; it had little support among DYS staff, and next to none among the leadership. Due in part to a strong tradition of institutional autonomy, DYS leadership did not succeed in defending the system against change. In fact, a leadership breakdown was the catalyst for legislative reorganization of DYS and a search for a new director.

The thrust of the campaign for change was more humane treatment for children, not a set of specific reforms. This thrust was sustained in the Reorganization Act, which broadly charged the department with improving services to youth, and in the composition and activities of the search panel, which sought a commissioner qualified to upgrade the department. The role of the commissioner, then, was all but explicitly defined as that of an outside change agent who would reform the department from the top down. The mandate of the new commissioner and his assistants, however, was *not* necessarily to close institutions and to develop radically new systems for the prevention and treatment of delinquency, but simply to better the quality of services to youth committed to the department.

**Trial Changes.** When Miller came to DYS, he found an agency in turmoil, divided internally by critical reports and external political conflicts. He found massive public support from reform groups and professional organizations, and encountered high expectations from the press and the legislature for a professional upgrading of the system and for shifting the emphasis of the department away from primarily institutional services to community-based programs. However, Miller found no funds for his four legislated assistant commissioners, and no funds for experimentation, training or research. Meanwhile, political appointees were still in command of the institutions.

During his first year in office, Miller attempted to prepare the system for change by hiring consultants to provide staff training and to introduce new concepts. He was supported in his efforts by many of the younger staff in the department. His aim was to introduce therapeutic community concepts within the institutions. He invited Dr. Maxwell Jones, a British expert on the therapeutic community model, to start a pilot training program at the Shirley Industrial School for Boys. Therapeutic community concepts, intended to alter the traditional passive role of the "inmate" or "client" through a process of active resocialization, in which roles are broken down and relationships become more equalized among staff and residents, were introduced.

Introducing these concepts in the Shirley structure brought immediate polarization, created staff tensions, and resulted in mass escapes. The older staff, who were by and large unskilled, found these new concepts a threat, and a challenge to their authority. The new staff had difficulty integrating these concepts into the daily operations of the institution without further training and support. This resulted in a number of legislative investigations and further staff entrenchment; hence Miller's initial effort was unsuccessful. He would later become aware that he had to change the system "without blowing it."

In mid-1971 he decided to slowly phase out the Shirley facility. This decision was made with the support of his assistant commissioners, and was accomplished by moving several of the cottages to other institutions and by using staff housing to operate group homes.

The Maxwell Jones training sessions provoked further resistance. They symbolized the beginning of a strong and visible staff alienation, which created additional pressures on the system. Some of this resistance became overt as in the writing to state legislators and the press, as well as covert sabotage as inducing runaways, work stoppages, misuse of sick leaves and early retirements. However, these staff confrontations had a limited negative impact on the department, because they were skillfully used by Miller to elicit sympathetic support from the press and reform groups.

Lacking resources and middle-management personnel, Miller's first year, despite its chaos, was effective in three different ways. First, he provided the rhetoric and the tone for later reform through his public appearances, press releases, and lectures around the state. During his lectures, Miller was very often accompanied by youngsters from the institutions, who described their experiences and attacked the system they had been a part of.

Second, he used his administrative power to change and to rotate top administrators in the different institutions. Shirley's administrators were changed several times, as well as those at Bridgewater and Lyman. These changes broke staff opposition and kept the process of change on the move.

Third, he introduced humanizing effects to the system through administrative orders. He prohibited staff from striking children, and put a stop to the excessive use of lock-ups, haircuts, marching, or imposing silences. Despite staff resentment, these measures had a certain degree of success, especially in those institutions where changes in administrations had taken place. Lastly, Miller closed down the maximum-security unit at Bridgewater in the late spring of 1970. Even though this was expected, the action was extremely significant in several ways. First, there was no alternative institution available to take its place, and Miller actively began to advocate that there was no need for one to take its place. Second, Bridgewater had been the "end of the line" for juvenile offenders and had always been used as the ultimate threat by the other facilities in the division. Without this threat, institutions were forced to find better solutions and to operate more effectively and independently. Most importantly, this decision provided a direction for the "new" department. Miller discovered the strategy he was to use in the future—that the closing down of an institution can work without insurmountable problems.

On the program level, Miller had few community-based innovative successes to show for his first year in office. The Mary Knoll facility at Topsfield, which was to be used as a teach-in center, faced so much community opposition that it did not get off the ground. Therapeutic community concepts had created staff turmoil, funding for parole volunteers and other community-based programs did not materialize.

**Incremental Changes and Innovations.** With the appointment of four professionally trained assistant commissioners, each in charge of his respective bureau, the department moved into the second year, which was to see major innovations and program changes. The highlights are as follows:

1. On the institutional level, several structural changes were introduced, all geared to create a decentralized cottage-based system, and to promote staff and youth involvement in the decision-making process.
2. Oakdale, a custodial-oriented institution for the youngest youths (aging from nine to eleven) was closed in March 1971. After half the children had been placed in private residences, the remainder were transferred to the Lancaster School for Girls, where they became involved in a unique and interesting program designed for them by the staff and girls at the school. The young boys' presence at the school created a number of program alternatives for the school, and mutual involvement of the girls in working with the boys' program.
3. With the availability of a federal grant, a staff training program was initiated. Several teams, which included both the old and young staff, received training in counseling and operating a group home. The training sessions also prepared the staff to work with the hard-core youngster in the care of the department.
4. Extensive group-home experimentation began in early 1971. Hyde Park House, a self-help center, opened in Roslindale, housing nine youngsters. Six group homes were started on institutional grounds using available staff housing. Group homes such as "Mary Lamb" and "I Belong" were extremely successful in producing effective programs, and served as an example for additional programs in the department.
5. A parole volunteer program was funded, giving the parole operation a much needed boost.
6. Western Massachusetts received a strong impetus toward the creation of program alternatives from the involvement of the University of Massachusetts, which provided the Westfield Detention Center with on-going consultation, student volunteers, and increased staff training.
7. Regionalization began to take hold. Seven regional directors were hired to reorganize staff to man the regional offices.

*The Closing Down of Institutions.* Despite these changes, Miller and the department were under increasing pressure from different directions. The hiring of new and young staff at the institutions increased polarization with the "old guard," building up more and more opposition. Institutional staff opposed to the new approach became demoralized, restive, and fearful about losing their jobs. Most important, the youngsters themselves were caught in the middle—between dying institutions and alternatives yet unborn. Services to them suffered accordingly. Staff continued to be underpaid, and most lost hope for advancement when the department decided to pursue purchase-of-care services from outside, private groups. Changes at the institutional level increased runaways, and with them increased opposition from the local communities and pressure from the legislature. In addition, there was a growing bureaucratic force exerted on the department from the Administration and Finance Office because it regarded the changes in youth services as chaotic and administratively lax.

The decision to close the institutions was made amid all these pressures. Despite the havoc it initially created, the shutdown was extremely successful in defusing the bigger threat, that of staff unrest, of political opposition, and of local-community resistance.

The department abandoned gradualism, for it only provided more time and excuses for political opposition to form in the legislature. During the January 1972 legislative recess, Miller used his commissioner's discretionary powers to officially close the institutions. Youngsters who could not be immediately paroled, placed or referred to community programs were housed temporarily on the campus of the University of Massachusetts.

This operation was called the JOE II conference, and was essentially planned and executed by a core group of the university's volunteers and regional DYS staff. The operation, in spite of many administrative problems, was successful, in that it made the closing of the largest (and oldest) institution, the Lyman School for Boys, relatively painless for the youngsters involved, since this method eliminated staff opposition and sabotage. The 100 youths, who stayed for about a month on the university campus, were matched with youth tutor-advocates while arrangements were made for them to be placed in community-based programs, preferably in their home regions.

The closing of institutions was an act that overshadowed all other incremental accomplishments and changes. It had a very important psychological impact. First, it set the tone and clearly defined the task for the year 1972. After initial staff bewilderment and surprise, energies were released toward the creation of community-based alternatives. Groups began to come up with proposals; resources were found; and children filled these placements at an accelerated rate. There was a new goal, a new task, and a new hope. Second, it gave Miller and the department national recognition. Numerous newspaper articles and several television networks covered the series of events, and the department was described by them as a bold, action-oriented agency willing to take risks to ameliorate the deplorable conditions of training schools for youthful offenders. In professional circles, this action was described as a new breakthrough in providing services for youth in trouble. Third, the drama involved in the closing of the oldest training school in the country, Lyman, effectively attracted public attention and brought about much public debate and edification. Finally, the closing of Lyman symbolized the end of punitive and repressive institutions even though other facilities in the state remained open waiting to be phased out in the near future. It was as if all the institutions had been closed.

In retrospect, this move succeeded for several reasons:

1. The University of Massachusetts and the western region of the DYS provided a good cushion to absorb youngsters, and moreover proved to be a rich resource for program alternatives.
2. Forestry camps and Outward Bound type programs were very effective in handling and providing programs for our youths.
3. Detention centers were still available to accommodate youngsters who were awaiting placements or were in need of them.
4. An intensive-care unit, Andros, was immediately opened at Roslindale. This unit, which later was staffed primarily by ex-offenders, was able to work effectively with hard-core youngsters, and thus gave the court the assurance that the dangerous youngsters were not in the streets.
5. The publicity that the closing of institutions generated caught the attention of many groups who proved to be resources for the department, and were the subsequent developers of its alternatives.

However, the closing down of institutions did not lack critics from outside and inside the department. Opponents of reform talked about an increase in the crime rate and the loss of community protection. The old guard staff was concerned with job security and other vested interests. Supporters of reform were afraid of a possible backlash over critical incidents that might set reform backward. There were others within the agency who doubted the department's administrative capabilities to withstand such a change and feared further bureaucratic entanglements.

**Creation of New Alternatives**. Today, twelve months after the department's catalyzing decision, the new approach of DYS is generally functioning quite well. The approach has three major thrusts: (1) Therapeutic and humane homes rather than custodial and punitive institutions; (2) small community-based residential and nonresidential programs instead of the large institutions; (3) purchase of services from private community groups rather than state operation of all programs.

What has evolved is a network of projects that are publicly supported and supervised, but privately operated and coordinated on a regional basis through the department's regional offices.

Approximately 1200 youths are committed each year to the care of the department. This figure fluctuates, and is declining in the face of increased court referrals (referrals put the child in the temporary care of the court, but do not result in the stigmatizing "criminal record" attached to commitment); presently, department committed and referred youth occupy the following placements: 500 are in group homes; 190 are in foster homes; 150 are in specialized residential placements (private schools, private psychiatric hospitals, etc.); 600 participate in day-care programs, which may be educational, recreational, or involve individual or family counseling.

The department contends that fewer than 5 percent of the youths placed in its care required security surroundings. For those youths who do require high security, the department purchases services from a private organization that occupies one of the old detention buildings owned by the state. This program treats approximately 35-40 youths at any one time.

In detention (youths awaiting trial), the department has greatly reduced populations within closed facilities, and aims to eliminate closed detention for all but the most severely disturbed.

The department has developed shelter-care detention facilities, structured much like small group homes, which support detained youth pending trial and assist in pretrial casework investigations. Neighborhood YMCA facilities are being used to establish local detention programs manned by department personnel. And foster homes have been rented to provide spaces for a certain percentage of detained youths. All these services have been established regionally according to need, and may face expansion in the future. As of January 1973, the department operates 10 shelter-care detention facilities, cooperates with 5 local YMCA programs, and uses 21 foster placements for detention. It should be noted that with the cooperation of the courts and court liaison personnel, some youths are sent home as an alternative to what in the past would have been to closed detention.

For those youths who need residential care, possibilities include short-term group homes (3-4 months), long-term group homes (1-2 years), drug halfway houses, foster homes, private boarding schools, and intensive private psychiatric hospitals. Many youths do not need residential programs, and can function successfully with the day-care counseling and support. Others need only jobs or job-training, or special educational help.

Group homes provide the largest share of residential treatment. With few exceptions, they offer group and individual therapy, and a limited number supply family and casework therapy. All group homes offer an educational program in some form. A large portion operate their own on-grounds schools with private tutorial assistance. The remainder utilize existing schools in the community with or without providing private tutorial assistance. Vocational training and employment is emphasized in some.

The thirteen LEAA funded group homes comprise a separate category of short-term care. All have some form of group, individual or family therapy. All emphasize education and provide individualized tutorial assistance. While some operate schools on their own grounds, others use local schools. All provide some form of recreational program.

Group homes often specialize in particular problems, and are contracted accordingly for particular children. Twenty-seven group facilities specialize in emotionally disturbed youths across a wide range, from mild disturbances to severe emotional disturbances and character disorders. Seven group homes specialize in mentally retarded youngsters, and fourteen specialize in drug rehabilitation. In the latter category, treatment modalities range from the Synanon treatment model to primal scream therapy. Nearly all the drug-therapy programs either provide individual, group, or family therapy. Fourteen residential schools and academies are used for the specially academically talented youths in the care of the department. Three homes provide services for girls whose needs may include support during pregnancy, and placements are arranged with the American School for the Deaf and the Devereaux School for the handicapped and multihandicapped.

From May 1972 to October 1972 the number of foster-home placements used by the department more than doubled, from 85 to 189 homes. This increase reflected not only the department's overall intention to expand foster placements, but was partly a function of several new uses of foster-care treatment. Under the Equal Employment Act (federal funding), the department hired eighteen people to make their homes available, with foster care, for both committed and detained youths. And twenty-one foster homes have been developed for youths awaiting trial, as an alternative to closed detention.

Nonresidential placements, as of October 1972, served 616 youths across the state. These services vary from community-college educational programs to intensive counseling, and may occupy from a few hours to an entire day, one or more days per week. Some of the programs are intensive summer programs, which provide follow-up work once the children are back in the regular public school session. Examples of the programs utilized include Neighborhood Youth Corps, Catholic Charities, local drug councils, and others. One of the most successful programs purchased by the department in this area is the Community Aftercare Program, a private nonprofit corporation that provides counseling and activities directed by university student volunteers. This program is particularly active in the metropolitan areas where there is a large resource of university students, and many needy urban children that will benefit from their services.

*Current Status and Future Directions*. The DYS has now successfully captured the national spotlight. Its image has improved radically. It has also moved from a secretive and inward looking department to an open and visible agency. The new role the department has written for itself is one of an advocate for its youths. There are many new groups, both professional and paraprofessional, working with the department, thereby improving its professional image.

The purchase-of-care arrangement forced the department to totally restructure its role and function. It moved away from service delivery as its major function to assume the role of a monitor and evaluator of the services being provided.

The role of the youngster in the department's care has also changed radically, moving from the role of "inmate"—the passive recipient of rules and "treatments"—to a legitimate role as a client in a system with rights and partnership. Placement decisions now involve the youth. Their constant presence in the central and regional offices is indicative of this new involvement, and thus they have become an active part in the decision-making process.

The department's planning unit anticipates that the number of youth committed to the department in 1973 will remain at about the same level—approximately 1,000 youths—primarily as a result of DYS efforts to divert youths through court liaison officers, using LEAA "impact funds" to implement court-based diversion and referral. The department projects that the number of youths referred to DYS will increase from about 350 in 1972 to 900 in 1973.

The number of youths discharged from DYS is projected to remain about the same as in 1972, reflecting the new department policy to keep youths on an inactive list, rather than discharging them. (This retains departmental jurisdiction over a youth to the age of twenty-one.)

The current "mix" of placement resources faces expansion in the area of intensive, foster- and day-care programs; secure detention and group care resources are expected to be decreased, and forestry, shelter-care and foster-care detention will remain at their current levels. The program mix (see Table 14-1) will broaden the types of services available, but stay within the fiscal constraints imposed by the state (the department's projected budget, 1973, for purchased services, totals $8,347,000).

It is important to note from the figures in Table 14-1 the drastic shift in focus away from the institutional system. The reform school, in effect, forced

**Table 14-1**
**Planned Shift in Available Treatment Slots, 1972-73**

|  | 1972 | 1973 |
| --- | --- | --- |
| Foster Care | 200 | 500 |
| Intensive Care | 36 | 70 |
| Group Care | 500 | 200 |
| Day Care | 600 | 1000 |
| Secure Detention | 95 | 45 |
| Forestry | 30 | 30 |
| Shelter Care | 125 | 125 |
| Foster Care | 100 | 100 |
| Totals | 1,686 slots | 2,070 slots |

"intensive" treatment on all the children, though the effects more closely approached intensive *mis*treatment. Now, more than 50 percent of the children under the department's care at any one time will be receiving day care. Nearly 25 percent will receive foster care, and only approximately 5 percent will receive intensive, confined treatment. By limiting closed detention, the department forces expedient placement of youth. By limiting intensive treatment alternatives, the department forces courts and placement personnel to seek treatment plans across the spectrum of possibilities before incarceration is considered. And by more than doubling foster care the department makes more available the most individual and personalized placement alternative.

*Opening the System*

Miller's first year in office is noted for his effort to "open" the system—loosening up the existing rigid structure in order to make it more amenable to change.

In approaching this task, Miller had several liabilities and obstacles: (1) He was an outsider to the system and lacked support within DYS; (2) his resources were limited by lack of funds; (3) years of institutional autonomy almost precluded any central authority's public-relations intervention.

Several important strategies were employed toward this end. The first of these was to increase public relations through the use of the mass media. During this early period Miller made many local television and radio broadcasts and was interviewed often by the press. He continually cast himself in the role of the agent of outside change. He exposed and criticized the wrongs of the system explicity: "We must eliminate the little totalitarian societies which dominated the juvenile institutions in the past. Most of the units were set up so that their successful kids could only function in a dictatorship." At the same time he was vague about the changes he was planning to implement. In this way he gathered support for himself while depriving his opponents of a focus for opposition, keeping himself on the offensive. His image developed as one of a reformer and a sensitive advocate for the needs of youth. He also exposed the internal conflicts and the staff sabotage to the press and public. He made the inner workings of the department publicly visible, and let the press and the public know that he was as concerned as they were about exposing the problems that existed.

The result of this continuing dialogue with the public through the media was a general increase in understanding and support of Miller and his philosophy. It helped to make the public more aware of the department and its functions, and it improved immensely the image of the department in the public mind. It also changed somewhat the image of a juvenile delinquent from a criminal to a victim. By exposing the injustices and brutality, more people became aware of these institutions, more people were made aware that children were being victimized instead of rehabilitated. He made the public feel responsible for allowing this sort of treatment to exist. "You can control runaways, you can produce 'model institutional' kids by brute force and fear if that's what you want, to reassure legislators, the police or the community. Lock doors, handcuff kids to their beds—and you'll have no runs. But they will react when they get out; they have learned to con the adults." Thus a new voice came to be heard at DYS, the voice of the concerned public. Once Miller exposed the injustices of the system, he was obligated to correct them. He had the support of the public in doing this.

Whereas the institutions were previously autonomous, now they were becoming accountable to the central administration. Miller began to ask for written reports of any cases involving force or brutality. In the Boston *Sunday Globe* of March 8, 1970, he complained of the existing system: "A staff member alone was often judge, jury and prosecutor in regard to particular incidents, with facts often grossly distorted to protect the staff. From now on, I will ask for state police investigation in cases of obvious brutality." Using his authority, more actors became involved in the transaction between the staff and the youth. It is no longer a closed and arbitrary system.

**Youth Involvement.** Another useful strategy employed was the involvement of the youths in decisions affecting their lives. He toured the institutions, often appearing unexpectedly. He went directly to the young people and listened to their grievances. He found out what was really going on rather than what the staff wanted him to know. And he gave youngsters a feeling that they had an important advocate, encouraging them to call him or come to his office. Institutionalized youngsters became an important source of information to him and his staff. By making himself accessible to the resident of the institution, he was in fact breaking down the institutional hierarchy. The youngsters began to realize they had some recourse if they were mistreated, while the staff realized they were accountable for their actions.

One of the costs of this change was the insecurity it wrought among the staff. They were robbed of their former means of discipline without any feeling of support from the administration. This at times caused conflict, resistance, and even sabotage. It also presented problems to the middle-management personnel who had to deal with the disgruntled staff at the institutions, and to try to implement all the new policies. So in terms of staff unrest, the cost of this change was great.

However, all of these strategies—the use of public relations, divesting the institutions of their autonomy, the breakdown of the hierarchy, and listening to the grievances of the young people had the result of opening up the system. The staff at the institutions were now accountable to many segments of the population—the young people, the public, and the central administration.

**New Concepts.** Miller's attempts to open the system by introducing innovative therapeutic methods were not very successful. The training sessions administered by Dr. Maxwell Jones created staff polarization and resulted in mass runaways.

It is important to note that these concepts proved to have many limitations for application to antiquated institutions that lacked programs, resources and progressive young staff members.

A few months later, in mid-1970, another attempt to change was made at Shirley School. The "guided group interaction" approach was introduced by Harry Vorath. This is a modified version of the Maxwell Jones approach, though more structured and geared to institutional settings. This approach was adopted by a group of staff from Shirley School, and was used in running an intensive-security unit at Oakdale.

Another approach that was tried in collaboration with Dr. Mathew Dumont from the Massachusetts Department of Mental Health was the self-help group. The department explored these self-help programs as an alternative that would provide massive change inside the institutions. The idea was to turn over several institutions to existing self-help groups which needed space for their own operations. They would in turn accept DYS youngsters into their programs. These groups held high promise for radically altering service delivery practices in the department for several reasons: (1) They have a high degree of success in terms of their acceptance by the community, the public, and the legislature because they are clean and well-structured; (2) they provide therapeutic environments for those residents interested in introspection and change; and (3) they maintain themselves on a minimal budget because of the strong demands exerted on the residents. Despite these high hopes, however, the outcome actually proved to be very limited for DYS for two reasons. First, all of these groups were able to work with only a limited number of DYS youngsters. They have high expectations and exert tremendous pressure on the residents. In order to continue they had to work with motivated children, and thus the attrition rate was very high. Second, these programs have an authoritarian approach, which proved to be at odds with the department's emerging approach of humanism, permissiveness, and equalitarianism. Because of the high visibility of the department and its many detractors, it was difficult to support new programs before they proved themselves viable. Although all of these new programs had only limited practical success, they were useful in as much as they challenged the old system and demonstrated that many possibilities exist in the treatment of youth.

**New People.** The youths have been a source of support for the new system. Many of them have gone to lectures and spoken of their experiences in the institutions. Their stories of brutality present a very convincing case against the old system.

Other groups of people, both interested in and capable of helping in the DYS reform movement, began to emerge. Most notable among these are the groups of ex-offenders. Since the closing of the institutions, several groups of ex-offenders have become involved in providing services for other youngsters. First among these is Libra Inc., a self-help group, which was given a contract by the department. Andros, a program geared to deal with the hard-core delinquent, is primarily staffed with ex-offenders. It has been in operation for over a year and has proved to be very successful in working with the most violent and aggressive youths in the department's care.

Two other groups, Self-Development Group Inc., and the "Medfield-Norfolk Project," have worked very closely with the department, whose policy has been to encourage these groups to provide leadership. The association has proven to be mutually beneficial. The groups have provided good services because of their prior experience and their ability to relate to the young people. The benefits for the groups have included an opportunity to prove their ability, and the opening of a new job market for ex-offenders. This policy has extended to DYS graduates, who have been hired by the department for a variety of roles and are providing meaningful insight and other sources of help for the department.

Self-help drug groups have come to assume a more important role since the closing of the institutions. Presently, two programs, Transition House and Spectrum House, are operating on DYS grounds. Many more self-help groups have been receiving financial support from the department by the placement of DYS youngsters in their programs.

Another segment of the public that has become actively interested in DYS are colleges and college students. Several universities and colleges have developed associations with this department. First and foremost is the University of Massachusetts School of Education, which has developed three different programs: JOE I, JOE II, and MARY. These programs have involved many students as volunteers, work-study students, and some have even been hired and become department personnel. North Shore Community College, AIC, Springfield College, and others have developed nonresidential summer programs for department's youth. In this way, students have been instrumental in developing innovative programs for the youngsters, while creating new roles for themselves.

Several of the residential and nonresidential programs affiliated with the department are using work-study students as well as student volunteers; most notable among these is the CAP program, which uses mainly students for their operation. Various students are using DYS as a field assignment. Most recent is the use of student volunteers to evaluate programs from which the department is purchasing care.

Among the traditional agencies, some have been willing and able to revise their practices and develop new intake policies in order to accept placements from DYS, while others have not. The Family Service Agency and YMCA, for example, have traditionally excluded DYS juveniles from their intake on the grounds that they are "unworkable," "psychopaths," or "in need of institutional confinement." However, recently their need for funds and their willingness to experiment have resulted in a change in that policy.

Some traditional programs such as McClean Hospital and the Judge Baker

Clinic have been unable to work out an agreement with the department because their traditional approaches and practices stood in the way. They were also turned off by DYS's lack of "professional standards." On the other hand, HRI, a new and aggressive private psychiatric hospital, was able to change its practices in order to accommodate the department's needs, and thus has developed a working relationship with the department. In opening its system, the department has helped others to open up theirs.

Another way that new people have been introduced to the department is through a tremendous turnover of staff. A recent look at the staff statistics shows that 62 percent of the current staff members have been hired since Miller took office. Many of the older employees left the department because the old staff had no sustaining hold or power to resist the changes being introduced. The new staff members generally were attracted to the department because they were interested in its liberal outlook, and tend to agree with its central direction. The process of change has attracted more progressive people who will tend to continue this process. Thus the new staff is both a result of, and eventually will be a continuing source of, change, rather than resisting it as the old staff had done.

In summary, Miller's first year in office was used mainly to "loosen up" the system by introducing new concepts, practices and people. Therapeutic community concepts had limited impact because of staff polarization. More impressive are the results of introducing and involving new people with the department, which seeded more intensive program collaboration for the future.

Miller used the press very effectively in exposing the old system, legitimizing children's role in the new one, and breaking down institutional isolation and autonomy. Other strategies, such as breaking the institutional hierarchy by going to the youth, the creative use of his role as outsider to the system, and the periodic show of humane authority by introducing changes in "form" (no haircuts, no lock-up, etc.) rather than content—proved to be effective tools that are replicable elsewhere.

*Changing the System*

Introducing new concepts, ideas and people into DYS caused the loosening of its rigid structures and the creation of a more favorable environment for change. However, "opening the system" alone could not account for the massive deinstitutionalization and the creation of new and humane alternatives in the three years since the Reorganization Act. One has to conceptualize the different processes and strategies that brought about the changes in the system. In the following discussion we will attempt to isolate these elements, realizing that this study is only a beginning to the deeper analysis that these processes require and warrant, and hopefully will receive in the future.

The changes that have been introduced in the DYS have been massive and dramatic, and especially unusual for a state bureaucracy. This holds true despite the many elements present that made such a change possible, e.g., the mandate for change as expressed in the Reorganization Act, support of local interested groups, and the definite commitment of a governor who expressed his support frequently. A department of youth services is usually controlled by many groups, which exert strong pressures to resist change. First, within the state government, there is the legislature, which controls the budget, and the governor's executive office, which exerts bureaucratic controls. Second, there are also other agencies of the criminal justice system: the police, the courts, and probation. Third, internally the department is comprised of staff who can exert controls through their unions or political influences. And finally there is the general public, the communities, and the press.

All of these pressures are usually drawbacks; however they can become assets if properly informed. It is these alignments and realignments that determine the degree of flexibility and support available to the commissioner in his efforts toward change. These forces, when they are exerted to maintain the system, work to deprive the commissioner of his authority, thus making any action for reform extremely difficult. This was not allowed to happen at DYS. Opponents of reform were put into a defensive position, and forced to explain and defend indefensible situations. On the other hand, the department continually broadened its base of support, thus moving into a less defensive, more powerful offensive position. This power was gained by depriving staff and institutions of their autonomy, cutting into the power of the bureaucracy and patronage systems of the government, and building upon the growing relationships with outside forces. Similar strategies were also used with the police, the courts, and the communities. This realignment meant involvement of youngsters, staff, new groups, and private groups from whom the department was purchasing care.

The question that needs to be answered here is how this happened—what were the different strategies used by Miller and his staff to bring about this process? The following is an analysis of the strategies and approaches employed by Miller and his associates in order to effect change.

**Flexible Agenda.** It is more accurate to describe the change process in the department during the past three years as *emergent*, rather than *planned*. These changes were often determined by chance, imagination, opportunity, and personal style, primarily the commissioner's. The strategies used depended largely upon options and solutions that arose spontaneously, and which the department was flexible enough to try. These options increased with the opening of the system and the introduction of new actors into it.

Frequently the department would adopt a new approach as soon as it proved useful or successful. In the same way, if a program was attempted and proved infeasible it was immediately abandoned or modified. Two examples will illustrate this matter:

1. There was an early policy decision to open group homes, which would be run by the department. However, in the process of establishing these homes it became evident that the department's flexibility would be enhanced by contracting these services, rather than operating them directly through the department, and thus the policy was changed. This change from the department's traditional role of providing services exempted DYS from bureaucratic entanglement and the intricacies of staff training and retraining. Although this change in policy created some staff alienation, it ensured quick and efficient movement toward meaningful community-based alternatives.

2. Another example of the department's flexibility is in the case of the CAP program, a nonresidential after-care program. CAP began as a small operation when institutions were closed, and proved to be extremely successful in working with groups of youngsters in storefront operations in the community by providing jobs, counseling, and opening recreational activities. The success of the program encouraged DYS to increase the number of referrals from 20 to 175 in only one year.

**Shotgun Approach to Change.** Another approach used by Miller was to invite many different programs and ideas into the department in the hope that some projects would be successful. Such a shotgun approach to change gave the department the flexibility to try out a number of options (in many different directions) and experiment, with a limited amount of resources. This approach was also consistent with Miller's belief that the old system was destructive and "insane," and that "any new alternative will be better than what we have."

Thus, the department's lack of a plan proved to be helpful, in that it made it flexible enough to find opportunities and use them when they arose. Different approaches were tried, each with limited success. When the therapeutic community concept failed, "guided group interaction" was tried. When this showed a limited success, the department introduced the "self-help group" concept into the institutions. Cottages were closed when the occasion arose and staff were constantly rotated, some for the purpose of training and others for the purpose of starting new programs or assuming new responsibilities. Programs that proved themselves were claimed as new and innovative; and those that did not work were terminated. In this manner, there were always a few good programs that met the criteria of being humane and effective. These were the ones the department could point to as successful.

This shotgun method also explains to a great extent the diversity of the new alternatives. The programs covered a broad scope, and were developed by a wide range of agencies—traditional and nontraditional, as well as educational institutions, and even recreation organizations such as the YMCAs.

This approach posed difficulties for the opposition, because the changes in the department were so constant that it was impossible for them to focus an attack on any particular program. However, it also posed difficulties for the department. Much of the older staff were alienated because they felt unsupported, and could not understand the department's changing direction. There was also a considerable amount of confusion and wasted effort in the central office, because many of the changes were made without enough staff involvement, especially those decisions made by Miller alone. (Some of the younger staff saw this movement strictly as opportunism, lacking any real commitment to programs for youth.) Changing directions sometimes meant abandoning programs run by new staff who supported Miller. The most striking example of this situation occurred when the decision was made to close the institutions. Several good programs that were being run by the department within the institution had to be disbanded in favor of contracting with outside groups, which resulted in some new staff antagonism and anxiety.

Despite the turmoil and staff anxiety caused by this course, the shotgun method was effective and necessary, given the limitations of a public bureaucracy.

**Avoidance of Conflict**. By espousing a direction rather than a program, Miller was able to avoid confrontations on specific issues with staff, communities and the legislature. Thus he could gather followers and maintain the department's visibility to the press, the rest of the bureaucracy, and the public, without confronting directly the most rigid and intractable forces in the system. By denouncing in general terms the institutional failures, Miller was never forced to explain specifically his plans to ameliorate these conditions; neither was he compelled to specify the cost of these changes to staff and other vested interest groups.

In effect, Miller's ability to articulate institutional failures forced the defenders of the old system into an impotent position. Who could argue, for example, with a call to "open up" institutions and "make them responsive to new ideas." Who could attack Miller's practice of visiting institutions spontaneously and talking with youngsters? Or how could anyone counter the following argument: "If you continue to turn out more criminals after treatment, something is obviously wrong." By placing himself on the side of justice and humaneness, he made it difficult for detractors to criticize him publicly for fear of placing themselves on the side of injustice and inhumanity.

Within the department, at the institutions, similar strategies were used. Staff were promised a place in the new system without being told specifically what that place would be. After isolating several key personnel who were resistant to change in the institutions, Miller promoted a few staff members who showed by their commitment or rhetoric that they were willing to support him. These promotions created a feeling among the staff that the system was open to them, and promotions were possible. This new sense of security among some of the older staff made it possible for some alliances, which were necessary in order to work out compromises and thus achieve specific objectives. Also, several of the newly promoted staff members proved instrumental in dealing with local conflicts. They were able to present and defend new programs to communities and legislators in a manner that made them more acceptable. All of these personnel maneuvers had the temporary effect of dispelling conflict.

However, conflict could not be postponed indefinitely. Staff became increasingly resentful because the promotions they hoped for did not materialize; constant changes were occurring, and there was a lack of communication and support from the central office. Despite all of Miller's strategies to avoid conflict with the staff, the personnel in the field were becoming increasingly alienated. This set the stage for increased opposition and conflict, which would probably have eventually erupted. However, the cataclysmic step of closing institutions scattered the opposition and irrevocably committed the department to a new approach that was more than experimental; it was definite, permanent, and all-encompassing. This is how Miller was able to avoid conflict over relatively minor issues long enough to effect a change that was so immense in its proportions that it practically defied opposition.

**Support from Outside.** The lobby for change was present even before Miller came to the department. It consisted of the media, professional associations, the legislature, and other interest groups.

Lacking centralized control over these institutions, Miller's first efforts were to broaden the base of decision-making by bringing the public and the press into the debate. An example is Miller's policy decision to eliminate the "lock-up."

Miller recognized that a memo to this effect would not make the change. So he publicized the decision at a series of press conferences. In a surprise visit to the institutions, he discovered that lock-ups were still used. A series of discussions and negotiations with individual superintendents at the institutions produced a modified policy statement—lock-up would be used only in extreme cases, and then only with the expressed permission of the commissioner. The policy was clarified, modified, centralized and adjusted, but became clearly the responsibility of the central office.

The press was also used to document the failures of the institutions and to dramatize the changes introduced in the department. For example, long after Bridgewater was closed, the physical facility was used as a showplace for the press, to dramatize the plight of the youngsters who had been incarcerated there.

When Shirley School had already ceased to be used as an institution, the press and the public were invited to a ceremony to destroy the "tombs," or solitary confinement cells, which were a symbol of the old, punitive system. Most dramatic was the closing of Lyman. Attention was drawn to the fact that Lyman was the first training school in the country to open and the first to close. The impressive scene of moving all of the youngsters in one day hid the fact that several programs continued on the institution's grounds for many more months, that Lancaster School for girls was still in operation six months later, and that other institutions had been phased out prior to Lyman.

The practice of dramatizing the changes served several purposes. It maintained the momentum for internal changes, and it attracted outside resources to make the change possible. But foremost, the drama kept the press interested and thus the public informed. These dramatic actions created in the public mind the image of an aggressive, active, forward-moving public agency, and showed the closing of institutions to be consistent with success and progress.

Outside groups such as ex-offenders, universities, and child welfare agencies proved indispensible in the development of new alternatives, because they had no stake in maintaining the old system. These groups were willing and able to make decisions and take actions which DYS staff were unable and unwilling to make because of their vested interest. A perfect example is the University of Massachusetts involvement through the JOE II program, which made possible the closing of Lyman School. DYS staff, and especially workers from Lyman, were incapable of making a commitment to close the institution in which they were working. They were interested in developing a rationale for keeping the school open and thus maintaining the status quo.

It is important to note that the University of Massachusetts and other agencies provided the temporary *structures* necessary for the changeover from institutions to community-based programs. On the regional front, many groups, some new private as well as some public agencies became a vital resource for the department's new community-based operations. Most of these agencies needed this new venture partly because of their dwindling resources and partly because of their desire to become involved in a new field. The department ultimately signed contracts with only a small portion of the agencies that submitted proposals. However, the interaction with these agencies served to orient them to the functions and needs of the department, and to significantly increase the consideration given to the problems of youth in trouble throughout the state.

**Change for Change's Sake**. The philosophy that was espoused and acted upon by Miller was that change is an end in itself, and that chaos and turmoil are an unavoidable by-product of social change. He believes that a firmly entrenched bureaucracy "can chew up reform much faster than reformers can dream up new ones." This is why constant change itself is as relevant as the direct consequences of that change. The idea was that significant change can only occur within a system after the destruction of the foundation of that system. Thus, destroying a system *before* creating alternatives to it was a characteristic mode of action for the department. For example, Miller undertook immediately the destruction of the internal control system of the institutions, leaving the system vulnerable, confused, and searching for new controls.

The most dramatic example of the effect of this change was when the decision was made to close the institutions. Despite the confusion that this decision wrought within the bureaucracy, it did force the staff, the regional offices and the communities to develop immediate alternatives. Thus this action shifted the responsibility from the department into the community.

This strategy of "change for change's sake" allowed DYS to accomplish rapid and massive alterations, but the costs were high. Within the staff, many committed and experienced people were unable to cope with the changes. Many have left, and the turnover has been costly. The quality of new services has been affected by this strategy. Some of the programs appeared overnight, without time for careful planning. Other existing programs with no prior experience in dealing with DYS youth had to suddenly accommodate themselves to these youngsters. Furthermore, the lack of management, and administrative and technical expertise within the department left many programs to improvise and find solutions on their own.

The shift involved moving away from institutional fiscal management to a flexible purchase-of-care arrangement, which caused the administration to lag behind the services. As a consequence, newly founded programs with limited financial resources often did not receive payment for weeks. This impaired their functioning and the delivery of services.

Despite the problems created by this planned-unplanned approach, based on its overall effectiveness and its innovativeness, it warrants merit and further study. This is especially true since the "planned change" approach has long proved ineffective in dealing with entrenched bureaucracies.

**Institutionalizing the Changes**. Miller's main fear was always that a series of critical incidents, radical change in the political climate, or a temporary loss of public support could negate the changes the department has accomplished. To insure that a succeeding administration could not retreat into the old institutional pattern, several steps were taken to block this regression. Some institutional properties were made available to correction, mental health, and private groups. However, most of them are still under DYS's administrative control. Miller also attempted to organize the private sector that is now providing care for DYS youth into an aggressive advocacy lobby for children. However, this lobby can also become self-serving and too involved with maintaining their status quo.

The department's future plan also called for converting a large number of staff positions into monies for the purchase of care, a step that would insure inadequate staffing for the maintenance of large institutions.

Despite these efforts, little attention was paid by Miller to establishing the administrative mechanisms needed to insure that the new system functions as desired. As a consequence, DYS may be headed for an administrative crisis. Lacking adequate fiscal controls, department spending is estimated to be much higher than the budget permits, and at the same time many services rendered could not be paid in time, due to numerous bureaucratic entanglements caused by the changeover. These and other problems in the system, such as lack of role definition, accountability, and delineation of responsibilities in the main and regional offices, is hurting new programs and making the quality of these new services to youth not what they could be.

Finally, the question that most reform-minded people are concerned with is whether the changes in DYS are here to stay, and if so, whether the process of experimentation and change in the department will continue, even on a less dramatic scale.

It is too early to answer these questions. Miller's departure before the changes have taken hold, however, especially while the department is still struggling with fiscal and administrative problems, could definitely force the department to a defensive posture, rendering it unable to maintain an advocacy role for the youth in its charge.

*Summary, Conclusions and Implications*

The sudden closing of institutions by the Massachusetts Department of Youth Services was an almost totally unforeseeable event. It was not a gradual process that was planned over a period of years. It was, rather, the climax of a series of events that continued to broaden the base of support for change, while reducing the number of possible alternatives. The climate for change began to develop in the 1960s when the quality of care in the institutions had reached an all-time low. The system had been failing children for many years. Many staff, lacking professional skill, had turned to excessive use of punishment in order to control their charges. This situation was brought to the attention of the public through the media. Criticism and attack came to a boiling point with the release of several investigative reports, especially the thorough study made by HEW. The public and the legislature became alarmed, and the time was ripe for the governor and the legislature to act.

The director of the department resigned in 1969. The legislature passed the Reorganization Act, which provided for the appointment of a new commissioner and four assistant commissioners of his choosing, and set a new professional tone for the agency. It broadly empowered the new department to "establish necessary facilities for detention, diagnosis, treatment, and training of its charges, including post-release care." While these powers in themselves did not mark a major new thrust, the language of the Act later proved sufficient grounds for Commissioner Miller and his assistants to implement a noninstitutional system, although this was not the overt intention of the bill.

Miller was chosen as commissioner because of his training and experience. He had experience in both theory and practice of youth service operations. The appointment of Miller in turn led to a further upgrading of the staff of the department. The personnel and ideological changes in the department, *coupled* with continued publicity in the media, and the resulting surge in public concern over the quality of care of children, increased and reinforced the climate for change. During his first two years as commissioner, Miller and his assistants tried many new programs within the existing system. There was increased staff training, made possible by federal funds. One institution was closed, others were decentralized into a cottage-based system. Some group homes began to develop as alternative placements for youth. A productive liaison was established between the University of Massachusetts and the Westfield Detention Center. And the process of regionalization within the state began.

The gains made by implementing these changes at first were outweighed, however, by the problems caused by them. The institutional system was so deeply entrenched that any change had to be massive in order for its effects to be significantly felt. So the changes were not great enough. And yet every new measure that was introduced was resisted by the older staff, who were justifiably fearful of their positions or of changing their long-accepted roles. For them the changes were too great, and they fought them.

There was also a certain degree of loss of control caused by the newness of the programs. Runaways temporarily increased, causing a reaction from local communities and the legislature. Thus all of the changes brought about, opposition from the staff, the legislature, and the public, while only minimally improving the services rendered by the department. The climate had been ripe for change. Many changes and alternatives were tried within the system, but were not initially successful. There were no viable alternatives left. The closing of institutions was a decision that went further than most people anticipated, and it came much sooner than anyone expected.

Once the institutions were closed, alternative programs began to develop; it would, however, be erroneous to assume that these alternatives developed automatically merely as a result of this closing. Actually the potential for these new programs was created as a result of the entire change process the department had gone through, i.e., opening the system to many outside groups, building bridges to universities and colleges, and introducing volunteers into the system. Also, the department's constant search for alternatives within the institutions prior to their closing, and its flexibility and readiness to take advantage of any options available, were a foreshadowing of rapid development of programs later on.

Thus the elements had been present for quite a while, and the closing of institutions served as the squeeze that triggered this reaction. This catalyzing factor is what makes the Massachusetts experience unique and innovative as a social-change phenomenon. By closing institutions, the DYS forced its alternatives to occur, resulting in massive and immediate change rather than a gradual and prolonged process.

It is too early to evaluate the effectiveness of the new alternatives. But they certainly cover a wide range of programs, involving many more actors and approaches. They are noncustodial in nature; they provide a variety of residential and nonresidential community-based programs privately run and regionally supported by the department through its regional offices.

The Massachusetts experience suggests new approaches to change in public bureaucracies. These agencies, characterized by a lack of autonomy, invite timidity among its staff, thus setting the stage for its exploitation by other government groups such as the legislature, and in turn the exploitation of its charges by the department staff. Such agencies must develop strategies that allow them to establish freedom and control over their operations. One way to increase this autonomy is by negotiating with legislators and other branches of government. DYS's leaders increased its autonomy by opening the system to the public, the media, the youngsters in its care, thus creating its own power base of support and lobby. Miller, as an outsider to the system, acted as a change agent and was able to use existing support within the system and at the same time infuse new ideas, approaches, and groups into it.

The changes introduced in DYS were the product of an *emergent* rather than a planned approach. Strategies outlined earlier—i.e., flexible agenda, shotgun approach, avoidance of conflict, change for change's sake—created opportunities within the department to achieve massive changes. Also, the constant forcing of options, rather than waiting for alternatives to emerge, created an agency with an aggressive image that discouraged opposition by throwing opponents off balance and gaining public recognition and confidence.

However, the cost to staff created by these strategies was enormous; the department's fiscal and management operations were constantly lagging behind programs, creating the possibility of administrative crisis. Also, the three years of changes thrust the department into turmoil with a continuous sense of crisis and the possibility of a complete setback very imminent.

Despite their possible negative results, these strategies hold a promise of replicability in most other human services agencies. Common problems demand common solutions. The departments of Mental Health, Corrections and Welfare suffer from the same excessive bureaucracies, inflexible operations, which stigmatize their clients, rendering them passive and helpless. This problem is common to many service bureaucracies throughout the country. As with DYS, these agencies need to become much less bureaucratic and humanize their operations. However, this has to be done when the public and the legislature are *not* willing to invest more funds in these departments. More money simply increases bureaucratic power. DYS is providing a model for achieving change through management rather than the commitment of new resources, and instead of investing more money in traditional professional and custodial groups, it gave the clients a voice, and brought in volunteers, students, and new groups to help change the system.

Finally, the DYS reorganization held the promise, if it did not achieve the result, of eradicating the double standard that society set up in dealing with the less advantaged and less powerful, thus increasing their democratic participation in the decision-making process. The reforms resulting from the reorganization have not come from an elite group of professionals or philanthropists, but from those who have the most to gain from reform. The Massachusetts experience has produced change by redefining and redistributing power in a way that allows growth in people and enhances their humanity.

# About the Contributors

**Benedict Alper** is a visiting Professor, Department of Sociology, Boston College.

**Yitzhak Bakal** is an Assistant Commissioner, Massachusetts Department of Youth Services.

**Robert B. Coates** is a Research Associate, Harvard Center for Criminal Justice, Harvard Law School.

**Larry Dye** is Assistant Professor, University of Massachusetts School of Education, Amherst.

**Dean L. Fixsen** is a Research Associate, Achievement Place, University of Kansas, Lawrence.

**Robert M. Foster** is Deputy Commissioner at YDDPA, HEW, Washington, D.C.

**Ira Goldenberg** is a Professor at Harvard University, School of Psychology and Public Practice.

**Martin Gula** is a Specialist on Group Care, Office of Child Development, HEW, Washington, D.C.

**John M. Martin** is Associate Director, Institute for Social Research, Fordham University.

**Alden D. Miller** is a Research Associate, Harvard Center for Criminal Justice, Harvard Law School.

**Jerome G. Miller** is a former Commissioner, Massachusetts Department of Youth Services.

**Lloyd E. Ohlin** is Director of Research, Harvard Center for Criminal Justice, Harvard Law School.

**Elery L. Phillips** is Research Director, Achievement Place, University of Kansas, Lawrence.

**Howard W. Polsky** is a Professor, Columbia University School of Social Work.

**Herbert C. Shulberg** is Associate Director at United Community Services of Metropolitan Boston.

**Frederick Thacher** is a Director of Community Care System Inc., Waltham, Massachusetts.

**Carole C. Upshur** is a Program Planner, Governor's Committee on Law Enforcement, Boston.

**Montrose M. Wolf** is Director, Division of Child Development, University of Kansas, Lawrence.

# Index

Achievement Place, 107-14
*Achievement Place Novel*, 109
Acting-out behavior, 19, 20, 21, 22, 26, 27, 28, 119-20, 127, 145
*Adolescent Girl in Conflict* (Konopka), 23
Adult Manpower Training Program (OEO), 46
"Advocates," 120-1, 128, 132-4, 135-8, 140-1, 147
Advocates for the Development of Human Potential (Univ. of Mass.), 123-4
Albee, G., 44-5
Alinsky, Saul D., 83
American International College (AIC), 169
American School for the Deaf, 164
Andros, 162, 169
Argyris, C., 54
Attica, 119
Attorney General's Advisory Committee on Juvenile Crime, 155
Augustus, John, 33

Bard, Morton, 45
Barker, R., 46
Bertrand, Marie, 25
Blos, Peter, 21
Boston College, ix
*Boston Globe*, 155, 157, 167
Boy offenders, 19, 20, 21, 24, 25, 26, 28, 142, 143, 144
Boys United: Resources, Neighbors (BURN), 72-3
Bridgewater Juvenile Guidance Institute, 153, 156, 159, 174
Brown, C., 53

Carnegie Foundation for the Advancement of Teaching, 117
Catholic Charities, 164
Child welfare, 14
"Clarion," Mass., 72-3
Clark, K.B., 53
Closing Down of Institutions and New Strategies in Youth Services" (conference), viii, ix

Coeducational programs, 28, 103, 132, 160
"Colonialist" interpretation of adolescence, 52-3
Community Aftercare Program (CAP), 164, 169, 172
Community Mental Health Centers Act, 15
Community residential youth centers. *See* Group homes
Community service systems, 13-7, 26-8, 151, 162, 175
Conferences, viii, ix, 121, 127-48
Correctional institutions: costs, 13, 16, 33, 37, 114, 123, 155, 165; discrimination against the disadvantaged, 11, 12, 43, 155; reform movement, 94-104, 155-8; staffs, 89-92, 154, 155, 158-9, 161, 170, 173; statistics, 14, 15, 28, 37, 155, 162-4, 165-6; treatment of inmates, vii, 26, 88, 93, 94, 154, 155, 159
*Cottage Six* (Polsky), 93
Coughlin, John, 153, 156

Data collection, 68-9, 129-45
Day-care programs, 163, 166
Deinstitutionalization, xii, 119-20, 121, 127-48, 151-80; and bureaucratic opposition, viii, xii, 4-5, 12, 60-1, 101-2, 134-5, 153, 155, 156-7, 159, 160-1, 171; and community resistance, viii, xii, 15-6, 67-87, 160, 161; and professional staff opposition, 158-9, 161, 173, 174
Demont, Mathew, 168
Detention centers, 153-4, 162, 163
Devereaux School, 164
Double standard. *See* Sexist society
Drug addiction, 35, 163, 164, 169

Eastmont Training Center (Montana), 15
Eisenhower Commission Report, 152
Equal Employment Act, 164
Ex-offenders, 162, 168-9

FBI, 4

"Family" homes, 80
Family Service Agency, 36, 169
Federal Children's Bureau (HEW), 14, 155-6
Fordham Institute for Social Research, ix
Foster homes, 14, 15, 80, 142, 144, 163, 164
Frank, Lawrence, 22
Friedenberg, E.Z., 52
Friends of Youth Association, 156

Gardner, Henry J., 88
Girl offenders, 19-29, 87-104, 142, 143, 144, 145, 164; and coeducation programs, 28; and community service systems, 26-8; and family dynamics, 20-2; and the female role, 22-4, 27-8; and sexist society, 24-5; and training schools, 25-6. See also Industrial School for Girls
Goldenberg, I.I., 54
Golden Gate Mental Retardation Center (San Francisco), 14
Goodman, P., 53-4
Gordon, J., 53
Governor's Management Engineering Task Force, 155
Group encountering, 62. See also Resident participation
Group homes, 14, 16, 49, 51, 59-66, 67-84, 107-14, 142, 144, 151, 160, 163-4, 172; and community resistance, 67-84; naming of, 72, 73, 79-80; and private service agencies, 68, 74-5, 151, 162, 172, 175; successes and failures, 68-84. See also Achievement Place

Halfway houses, 16, 49, 51, 67n, 103, 151, 163. See also Group homes
Hampshire College, 132
Handicapped offenders, 164
Hard-core offenders, 154, 162, 169
Harris poll, 67n
Harvard Center for Criminal Justice, 26, 129, 157
Health Services and Mental Health Administration (HEW), 36
Homosexuality, 28, 93-4
Horner, Matina, 22-3
Howe, S.G., 87-8

Human Resource Institute (HRI), 170
Human services programs, 39-47: diagnostic centers, 42; information and referral centers, 42; multi-service centers, 42-3; service networks, 43; personnel and training, 43-6; research, 46
Hyde Park House, 160

Illinois Family and Children Services, 151
Industrial School for Girls (Mass.), 87-104: cottage life, 92-3; facilities and staff, 89-92; history, 87-9; homosexuality, 93-4; reform, 94-104
Institutionalism, xi-xiii, 53-4, 94-5, 153-5
Intensive-care units, 162

Job Placement Services, 36
Joint Commission on Correctional Manpower, 67n
Jones, Maxwell, 158, 159, 167, 168
Judge Baker Clinic, 169-70
"Juvenile Delinquency" and society, xii, 3-7, 10, 25, 26, 37, 49-55, 145, 154, 165, 166
Juvenile Delinquency Prevention and Control Act, 15
Juvenile Opportunities Extension (JOE), 119-21, 128-48, 161, 169, 175

Kansas, 107, 114
Kelly, J., 46
Kennedy Research Center at Peabody College (Tenn.), 15
Kerner Commission Report, 53
"Kimberly," Mass., 73-4
Konopka, Gisela, 23, 24
Kovar, Lillian, 21
Kozol, J., 53-4

Laing, R.D., 5-6
Lancaster Industrial School for Girls, 145, 153, 160, 175
Law Enforcement Assistance Administration (LEAA) of the Justice Department, 14, 42, 163, 165
Leach, Edmund, 5
Levine, Murray, 54
Libra Inc., 169

Liebow, E., 53
Lock-up. *See* Solitary confinement
Lyman Industrial School for Boys, xi,
   120-1, 128, 1131-2, 140, 141, 144,
   145, 153, 159, 161-2, 174-5

McClean Hospital, 169-70
McIntyre, D., 54
Maloney, Frank, 157
Mary Knoll (Topsfield, Mass.), 160
Massachusetts Act of 1855, 88
Massachusetts Administration and
   Finance Office, 161
Massachusetts Association for the
   Reintegration of Youth (MARY),
   121-2, 169
Massachusetts Committee on Crime
   and Youth, 156, 157
Massachusetts Conference on Social
   Welfare, 156-7
Massachusetts Department of Edu-
   cation, 153, 157
Massachusetts Department of Mental
   Health, 80n, 168
Massachusetts Department of Proba-
   tion, 143
Massachusetts Department of Youth
   Services (DYS), ix, 49, 67-84,
   117-24, 127-48, 151-80; and com-
   munity resistance to group homes,
   67-84; and institutional reform,
   151-80; and National Conference on
   Juvenile Delinquency, 127-48
Mead, George Herbert, 3
Medfield-Norfolk Project, 169
Mental health profession, 49-52
Mental retardation, 14-5, 164
Mental Retardation Facilities and
   Community Mental Health Center
   Construction Act, 15
Michigan, 14, 15
Miller, Jerome, 49, 118, 119, 120,
   127, 151-2, 155, 157, 158-61,
   166-7, 170-9
Monohan, T.P., 21
Montana, 15
Morris, Ruth, 24

National Conference on Juvenile
   Delinquency Prevention and Treatment Programs, 121, 127-48: daily
   routine, 133-4; evaluation, 134-41;

goals, 129-31; group leaders, 121,
   128, 133-5; outcome data, 141-5;
   placement, 120, 141-4, 148; plan-
   ning and lead time, 146; selection
   and training processes, 131-3, 147
National Institute of Mental Health
   (NIMH), 42
Neighborhood Facilities Program
   (HUD), 15
Neighborhood Youth Corps, 164
News media, 155, 156, 157, 161, 166,
   170, 174
New York (State), 14
North Shore Community College, 169

Oakdale Residential Treatment Unit,
   153, 160, 168
Ohlin, Lloyd, 157
Orphanages, 14
Outward Bound, 162

Palm Beach County, Florida, 14
Parent Teachers Association, 156
Parole systems, 154, 160
Police, 45
Polsky, Howard, 93
President's Commission on Law
   Enforcement and the Administration
   of Justice, 152
Primal scream therapy, 164
Prison reform, 119
Protestant Council, 77, 81, 83-4

Recidivism, xii, 4, 10-1, 13, 33, 123,
   142-5, 152, 155
Reform schools. *See* Correctional
   institutions; Training schools
Regionalization, 160, 162
Rehabilitation models, 10, 46, 49-56,
   80, 103, 107-14, 128, 154, 158:
   clinical, xi, 49-52, 56; ecological, 46;
   guided group interaction, 168, 172;
   social action, 52-6; teaching-family,
   107-14; therapeutic community, xi,
   158-9, 160, 162, 167-8, 170, 172;
   training school, 154; youth advocacy, 128, 141, 145, 147-8
Reiss, Albert, 24
Reorganization Act (Mass.), 157, 158,
   170, 171, 177
Resident participation, 59-66, 101,
   102, 108, 109-14, 123, 138-40, 151,
   160, 165, 167

Robey, Ames, 21
Roslindale Detention Center, 154

Sarason, S.B., 54
Sargent, Francis W., 156, 157
Scott, Edward M., 23
Self-Development Group Inc., 169
Self-government, 108, 109-14
Self-help programs, 160, 168, 169, 172
Sexist society, 19, 20, 24-5, 26, 27-8
Shirley Industrial School for Boys, 119-20, 127, 153, 158-9, 168, 174
Soledad, 122
Solitary confinement, 26, 88, 89, 92, 93, 94, 154, 155, 159, 174
South Huntington Avenue Detention Center, 153
Spectrum House, 169
Suicide, 24, 25
Synanon, 164
SZEP, 155


Teaching-Family Handbook, 108
Teach-ins, 119, 160
Tennessee Department of Corrections, 15
Training schools, vii, ix, 11, 25-6, 87-104, 153-4. See also Correctional institutions
Transition House, 169

U.S. Department of Health, Education and Welfare (HEW): Office of Education, 36; Report on Mass. Dept. of Youth Services, 155-6, 157, 177
U.S. Department of Justice, 42
U.S. Department of Labor, 36
United Way, 36
Universities, 44-5, 117-8, 122-4, 135, 136, 138, 140, 141, 145, 147-8, 164, 169

University of Massachusetts, 117-24, 127-48, 160, 161, 162, 175, 178; and the Mass. Dept. of Youth Services, 118-9, 123-4, 162; and the National Conference on Juvenile Delinquency, 121, 127-48, 161. See also Advocates for the Development of Human Potential; Juvenile Opportunities Extention; Mass. Assoc. for the Reintegration of Youth
University of Massachusetts Conference. See National Conference on Juvenile Delinquency Prevention and Treatment Programs
University of Massachusetts School of Education, 169

Vedder, Clyde, B., 21
Video-tape, use of, 110
Volpe, John, 155
Volunteer personnel, 119, 128, 132, 160. See also "Advocates"
Vorath, Harry, 168

Weber, Max, 92
Westfield Detention Center, 119, 121, 128, 131, 132, 133, 134, 144, 145, 154, 160, 178
Williams, W., 46
Wood, Robert C., 117
Worcester Detention Center, 154

YMCA, 163, 169, 172
Youth-adult alienation, 10, 37, 52-3
Youth Development and Delinquency Prevention Administration (YDDPA) of HEW, 9, 33-7
Youth Services Board, 153
Youth Services Systems, 9-12, 33-7. See also Human services programs; Mass. Dept. of Youth Services

Zoning restrictions, 80